Entrepreneurship in the Hospitality, Tourism and Leisure Industries

About the Authors

Alison Morrison is a senior lecturer specializing in small business management and entrepreneurship at The Scottish Hotel School, University of Strathclyde. She has a M.Sc. in Entrepreneurial Studies and her Ph.D. thesis investigated small-firm strategic alliances. Since 1979 she has been an entrepreneur in her own right, owning and operating a number of restaurant and hotel businesses. In addition, she regularly undertakes consultancy projects for entrepreneurs both in the UK and internationally.

Mike Rimmington is senior lecturer and MBA Programme Director, School of Hotel and Restaurant Management, Oxford Brookes University. He is a graduate of Durham University Business School. He has taught entrepreneurship courses at graduate and undergraduate level for over five years in the UK, France and USA. Entrepreneurial activities have included the development and launch of innovatory graduate-level distance learning courses. These now recruit students world-wide.

Claire Williams is a lecturer in Marketing and Hospitality Business, School of Leisure and Food Management, Sheffield Hallam University. Her M.Sc. thesis at Virginia Polytechnic Institute and State University investigated the link between hospitality entrepreneurs and business strategy. She has been involved in the creation and operation of several entrepreneurial ventures including a property company and, most recently, Churchill's Fine Sandwich Emporium.

Entrepreneurship in the Hospitality, Tourism and Leisure Industries

Alison Morrison
Mike Rimmington
Claire Williams

OXFORD AUCKLAND BOSTON JOHANNESBURG MELBOURNE NEW DELHI

Butterworth-Heinemann
Linacre House, Jordan Hill, Oxford OX2 8DP
225 Wildwood Avenue, Woburn, MA 01801-2041
A division of Reed Educational and Professional Publishing Ltd

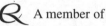 A member of the Reed Elsevier plc group

First published 1999

British Library Cataloguing in Publication Data
A catalogue record for this book is available from the British Library

ISBN 0 7506 4097 9

Typeset by Avocet Typeset, Brill, Aylesbury, Bucks
Printed and Bound in Great Britain by The Bath Press, Bath

Contents

Foreword

The late John Paul Getty, one of the greatest entrepreneurs of the immediate post War years once said that a lasting personal relationship is only possible if you are a business failure. Whilst this may not be altogether true, it does underline the uncompromising commitment required to make a success of a business, almost to the exclusion of all else.

The authors carefully examine the motivation of entrepreneurs, analyse the main drivers of entrepreneurial behaviour and establish the factors which lead to business success. Though entrepreneurs are by nature activists, taking time to read and reflect on this book would greatly increase their chance of success and reduce the possibility of failure. Both individual entrepreneurship and corporate entrepreneurship are examined. Although the latter is seen to be quite different as the corporate environment implies a greater level of bureaucracy and no individual financial risk.

Whether the entrepreneur is born or made will always be difficult to establish. What entrepreneurs share is a certain restlessness, abundant energy, a capacity to inspire, intelligence and personal and critical values. They have the ability to challenge established procedures and assumptions, an unwillingness to take no for an answer, and a certain impatience to get the job done.

Whilst successful entrepreneurs come from varying backgrounds and environments, an upbringing where parents are self employed or in business does give a certain conditioning. Many successful entrepreneurs come from families where the parents have been entrepreneurially successful, Rupert Murdoch is a fine example. Being brought up with a work ethic and being raised in a business environment does grow some ability and skill but the drive which is required must be inbred.

Money per se is not necessarily a motivator. There are never ending examples of successful entrepreneurs who have created wealth far in excess of their own, or their families needs, but are driven on to even greater things. Although by then it is the enjoyment of the game or the thrill of the chase which may be the main spur.

Entrepreneurs, by their very nature will succeed whatever the constraints of the environment they work in. In countries where the economic structure and taxation regimes are hugely unfavourable entrepreneurs still survive, and find their way round the difficulties. Italy is such a country; Italians are probably entrepreneurial by nature and in spite of the draconian bureaucratic controls, anti-employer labour laws, high levels of taxation and huge state enterprises, they have managed nevertheless to flourish.

But the most entrepreneurial environment is that of the USA where belief in the free market, liberal labour laws and an admiration of business success spawns a continuing multitude of entrepreneurs. In the UK the structural reforms that took place in the early 1980s under Mrs Thatcher were followed by a huge increase in start ups of small businesses. Many were destroyed in the economic recession of the early 1990s but many more have emerged since and are responsible for the decrease in unemployment which has taken place in the UK when compared with the rest of Europe.

It is interesting to examine the behaviour of management teams that carry out management buyouts prior and post the transfer of the business. From being competent executives running a business well, they become galvanized into a form of action which would not have been contemplated in their previous state. They are much more exposed than in a corporate environment where adequate performance is often acceptable and where failure can often be fudged. Now there is nothing they can hide behind other than the success or failure of their own efforts. The criteria for establishing what might be acceptable costs changes considerably and their success is driven by a need to advance profitability quite dramatically in the short term. The environment is no longer a cosy and comfortable one, praise for success and blame for failure are lavished more directly by the outside world. Apart from monetary considerations the satisfaction to be derived from successful endeavours is greater because it is more clearly associated with their own efforts.

Whether a business has to achieve a certain size before the owner can be considered entrepreneurial is a mute point. To leave the security of a regular job to invest what little savings that might have been accumulated to open one establishment is an entrepreneurial exercise. The individual is taking a risk, the cost of failure however is not so enormous and if the enterprise fails the individual can go back to a job, somewhat chastened but with their experience enriched.

It is only when the entrepreneurial business reaches a certain size that it is noticed and the achievement recognized and admired. At this stage the risk undertaken is greater, there is more to lose and failure is very visible. As a business grows in size so management skills become more important and very often the entrepreneur does not have them or does not see the necessity for them, this is where they come unstuck. My father, Lord Forte, always said to me that his great concern in the early stages was when he moved from one unit to two. In the end he appointed his best employee as the manager of the first establishment and went to open the second one himself. Much to his surprise the first establishment improved its profitability under the control of the manager.

His later struggles were those of financing his expansion which was mostly from bank loans. When he bought the Café Royal in the late 1950s he went to the completion meeting without having found the purchase money. He took the seller, who was Bracewell Smith aside, told him he did not have the money and asked Bracewell Smith to lend it to him, which he did!

When buying the George V and Plaza Athenee in Paris, he had to deal with the majority shareholder and widow of the founder Madame Duprès. She had the reputation of being extremely difficult to deal with and had rebuffed a number of suitors including Maxwell Joseph. My father succeeded in making an appointment to see her in Paris. He turned up on the appointed day and she made the excuse that she was ill and could not see him. Undaunted, he sent her twelve dozen roses and a get well card. She saw him the next day, and he bought the hotels.

Charm was one of my father's strengths and he used it effectively to persuade people to back him, and staff to give that little bit extra. He clearly used it to great effect with Madame Duprès!

Not all entrepreneurs are charming, many are quite the opposite and positively abrasive, but all, if they are to be continually successful have to be people of their word. A reputation for straight dealing and maintaining promises is important. Word soon gets around if you are not. It is a quality which my father regarded as paramount and drummed into me from my earliest days.

As I said earlier, it is always hard to know if people can become entrepreneurs if they are not born as entrepreneurs. But I believe it is difficult to stop being an entrepreneur once you are one. When I worked in my father's company in my early years we were certainly entrepreneurs, but I believe that in the 1980s and 1990s the bureaucracy and regulations associated with a large public company meant one had to fight to keep that spirit alive. When Forte PLC was taken over in 1996 I could have retired on my profit from the high price we forced Granada to pay. Instead, I chose to invest it in setting up a new luxury hotel company, RF Hotels. Two years on we are already an established and profitable operator. I am making money and enjoying myself. So perhaps once an entrepreneur, always an entrepreneur.

Perhaps a key characteristic of an entrepreneur is a willingness to learn from others. The readers of this book will have that opportunity and, as a result, be well armed to go into the business world. Hopefully, they will make some money, enjoy themselves and add to the increasing success that the UK is experiencing.

Rocco Forte

Preface

The authors, as both university lecturers and practising entrepreneurs, were concerned that there was a dearth of texts combining an academically grounded and practical approach to entrepreneurship. This is particularly true within the context of the hospitality, tourism and leisure industries. So, with identified reader groups in mind we combined knowledge and expertise to write *Entrepreneurship in the Hospitality, Tourism and Leisure Industries* in the hope that it will assist in the teaching and learning process, inspire the next generation of entrepreneurs, and support the valiant efforts of existing ones.

Hence, the emphasis is on contextualizing associated theories and concepts within the hospitality, tourism and leisure industries. In this way, the realities of the operating environment and its relationship to academic findings are clearly illustrated. This is achieved through numerous industry-relevant short case illustrations which are interspersed throughout. Where these have been drawn from secondary sources, the sources are quoted alongside the illustration or, where more significant, along with the chapter references. When reported from our own experience or distilled from many sources, the source is stated as 'authors'. The case illustrations maintain a **reality check**, ensuring the applicability of the theoretical discussions.

For some time now, there has been widespread recognition that entrepreneurship is the engine that drives the economy of most successful nations. This has lead to an increasing interest in the phenomenon, spawning a whole range of questions which the text sets out to address. These include:

- What constitutes the process of entrepreneurship?
- What makes persons enter into that process?
- What environment do they require in order to flourish and reap the rewards of their personal initiative?
- What operational, management and strategic practices do they need to adopt to help bring about entrepreneurial success?

Undoubtedly, we currently live in a period of workplace revolution, of markets in transition within which, for those with entrepreneurial skills and mind-set, anything is achievable. Today, the hospitality, tourism and leisure industries present a wealth of opportunities – both for those creating their own ventures and for intrapreneurial employees. Such an environment is also dangerous! We are in an era that is as vibrant and exciting as it is challenging and insatiable.

Reader groups

With this environment in mind, the book was written for the following reader groups:

Teachers and students of entrepreneurship in general, and specifically for those interested in the hospitality, tourism and leisure industries.
Each chapter commences with a clearly articulated set of learning objectives, the attempt of which is to deepen and enrich the link between theory and practice by demonstrating the key principles of entrepreneurship. To this end, the approach has been to present theories and concepts, interspersed with industry short case illustrations to relate theory to practice. At the end of each chapter is a set of reflective questions designed to deepen understanding and learning.

Trainers and advisers involved in the stimulation and development of entrepreneurial firms.
Likewise, these two categories of reader should find the chapters on finance and business planning, operation and management, and marketing and strategy of particular relevance to the businesses they work with. For instance, these readers may be working for LECs or TECs, and despite all good intentions, are in effect distanced from the entrepreneurs. As such, the practical approaches should be of particular relevance to them in developing a depth of understanding of, and sensitivity to, the specific issues and challenges related to the hospitality, tourism and leisure industries. They will then be in a better position to identify and deliver training needs and to target timely and supportive advice.

Practising entrepreneurs keen to understand more clearly factors at work within the entrepreneurial process, and to entertain alternative approaches to management.
Trainers and advisers share common ground with this book's anticipated third category of reader – practising entrepreneurs. The content assists in providing clarity relative to the process in which they have become embroiled, and perspective to enable them to successfully navigate a course through the dynamic and challenging environment for enterprise. A framework within which to develop and focus operational, management, and strategic routes and techniques is provided. Furthermore, intellectual debate challenges some of the conventional thinking, rejuvenating traditional outlooks. The key issue for the practitioner (and adviser) is how to harness the energies and qualities of an entrepreneurial firm, while attaining the level of focus and control required to achieve business survival and growth. Moreover, the nature of the hospitality, tourism and leisure industries is such that the entrepreneur can easily become immersed in functional areas. The structure of the text helps to establish a framework of considerations against which to stimulate, measure, and guide the entrepreneurial firm without detracting from its many admirable assets.

Corporate entrepreneurs at all levels, and within all sizes, of organizations.

The fourth group of readers for which this book is intended is that of corporate entrepreneurs – employees within corporations. In today's dynamic and competitive environment, large organizations can learn much from the concepts associated with entrepreneurship. Both entrepreneurs and intrapreneurs relate to the outside world in a common language. Both are involved in making decisions about how to manage market conditions, quality concerns, customer relations, and value for money. Further similarity is expressed relative to the need to strive for competitive advantage in an increasingly crowded and aggressive market place. Provided a conducive organizational culture can be established and appropriate management procedures put in place, the benefits of entrepreneurship can be experienced even within large corporations. More than ever we operate in a business climate where uncertainty and ambiguity are the norm. The fluid, reflexive nature of entrepreneurial strategy recognizes these dynamics and harnesses them as positive, not problematic, forces. Thus, the stance adopted in this book is that the principles of entrepreneurship are generic, transferable to all types and sizes of organizations.

Main aims of the book

While this book is intended for the four groups of reader identified, broadly speaking it has five main aims. These are to:

1 develop a greater understanding of the process of entrepreneurship, entrepreneurs and the environment in which the process takes place;
2 provide students with a means of developing knowledge and skills to enable them to make an informed decision to proceed and develop their own ventures, or alternatively, to be more intrapreneurial within existing corporations;
3 support teachers in the process of developing the student, both in terms of their personal entrepreneurial skills and knowledge base;
4 enable trainers and advisers who work with entrepreneurial firms to better understand the nature and characteristics of these businesses and to address their specific training and advice inputs more accurately;
5 provide independent and corporate entrepreneurs with a set of concepts and constructs, grounded within the practicalities of the hospitality, tourism and leisure industries, which can aid their understanding of the process they are involved in and help them to be more effective.

Structure of the book

To this end the book divides into two parts. The first is concerned with concepts, principles, and the environment associated with entrepreneurship.

The second involves the entrepreneurial implications for the management of finance, business planning, operations management, marketing, and strategy.

Part 1: Concepts, Principles and Environment Associated with Entrepreneurship

This first part of the book focuses the reader on questions and challenges in respect of the process of entrepreneurship, the nature and characteristics of entrepreneurs, and the environment within which they operate. Here there is an attempt to answer the needs of students, and those other categories of readers who wish to acquire a broad overview of the issues which currently engage commentators on entrepreneurship. This part of the book places entrepreneurship in context, and provides a useful survey of reasons why the subject is of import. It presents an outline of subject content and pertinent issues. By concentrating on **issues**, rather than on a description of the place of entrepreneurship in the economy, students will then be in a better position to see how entrepreneurship as an academic discipline is identified.

Part 2: Finance, Business Planning, Operations Management, Marketing, and Strategy

The second part of the book addresses the practicalities involved in the creation and entrepreneurial management of the venture, once established. In this way academic theories and constructs combine with the industry-relevant short case illustrations, and practical proposals. This approach is designed to stimulate intellectual debate and challenge some conventional business practices. Through the prioritization of industry-specific operational, management, and strategic **practicalities**, underpinned by current research findings, the reader is focused on directly implementable approaches and issues.

Content issues

In the extremely multi-disciplinary arena which comprises entrepreneurship studies in the hospitality, tourism and leisure industries, there is a danger in believing that the more functional knowledge the entrepreneur possesses, the more equipped the person is to think and act strategically. This view fails to recognize the **interdependence** of the many parts which make up a business. Moreover, the **quality** of what comes out of this interdependence is what makes a business effective, entrepreneurial, and gives it the capability to interact productively with its environment. This book examines how such productive interaction, driven by the process of entrepreneurship, can be achieved.

Teaching and training

The approaches of those involved in teaching and training entrepreneurship are many and varied. However, what each has in common is the challenge of how best to help students of entrepreneurship to develop their skills and knowledge. This may require an attempt to:

- link theory and practice;
- raise awareness and put business concepts to use in the explanation of practice;
- encourage imaginative, creative, and innovative interpretation of conventional business practices;
- examine the relationship between entrepreneurship, the support environment and various providers of finance;
- investigate specifics of the interface between entrepreneurship and hospitality, tourism and leisure operations, management, and strategy;
- rejuvenate marketing and strategic management approaches.

These are but a few of the educational processes utilized by those charged with responsibility for entrepreneurship curricula. Embedded in the concern with process and content are a number of questions:

- What kind of practical advice should be given to aspiring entrepreneurs and current practitioners?
- What is the appropriate content of entrepreneurship education and training programmes?
- Are the learning needs of students and practitioners radically different?

The key issue is the stage of development of the entrepreneur. The student is at a stage most probably preparatory to entrepreneurship, while the practitioner is already immersed in the realities of the operating environment. However, both groups can gain from the holistic perspective of the entrepreneurial role within the big picture of entrepreneurship in Part 1, and the operational, management, and strategic perspective presented in Part 2. It is the contention of the authors that the academic development of potential entrepreneurs should be interlinked with, rather than divorced from, the experiences of practising entrepreneurs.

Part One
Concepts, Principles and Environment Associated with Entrepreneurship

1 The process of entrepreneurship

The objective of this chapter is to develop an understanding of what is meant by the process of entrepreneurship in both economic and social terms. Specifically, the chapter will:

* introduce and define the process of entrepreneurship;
* identify key participants in the process;
* develop understanding of entrepreneurship's contributing elements and features;
* consider the application of the process within the hospitality, tourism and leisure industries.

Introduction

Over the last two decades the business environment in the UK has undergone tremendous change. The result is a restructuring of economic and social systems in a way which has led to increased levels of business formation, innovation, new organizational forms, and more general shifts in attitudes and behaviour. This mirrored a transition from a managerial to an entrepreneurial society which was evident in the USA in the 1970s, and was described by Naisbitt (1982) as an **entrepreneurial explosion**. Timmons (1994) views the transition as a **silent revolution** which may affect the twenty-first century as much as, and probably more than, the Industrial Revolution of the nineteenth century. This revolution is revitalizing economies, creating millions of jobs and forging new prosperity. It is built on the back of dynamic fast-track companies driven by ambitious entrepreneurs. Such entrepreneurs are willing to take risks on the road to success. Across Europe entrepreneurs are launching businesses which grow at well over 25 per cent per annum, and are operating in all industry sectors (European Foundation for Entrepreneurship Research, 1996).

Embodied in this revolution is the process of entrepreneurship, central to which is the requirement for the personal initiative of the entrepreneur. Thus, according to Fass and Scothorne (1990) the process of entrepreneurship is recognized as being at the heart of an economic development task and driven by the motivations of individuals, who are seeking to satisfy their personal goals. As such, the ultimate aim of economic development is to create opportunities for personal fulfilment through economic activity. This implies a partnership between policy-makers and entrepreneurs in

---

Illustration: Cardiff docks, process of entrepreneurship

The rapid metamorphosis of the old Cardiff docks into four square miles of commercial, industrial, housing and leisure development is revitalizing a region which has witnessed a large decline in traditional industries. The success of Cardiff Bay depends on the skilful integration of a strong supply-led tourism strategy working at local, regional and national levels. Central to the process has been attracting and securing investment from a wide range of entrepreneurs in visitor attractions, restaurants, water sports activities, bars and hotels. By the end of 1996 Cardiff Bay had attracted £8000 million private capital and the Bay already generates an estimated £144 million a year for Cardiff. It is forecast to attract two million visitors a year by the year 2000 and is expected to create 30 000 jobs throughout South Wales.
Source: Cramer, 1996

---

order to achieve economic renewal and prosperity. At a local level, the above illustration shows how this process was approached in Cardiff.

However, it is considered important to temper the euphoria of the entrepreneurial revolution with the reality of why people are turning to entrepreneurial careers. Such people are, in fact, 'buying' personal independence and control through the process of new venture creation. In this respect, entrepreneurship may be seen as an aspect of the theory of choice (Reid and Jacobsen, 1988), where people are **pulled** towards entrepreneurship. The universal truth of this interpretation in a situation of substantial change in labour markets is questionable. Such restructuring has effectively **forced** some to **choose** entrepreneurship, as the only alternative is not to have a job. In this scenario individuals may also be **pushed** into entrepreneurship through the lack of alternative employment opportunities. This moves discussion of entrepreneurship into a choice between earning money or not having gainful employment. Thus, it is important to recognize that the route towards entrepreneurship may be varied – a response to a crisis situation or exploitation of a market opportunity, or both.

Definition

There is no universally accepted definition of entrepreneurship. Attempts have traditionally been made to describe it relative to: an economic function; ownership structure; degrees of entrepreneurship; size and life-cycle of firm; and a resource base. These descriptions are outlined below.

Economic function

Economists are attracted to the subject of entrepreneurship because they see it as a means of stimulating the economy through the harnessing of personal initiative in the creation of firms and jobs. Thus, it is seen as an economic function. In these terms Cantillon (1755) stated that entrepreneurship entails

---

Illustration: Stoke-on-Trent, co-ordination of factors of production

Stoke-on-Trent has achieved considerable success as a city-break tourist destination. This is a result of the potteries, hotels, restaurants and coach-tour firms coming together to produce an attractive package, which has been successfully marketed. A wide range of customers are attracted. Potters from overseas, collectors, and some foreign tourists, travel to Britain for the area known as the Potteries before all else. Most foreign tourists arrive on organized coach parties. Empty-nesters (couples whose children have left home) dominate the domestic weekend-break market. Alton Towers' visitors and the Staffordshire Moorland's holiday-makers pop into the Potteries for a day of tableware tourism and shopping. Forty-odd factory shops and museums are dotted all around the Potteries conurbation of six towns that is the City of Stoke-on-Trent. Thus, capitalizing on the enterprise of the entrepreneurs of days gone by, such as Josiah Wedgwood, today's entrepreneurs are taking the initiative, stimulating the process of entrepreneurship. Locally, this is resulting in job creation, tourist expenditure and environmental improvements.
Source: Dixon, 1996

---

bearing the risk of buying at a certain price and selling at an uncertain price. Implicit in this activity is a risk-bearing function. Say (1800) broadened this economic perspective to include the concept of the bringing together of the factors of production, within which the entrepreneur is primordial. This approach assumes an entrepreneur who responds to an outside force, which then impacts on the market system. Stoke-on-Trent is an illustration of how entrepreneurs co-ordinated to bring together the factors of production which compose tourism.

Ownership structure

Entrepreneurship has also been defined relative to ownership structure, represented as the creation of a new enterprise, which has the entrepreneur as the founder. This approach deliberately excludes firms which have a different ownership structure, such as the shareholder-owned corporate groups, charities, or public-sector organizations. It suggests that the process of entrepreneurship is not appropriate to, or applied by, such organizations. An

---

Illustration: bed and breakfast accommodation, ownership structure

Bed and breakfast accommodation appeals to tourists, especially those from overseas, because owners allow guests into their homes and give a great insight into the British way of life. In addition, as this type of accommodation is generally less expensive than hotels it is attractive to those travelling on limited budgets. It is estimated that there are more than 25 000 bed and breakfasts in the UK. By far the majority are run by the owner as a part-time activity or by retired people to supplement their income.
Source: Hyman, 1996

---

illustration of a firm with the owner as the founder is that of the bed and breakfast operation. As we will explore in the following chapters, such ownership-restricted views of entrepreneurship have now been largely superseded. Entrepreneurship is widely agreed to take place within all sizes and types of organizations.

Degrees of entrepreneurship

Efforts have been made to categorize the degree of innovative and creative behaviour which can be deemed to represent entrepreneurship. For instance, to what degree can the bed and breakfast illustration really be considered as an example of entrepreneurship? Is the originator an entrepreneur or a small-firm proprietor? Furthermore, many small-firm owners create the business then simply maintain it, providing a reasonably steady-state **lifestyle** income. Firms which have been inherited are often run by the next generation in the same manner as did their forebears. To what degree can these three categories, small firm, steady state, and inherited, be classed as examples of entrepreneurship? Dale (1991) proposes that the focus for the measurement of entrepreneurship should be on the degree of success achieved through the change initiated. Such measures could be related to growth factors such as market size, return on personal investment, number of employees, and increased diversity of products/services. If the degree of entrepreneurship is to be measured by apparent success achieved through the change initiated, then Groupe Chez Gerard offers a good illustration.

Illustration: Groupe Chez Gerard, degrees of entrepreneurship

Laurence Issacson and his partner Neville Abraham are, respectively, Deputy Chairman and Chairman of Groupe Chez Gerard, which celebrated its tenth birthday in 1996. The group owns ten restaurants, and serves around 11 000 customers per week. With a weekly turnover of £300 000 Groupe Chez Gerard has been remarkably successful in targeting its market and growing the business. The group employs 400 people, but expects to increase that number within three years to 800–1000 as it expands.
Source: Fox, 1996

Size and life-cycle of firm

Frequently, entrepreneurship is perceived as being associated with young start-up businesses. Many firms seem to start out as high energy, dynamic, small entrepreneurial businesses only to mature into a mirror image of the more sluggish, established corporate bureaucracies. However, there appears to be no loss of entrepreneurial vitality in the following illustration of Harry Ramsden's; despite having already developed so rapidly, the company shows no sign of reducing its entrepreneurial activity.

Illustration: Harry Ramsden's, size and life-cycle of firm

Harry Ramsden's, the Yorkshire-based fish-and-chip restaurant group started as one unit in Leeds. It was floated on the stock market in 1989. In 1995 turnover stood at £4 326 433, up 16 per cent on 1994, and operating profit at £1 303 019 was up 20.6 per cent. The group is stepping up expansion with a raft of franchises set to open across Scotland, the south of England, and resorts abroad. Separately, further overseas openings are expected following the deal with Compass Catering in 1996, which allows the contract-catering giant to use the Harry Ramsden's brand internationally in airport, railway and leisure outlets.
Source: Arnot, 1996

Resource base

Kirzner (1980) describes entrepreneurship as both a costless and a priceless resource from which economic development models can benefit. However, he emphasizes that it is not something which can be deliberately introduced. Entrepreneurship is a factor primordial to the very idea of a potential production process awaiting possible implementation. This is based on the assumption that, within our social and economic system, there is an initial stock of entrepreneurial resource waiting to be mobilized. This cannot necessarily be taken for granted and much energy has been devoted by government agencies such as the DTI, DfEE, TECS and LECS to the establishment of a climate which supports enterprise. This is explored further in Chapter 4. Certainly it can be argued that in the UK today there is no shortage of individuals who have the creativity and drive to capitalize upon entrepreneurial opportunities. This assumption was made by Leeds councillors in their plans to rejuvenate the centre of the city, as shown in the illustration below
.

Illustration: Leeds, entrepreneurship resource

Leeds is a city under the scalpel, as enlightened councillors and entrepreneurs shave off the vestiges of its Victorian manufacturing and retailing past to reshape it as a modern, commercial city with a vibrant continental-style café and night-life culture. Central to its success is the willingness of hospitality entrepreneurs to take up the council's exhortations to open pavement cafés, operate late licences and boost the diversity and quality of eateries and bars to keep people in the city centre after working hours.
Source: Lyons, 1994

These approaches generate a number of questions such as:

- What stimulates entrepreneurs to initiate the economic function?
- Is entrepreneurship the preserve of solely the owner/managed firm?
- If we accept that the process is about initiating change, how big is the degree of change required to be to constitute entrepreneurship?
- Can a firm, regardless of size or age, keep in touch with the youthful vigour and creativity that characterizes entrepreneurship?

- How can the resource of entrepreneurship be deployed efficiently within the UK social and economic system?

These questions are of vital significance, central to the content of this text, and will be addressed in the following chapters. Certainly, it is the view of the authors that entrepreneurship should not just be left to happen. The right macro- and micro-conditions need to be created. Entrepreneurs can be developed and supported towards achievement of business success.

Definition focus

It can be observed that it is not a useful pursuit to attempt to pigeon-hole the process of entrepreneurship relative to any one specific perspective. The process is much more holistic and dynamic in nature. At the heart are entrepreneurs, their persistent search for opportunities, and their efforts to marshall the resources needed to realize them. The essence of entrepreneurship is the initiation of change, through creation and/or innovation. This is described by Drucker (1986) as the effort to create purposeful, focused change in an firm's economic or social potential, plus the application of distinct entrepreneurial strategies and entrepreneurial management.

Curran and Burrows (1986, p. 269) contribute to this clarification by describing the process of entrepreneurship as:

> The innovatory process involved in the creation of an economic enterprise based on a new product or service which differs significantly from products or services in the way its production is organized, or in its marketing.

The importance of this characterization is that it moves the discussion away from the confines of small, owner-managed businesses to that of concepts and theories which can be applied to *any* economic enterprise. It progresses our understanding to a more all-embracing concept of entrepreneurship which has no reverence for size or ownership structure. This is very much the approach adopted by Drucker (1986, p. 16) who describes entrepreneurship as a process which requires:

> … above all application of the basic concepts, the basic techniques, of management to new problems and new opportunities.

Richard Branson, Virgin Management Ltd, supports this holistic concept of entrepreneurship in the following, very human, description (Anderson, 1995, p. 2):

> … the satisfaction of doing it for yourself and motivating others to work with you in bringing it about. It is about fun, innovation, creativity and the rewards are far greater than the purely financial. These were the goals with which we founded the Virgin Group and we have striven not to lose sight of them. Most of all, entrepreneurship is a state of mind. You do not have to run your own company, but you should try to look beyond the obvious and accepted in whatever you do.

This leads the authors to assert that the process of entrepreneurship has its foundations in both concept and theory, and person and intuition. Unquestionably, at the heart is a human creative act which initiates economic activity, and applies the associated management practices. Without such action there is no entrepreneurship. In this respect Kirzner (1979), believes the source to be within the human spirit which will flourish in response to uncertainty and competition. This spirit is described in glowing inspirational terms by Gilder (1971, p. 258):

> The spirit of enterprise wells up from the wisdom of ages and the history (of the West) and infuses the most modern of technological adventures. It joins the old and new frontiers. It asserts a firm hierarchy of values and demands a hard discipline. It requires a life of labor and listening, aspiration and courage. But it is the source of all we are and can become, the saving grace of democratic politics and free men, the hope of the poor and the obligation of the fortunate, the redemption of an oppressed and desperate world.

Such definitions present a somewhat biased, idealistic vision of entrepreneurship which assumes that all intentions of entrepreneurship are morally sound and socially responsible. Entrepreneurship is concerned with the initiation of change. As such, it challenges, and perhaps destroys, the established order and the complacency of traditional social and economic systems. Furthermore, Gilder (1971) emphasizes that one of the key principles of entrepreneurship is the absence of clear and fast rules. With no rule book to control the **game** which is entrepreneurship it is inevitable that there will be winners, losers and unruly behaviour. Consequently, it would be delusory to accept that all outcomes from the process of entrepreneurship will be positive.

Table 1.1 summarizes the different definition approaches and features discussed in this chapter. From this it can be concluded that entrepreneurship is about more than an economic function. The essence is the application of innovatory management processes, directed at bringing about change of both a social and economic nature. The key to unlocking the potential of entrepreneurship lies within the individual members of society, and the degree to which the spirit of enterprise exists or can be stimulated. Furthermore, without this personal initiative, originating in the spirit of enterprise, the process of entrepreneurship is a non-starter.

Types of entrepreneurship

As a consequence of reviewing these differing stances towards definition, it is proposed that the process of entrepreneurship can be regarded as having common applicability in all business domains regardless of size and ownership structure. However, a need is recognized to develop a more comprehensive understanding of the types of, and contexts for, entrepreneurship. A useful approach is that of dual segmentation, as illustrated in Figure 1.1. First, three clearly distinctive types of entrepreneurship are recognized. Second, the right-hand segment takes account of the particular contexts within which the process of entrepreneurship takes place. Each of these three

Table 1.1 Process of entrepreneurship: definition approaches and features

Approaches	Features
Economic function	• Personal initiative of entrepreneur • Risk-bearing function • Harnessing of factors of production
Ownership structure	• Creation of business with entrepreneur as founder
Degrees of entrepreneurship	• Size of firm • Personal financial risk • Creativity and innovation • Growth realization
Resource base	• Primordial to potential production process
Size and life-cycle of firm	• Association with young start-up firm
Consolidation approach	• Conditions of uncertainty and competition • Entrepreneurial management and strategy • Initiation of change • Innovatory process • Ownership, structure and size of firm irrelevant • Personal initiative through the spirit of enterprise

Sources: Cantillon (1755), Say (1800), Gilder (1971), Kirzner (1979, 1980), Curran and Burrows (1986), Drucker (1986), Dale (1991)

types of entrepreneurship can be practised within the identified contexts. Indeed, in recognition of the dynamism of the entrepreneurial process, there may be situations where the typologies are used interchangeably in response to different challenges, situations and needs.

The approach presented in this model is central to the definitional stance adopted in this text. It moves the parameters of definition away from being associated purely with new venture creation to encompass the management practices adopted within existing businesses which have the potential to sustain the initial entrepreneurial impetus. Furthermore, it is not the preserve of only **for-profit** organizations. Entrepreneurship has the potential to be applied across institutions of all types: commercial firms; charitable organizations; and public-sector-controlled hospitals, retirement homes and leisure centres.

Typologies and contexts

Typologies

• **Entrepreneurship**: Timmons (1994) defines entrepreneurship as creating and building something of value from practically nothing. It is the process of creating or seizing an opportunity, and pursuing it *regardless* of the resources currently personally controlled. This involves the definition, creation and distribution of value and benefits to individuals, groups, organizations and society at large. Traditionally, it has been associated with the solo entrepreneur intensely, directly, creatively and actively involved in the process. Such individuals face challenges of uncertainty, calculated

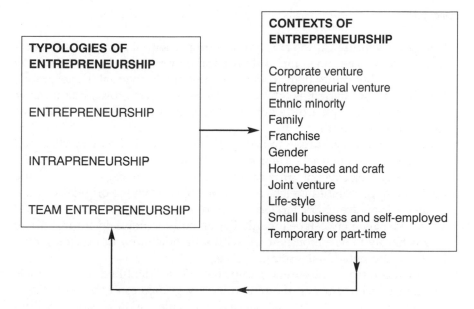

Figure 1 Entrepreneurship dual segmentation

risk-taking, and risk minimization. Typically they retain almost total control and remain at the centre of the decision-making web. A high premium is attached to nurturing strong but informal cultures. Employee integration tends to be on the basis of personal allegiance to proprietors (Goffee and Scase, 1996).

• **Intrapreneurship**: Within corporations the process of entrepreneurship may be initiated by dynamic employees who are motivated to be creative and innovative to the social and economic enhancement of their organization. In such a context, the process is termed as **intrapreneurship**. Currently, this is encouraged and fostered by the more enlightened and competitive corporations and other organizations. Successful intrapreneurship requires the appropriate organizational structures, cultures, relationships and operational practices which motivate employees to be more entrepreneurial in their day-to-day decision-making (Goffee and Scase, 1996). Instrumental to the permeation throughout the corporation of this approach is organizational learning and employee empowerment towards the revitalization of the business.

• **Team entrepreneurship**: This typology does not view the process of entrepreneurship or intrapreneurship as the preserve of the individual. Rather, it is seen as a capability and attitude whereby individual skills are integrated into a group, or team, becoming partners in the business's future evolution. This collective capacity to innovate becomes something greater than the sum of its parts. In other words, it provides a healthy synergistic effect. Reich (1994) argues that team entrepreneurship should be awarded a higher profile, given the current business environment. This downplays the myth of the lone entrepreneurial hero, and celebrates the potential of creative teams.

Contexts

- **Corporate venture**: As the embryonic entrepreneurial firm grows, owner-ship is likely to become more diffused and entrepreneurship may become a group quality rather than confined to any one individual. For example, Whitbread PLC started as a family business and has grown into a major corporation with quite different ownership and management structures from those at its birth.
- **Entrepreneurial venture**: A minority of firms in the UK may be classified as truly 'entrepreneurial'. Their owners/managers will be driven by the managerial objective of growth realization, and maximization of the potential opportunities which can be developed from the original venture created. They are characterized by innovative strategies and practices. Virgin Management can be regarded as an entrepreneurial venture – there seems hardly to be a month go by without a new opportunity being real-ized and presented to the market place.
- **Ethnic minority**: Entrepreneurship has been identified as a vehicle through which members of ethnic minority groups can overcome disad-vantage and achieve personal success. Examples of such groups within the UK are represented by African-Caribbean, Indian, Pakistani, Bangladeshi, and Greek-Cypriot communities. According to Deakin (1996) ethnic entrepreneurs have been successful in developing market niches which are 'ethnically protected', in which to excel. An obvious example is the wealth of specialist ethnic restaurants which are now common features of the eating-out scene in the UK.
- **Family**: A large percentage of smaller firms represent family enterprises. Very often the small hotel, visitor attraction, or activity centre will involve most of the family performing different roles. Within such firms, issues of importance are the social systems which exist and the question of succes-sion. The also family has an important role to play in terms of being a sup-plier of resources, such as finance and labour. However, examples of large-firm family businesses can also be identified, such as Forte PLC before its take over by Granada. Ownership is generally shared by the family, and control exercised by the senior or founding member.
- **Franchise**: The highly standardized nature of some products and services, and the strength of the brands involved, have resulted in franchising becoming a dominant feature of operations in the industry sector. Business format franchising entails the franchisor granting a licence to local operators (franchisees) to use the brand name, product, service and associated goodwill for a specific period of time. Franchisees are supplied with a complete, proven, business concept together with the unique **know-how**, thereby removing from the franchisee some of the uncertain-ties of setting up in business. Investment ranges from £2000 upwards, with average investment being £45 000. Industry examples are Uniglobe Travel, Rosemary Conley Diet and Fitness Clubs, Kentucky Fried Chicken, McDonalds Restaurants, and Pizza Express.
- **Gender**: It is often the high profile male entrepreneurs who are cast, and identified with, as role models. Consequently, there has been an increased emphasis on the encouragement of female entrepreneurship as statistics indicate a generally low business start-up rate within this group. For

example, female self-employment increased from 20 per cent of total self-employment in 1981 to 26 per cent in 1994. (DfEE, 1996). The level of female activity in entrepreneurship is influenced by a complex set of social and economic factors, and the influence of these factors can vary across different industry sectors. There are few high-profile examples of female entrepreneurship within industry, however an excellent example is the achievement of Prue Leith in developing her catering enterprise, eventually sold to Eurest in 1994 for £17 million. Anita Roddick was also an entrepreneur in the hospitality industry, before creating Body Shop.

- **Home-based and craft**: Within the hospitality, tourism and leisure industries, this represents a small, highly specialized segment. The restricted size is mainly due to the nature of the businesses in this sector with their fixity to the service provider's home, rather than the location of the customers. The most obvious example is that of the bed and breakfast operation. However, as a result of information technology developments, new varieties of home-based businesses are emerging, such as Internet marketing support, central reservations services, and bespoke tourist itinerary planning.
- **Joint venture**: This represents an arrangement whereby firms remain independent but set a up new organization jointly owned by the parent firms. This type of quasi-merger arrangement can be seen in consortia firms such as Best Western, Consort, Virgin Collection, and Pride of Britain. They are typically focused on a particular venture, project, or activity. Each will vary in terms of formality, ranging from a loose voluntary agreement to one which involves financial shareholding. Such arrangements are discussed in more detail in Chapter 7.
- **Life-style**: The majority of small firms within the UK can be termed **life-style** businesses. Their owners are likely to be concerned with survival, and maintaining sufficient income to ensure that the business provides them and their family with a satisfactory level of funds to enable enjoyment of their chosen life-style. Examples can be found in businesses such as the **way-of-life** hotel, and sports persons offering coaching or associated leisure activity packages. There is debate in the literature as to whether running such an organization is really entrepreneurship.
- **Small business and self-employment**: These businesses are often entirely dependent upon the talents and energies of the proprietors. Lacking in basic management skills, they tend to neglect market opportunities and instead choose to **trade** within a stable network of customers who will provide a regular and **satisfactory** return. They are not necessarily strongly profit-motivated and theories of rational economic calculation cannot satisfactorily explain their behaviour. Many use unpaid family labour, and employ no staff on a regular basis. These entrepreneurs sell to customers their personal skills, for example bed and breakfast, tour guide, or craft souvenir vendor. It is their detailed knowledge of trading opportunities, within a particular locality, which is often their strength.
- **Temporary/part-time**: This approach relates to entrepreneurship which is not a constant process, but one which can be applied as and when required. It emphasizes the temporal dimension, whereby an individual, or a firm, may be more or less entrepreneurial depending on the extent to which they have the inclination, or pressure upon them, to act entrepre-

neurially. This refers to management practices within permanent, established firms and to small-scale entrepreneurial activity. The latter is frequently evidenced in the submerged, or black economy, often associated with economic marginality rather than prosperity. Such firms often appear during periods of peak demand, such as the tourist season, and disappear into oblivion as the demand wanes.

The dual segmentation approach to the definition of entrepreneurship, described above, serves to explode the subject, introducing a wealth of dimensions which clearly reflects the diversity of the process. As such, it more accurately represents the reality of entrepreneurship. These dimensions are not intended to be all inclusive, but they do serve to introduce many of the issues which will be discussed further in subsequent chapters.

Participants in the process

The key role played in the process of entrepreneurship is reflected in the efforts and activities of the lead entrepreneur, intrapreneur, or team. This is in terms of the achievement of a fit between an opportunity identified in the market place and the resources needed to exploit it. What is particularly important is that we understand that the entrepreneurs do not function in a vacuum, untouched by the social and business systems in which they operate (Carson *et al.*, 1995). Specifically, success is dependent upon the relationships developed with the following participants in the process of entrepreneurship:

- family unit and social structure in stimulating and supporting;
- financial institutions and venture capitalists who are generally required to provide the resources to fuel the process;
- state participation through fiscal and legislative reforms which are designed to foster an environment for enterprise which is conducive to success;
- a built-up and active network for complimentary skills and management abilities in order to realize the business opportunity;
- private and public-sector professionals in the provision of business advice and professional support; and
- established evidence of successful entrepreneurship to act as inspirational role models.

This represents a meshing of formal and informal networks which play a vital role in stimulating the process of entrepreneurship. The formal network consists of the professionals in both the public and private sectors. Informal networks refers to the advice and support given by family and friends, colleagues and business contacts, and other entrepreneurs. This is often of greater significance than that received through the formal network. All of these participants are joined in a partnership which results in a re-engineering of social and economic systems within the UK.

Entrepreneurship elements

The participants discussed above are obviously important elements of the process of entrepreneurship. The lead entrepreneur(s) initiates the process, and the networks containing the other identified participants support and mobilize the creation of an opportunity towards its realization. This process is generally most vigorous in an economically and competitively exacting environment. The environment both challenges and stimulates the process of entrepreneurship, the key elements of which are summarized and described in Table 1.2.

Table 1.2 Key elements of entrepreneurship

Elements	Description
Change initiation	Capability to identify an opportunity for creation or innovation, and ability to turn it into a reality
Commitment to employees	Application of appropriate management practices and reward systems designed to exact employee loyalty, retention and efficiency
Creative resourcing	Ingeniously marshalling resources, of both a financial and managerial nature, from a complex set of sources in order to mobilize and realize the opportunity
Entrepreneurial learning	Motivation to acquire the necessary knowledge and expertise through relevant exploration and reflection, in order to excel
Innovation and creativity	Renewal of products or services by adding value through application of expertise and imagination
Knowledge leadership	Development of sources of management information to enable first-mover capability, and effective strategy formulation and implementation
Opportunity alertness	Continuous focus on emerging trends and opportunities to be captured and realized
Relationship management	Maintenance of effective teams, networks, and flexible management structures
Risk and uncertainty management	Evaluation of personal and financial risk elements, self-confidence and determination to succeed
Timing of action	Acting within a limited window in which an opportunity can be optimized
Vision and strategic orientation	Formulation of ambitions, and strategies to realize them

Sources: Kirzner (1980); Timmons (1994); Carson *et al.* (1995); Goffee and Scase (1996); Deakins (1996)

These key elements of the process of entrepreneurship are now illustrated within the context of the hospitality, tourism and leisure industries (page 16).

Change initiation

Illustration: Holiday Inn World-wide, change initiation

Kemmons Wilson founded what is now called Holiday Inn World-wide in 1952. In 1951 he and his family of five children decided to visit Washington on holiday. Everywhere they went, they found that while a room cost $6–8 each child was charged $2 extra. This annoyed Wilson and he vowed to develop a chain of hotels where children could stay free as long as they slept in the same room as their parents. Wilson's hotels would also feature free parking, air-conditioning, free in-room television and swimming pool. By the late 1970s Wilson and his associates ran a hotel chain of more than 400 000 rooms.
Source: Wolff, 1994

Wilson exhibited the capability to identify an opportunity for creation and innovation of a new concept, and turned it into a reality. Undoubtedly, his actions changed irrevocably the face of the international hotel industry. In today's world, perpetual, managed change is crucial to long-term survival.

Commitment to employees

Illustration: Browns restaurants, commitment to employees

Until 1998 Jeremy Mogford was the owner of Browns restaurants, a group of four located in the university towns of Oxford, Cambridge, Brighton and Bristol. As an employer, Mogford was widely regarded as being one of the industry's best and most enlightened. This was particularly well reflected in an exceptionally low turnover of staff, and the fifteen or more years with the company that many of them had served. Mogford attributes this remarkable stability to his policy of promoting from within, and to his management practices and conditions of service. The company trained staff and encouraged them to be involved with the business through monthly meetings, where policy and performance figures were discussed and ideas welcomed. As an incentive, staff received bonuses based on turnover and monthly results. After a year's service, they were eligible for accident insurance and after two years' employment they also got private health-care cover, plus a private pension plan to which both parties contributed. Senior managers were also given permanent health insurance. 'It is incredible just how many of the people who leave return to us within just two or three years. It's simply because they've compared us with other employers and realize how much we have to offer', said Mogford.

A commitment to the development of a more professional approach to management in the hospitality industry generally has also been demonstrated by Mogford's sponsorship of young hospitality graduates to study for the Cambridge MBA. Such altruistic behaviour is extremely unusual within the hospitality industry!
Source: Hardcastle, 1996

The management practices and reward systems, of both an intrinsic and extrinsic nature, applied by Mogford yielded rewards. They resulted in employee loyalty, employee retention, and enhanced the overall financial efficiency of his businesses. Furthermore, the employees developed a sense of personal ownership and attachment to the firm. Whilst in this instance progressive policies clearly yielded results, such commitment to employees is all too often absent within the hospitality, tourism and leisure industries. Since labour costs can be a very significant proportion of turnover, there is a great temptation to achieve high productivity through minimization of staff expenditure, rather than via maximization through increased labour effectiveness. Even in capital-intensive businesses, such as leisure and fitness centres, there is a temptation to take the human resource for granted since there is currently no shortage of people who want to work in such an environment.

Since people are such a key factor in delivering services, management and motivation of them is crucial to entrepreneurial success. So whether or not there is true commitment in the way demonstrated by Mogford, there must certainly be a commitment to ensuring that employees effectively perform their service delivery role.

Creative resourcing

Illustration: Highland Mysteryworld, creative resourcing

Laurence Young is the entrepreneur behind the development of the Highland Mysteryworld visitor centre on the banks of Loch Leven in Scotland, which first opened in 1996. It is owned by the Young family, under the company name of Glencoe Adventure. The investment of £1.2 million in the project came from the Young family's personal resources of £100 000, a bank loan of £600 000 (1.9 per cent over base interest rates), and £180 000 from a local development company, Lochaber. A further £350 000 was secured because of delays in planning permission. While the permission was being processed the European Union designated the Highlands and Islands as being worthy of receiving Objective One funding, some of which Young managed to secure for Highland Mysteryworld.
Source: Guild, 1996

There is no doubt that the Young family ingeniously marshalled the resources needed to mobilize the visitor centre project. Indeed, the resourcing was so creative that, in the end, the family's own investment amounted to a mere 8 per cent of the total. The importance of adequate resourcing is explored in more detail in Chapter 5.

Entrepreneurial learning

Illustration: Pied à Terre, entrepreneurial learning

Pied à Terre is the 35-seat London restaurant of Richard Neat. It opened in 1991 and achieved two stars in the 1996 Michelin Guide. When Neat describes his background in catering, his accomplishments seem incredible. He started out as a washer-up at a nearby Little Chef 'because it paid more money than a paper round'. But, at 15, he decided he was seriously interested in the industry and gained experience in the kitchens of Pennyhill Park, Bagshot. In 1984 Neat joined London's Savoy, moving to the South Lodge country house hotel in West Sussex in 1985. While there, he set his sights even higher. He sent seven letters to various gastronomic havens in France and one letter to Raymond Blanc, who was the only chef to respond. He spent two years at Le Manoir aux Quat Saisons, leaving in 1989 to work with Robuchon at Jamin for a couple of years. He then returned to England and worked under Marco Pierre White at Harvey's, Wandsworth, for 12 months before opening Pied à Terre.
Source: Afiya, 1996

Unquestionably, Neat had the sustained motivation to acquire the necessary knowledge and expertise to eventually establish his own restaurant. Furthermore, he was determined to learn to excel, not only in terms of his technical skills, but also in relation to his business-management capabilities. As we shall demonstrate, it is the combination of specialist creative and technical expertise together with business and management acumen that can combine so powerfully to bring about entrepreneurial success.

Innovation and creativity

Illustration: Planet Hollywood, innovation and creativity

Planet Hollywood is a themed restaurant concept which was the brainchild of entrepreneur Robert Earl and movie producer Keith Barish in 1991. They own the majority of the company, but investors include movie stars Arnold Schwarzeneger, Sylvester Stallone, Bruce Willis, Demi Moore and All Stars. The outlets sell burgers against a backdrop of movie clips, loud theme tunes, and other memorabilia including Charlie Chaplin's cane, Rocky's motorcycle and Judy Garland's dress worn in the Wizard of Oz. In 1996, according to The Sunday Times' eight annual survey of Britain's 500 wealthiest people, Earl was the richest man in leisure. The survey valued him at £350 million compared with £80 million in 1995. The increase is due to the success of the Planet Hollywood chain.
Source: Armstrong, 1996

It is easy to forget that, at the time, Planet Hollywood represented an extremely innovative product within the restaurant and leisure sectors. Through the application of expertise and creative imagination, value was added to the basic, traditional restaurant concept. In return the entrepreneur enjoyed substantial financial rewards and the satisfaction of achievement. In the seven years since the development of Planet Hollywood, there have been a plethora of themed concepts which have come on stream to compete with Earl's creations. We now have themes ranging from soccer to fashion. What is innovation today soon becomes commonplace as imitative concepts are attracted by success.

Knowledge leadership

Illustration: Massarella Catering Group, knowledge leadership

Jeremy Massarella, Financial Director of South Yorkshire-based Massarella Catering Group studies his monthly sales report and finds that giant sultana scones have leapt into the Best-selling Products Table at number eight, below top-selling semi-skimmed milk, which notched up sales of 3073 units. The availability of such precise figures is a result of the company's new central distribution system, which Massarella believes is key to the expansion plans of his family's catering business. He is hoping to expand the company beyond its current management of about 116 restaurant and café units, located in department stores, at factory shop sites, and in shopping centres. Such figures are a far cry from those generated in the early days of the company. In 1860, when the Italian Massarella family settled in South Yorkshire it set up what was to become one of the largest ice-cream manufacturers in Europe. This business was sold in the 1950s to J Lyons.
Source: Davis, 1996a

Two very different eras, but the principle in both is the same. Success has been achieved through knowledge leadership relative to the particular business contexts faced by the Massarella family. This enabled them to have first-mover capability, and effective strategy formulation and implementation. Initially this was through their specialist knowledge of ice-cream making. Today the central distribution and control system brings the possibility of sustained competitive advantage in terms of both operational consistency and effectiveness.

Opportunity alertness

Illustration: Spas, opportunity alertness

Allan Wheway, former owner of Champneys, the exclusive Hertfordshire health resort, is building a business restoring people to full health. He is doing this through encouraging indulgence in the pleasures of massage, facials, aromatherapy and reflexology. These therapies have traditionally been enjoyed by women, but Wheway is attempting to also convert men to the joys of self-indulgence. He has signed a deal with Whitbread, the brewing and leisure group, to establish day spas in at least thirty of its David Lloyd leisure clubs. They will be modelled on Britain's best-known example, The Sanctuary in London's Covent Garden. However, the new crop of spas will differ in that they will not be exclusive to women, and will actively target men.

Wheway recognized that many of the sports and leisure developments were neglecting the health and beauty dimension. He has therefore been alert to the potential added-value attached to the well-known Sanctuary name. His purchase of the original Sanctuary enabled him to capitalize on what effectively is a brand. The Sanctuary is ideally positioned to take advantage of the under-exploited health and beauty market.
Source: Bernoth, 1996

Wheway is clearly focused on, and alert to, the opportunities which are emerging from new life-style trends and changing social attitudes. Furthermore, he has progressed to capture and realize one such opportunity through a very timely acquisition and a joint-venture arrangement which enables him to realize the wider potential of a well-known name.

Relationship management

Illustration: Fat Jackets, relationship management

Chris and Sue Leighton aim to make their baked potato brand Fat Jackets as famous as McDonald's. Instrumental in achieving this ambition is the creation of an appropriate corporate image. Although the Leightons have incorporated most of their own ideas into the Fat Jackets concept, Coverpoint Catering Consultancy was employed to 'pull it all together'. In addition, Chris aimed to avoid any mistakes relative to customer perceptions of their proposed brand identity through research. He said, 'We talked to about 100 customers and catering professionals, as well as people who had previously written offering us ideas'. His research also included visits to fast-food outlets in the USA.
Source: Davis, 1996b

The Leightons are astute in their establishment and maintenance of effective networks of participants in their process of entrepreneurship. Putting together new business ventures demands the co-ordination of different areas of specialist expertise. Through their desire to keep in touch with all key players, the Leightons profited from the strengths of the consultants, professionals, other USA-based operators and even customers. These all combined in a synergistic way as a result of their nurturing of these important relationships.

Risk and uncertainty management

IIllustration: My Kinda Town restaurant group, risk and uncertainty management

The late American, Bob Payton, is best remembered as founder of the My Kinda Town restaurant group. However, in 1989 he moved into the broader leisure industry in the development of Stapleford Park in Leicestershire as a country house hotel. When he was asked if a feasibility study had been done prior to commitment to the project, he replied, 'Yes, but it was a bit of a waste of time because this was a first, it was a personal vision. Nobody had ever tried to do what we were doing before: consequently there were no similar models to draw from, and the study was of little practical help. It was necessary though to show to banks and funding institutions'. The main doubt raised by potential investors was that they perceived that Payton was an expert on pizza and burgers but he knew nothing about the leisure industry. However, Payton had the self-belief to persuade them that he was actually already in the leisure business, and feeding and sleeping people required essentially the same expertise as running a restaurant. He was therefore able to convince his

> backers that, whilst the venture did constitute a risk, he had the necessary expertise to make it a success.
> **Source**: Terry, 1988

Payton was aware of the elements of personal and financial risk, and uncertainty, involved in the new project. However, his strength of determination and self-confidence moved the project forward to become a reality. Certainly providers of capital look towards minimizing the risk they are taking and the track record of the entrepreneurial team is one of the main things that gives them confidence. Even so, with new rather than imitative concepts there is bound to be a strong element of uncertainty which needs to be acknowledged and managed.

Timing of action

> *Illustration: Macdonald Hotels, timing of action*
>
> Macdonald Hotels was formed in 1990 by Donald Macdonald, formerly Managing Director of hotels at Stakis. The company began by purchasing two hotels in Scotland and then made further acquisitions, including a number from The Rank Organization and De Vere Hotels. It also manages time-share resorts in Spain, under contract for Barratt Developments, and UK hotels put into receivership by the Royal Bank of Scotland. In 1996 it owned sixteen hotels and operated a further fifty-three under contract. Macdonald Hotels had a successful stock market flotation in 1996 which netted the three founder Directors a paper profit of approximately £40 million, from an initial investment of £500 000.
> **Source**: Daneshkhu, 1996

The success of Macdonald Hotels is undoubtedly linked to the fact that it began just as the recent economic recession took hold. The strategy was to take advantage of the emerging opportunities resulting from the financially precarious situation of many UK hotels. This took the form of offering to manage hotels forced into receivership on behalf of the Royal Bank of Scotland. As the economy edged out of recession, the window of opportunity began to close and the company redirected its strategy towards a policy of acquisition. However, the original momentum was established when Macdonalds took advantage of a finite window of opportunity. The business was developed based upon the need for receivers to continue to operate hotel properties until market conditions had recovered sufficiently for them to be sold on at a reasonable price. Timing was crucially important, as was the fact that Macdonald had spotted that seemingly dreadful trading conditions in fact represented a wonderful opportunity.

Vision and strategic orientation

Illustration: Jarvis Hotels, vision and strategic orientation

John Jarvis CBE FHCIMA, Chairman, Hilton Hotels, was sleeping in the luxurious first class compartment of the plane taking him from Shanghai to Hong Kong. A few hours earlier, he had successfully opened an 800-bedroom Hilton hotel in Shanghai. Despite this success he was feeling dissatisfied. His ambition had been to own a hotel and he had not yet achieved that goal. 'I thought, Jarvis this is really silly. All you have ever wanted was one hotel and here you are a Chairman of the strongest brand of hotels in the world. You haven't achieved your ambition and it is about time you did.' He came back to London, handed in his notice and asked the City for £50 million to buy hotels. This it pledged without qualm. Jarvis Hotels was founded in 1990. In 1996 it owned and operated sixty-two mid-market hotels throughout the UK. The hotels also offer conference facilities and a chain of Sebastian Coe health clubs. In 1995 the company made a profit of £23 million and had assets valued at £323 million. It was floated on the stock exchange in 1996 to fund future expansion and investment in existing properties.
Source: Murray, 1996

Unquestionably, Jarvis had an ambitious vision as many people do. However, he also possessed a strategic orientation which was instrumental to the realization of his vision. Furthermore, he was fully committed to opportunity pursuit and realization.

Features of an entrepreneurial firm

From these illustrations, it is possible to identify the features which distinguish an entrepreneurial firm from those of a more managerial **steady-state** firm. These features are shown in Table 1.3.

However, it is considered important not to identify a firm as either purely and exclusively managerial or entrepreneurial, rather that it represents a continuum with these types at each extreme. This reflects the diversity and dynamism of a heterogeneous grouping of business interests and objectives, as recognized in Figure 1.1. In this perspective, managerial firms see the future as an extension of the past, as such strategies are based on myths, rituals, legend, traditions. Entrepreneurial firms invent their own future with only a genetic reference to the past. Their culture is based on the value and identity of the individual, vision and direction, and values the spirit of enterprise. Thus, the entrepreneurial firm is not obsessed with goals, but with direction. It is not the destination that is important but the journey, and the thrill of travelling onward, past the original destination, stretching to out-do what was achieved yesterday.

McCrimmon (1995) describes such entrepreneurial firms as glorified by independence, creativity, improvization and rebellious opportunism, thereby appealing to the child in all of us. There is a seductive attraction about the vitality and energy which often epitomizes them. However, the sustainability of this frenzied vigour must be questioned. Is it realistic to

Table 1.3 Features of an entrepreneurial firm

Feature	Description
Knowledge and learning	A learning organization which is continuously committed to the acquisition of knowledge and expertise relative to both market and management information. This is in order to maximize the firm's potential and to excel within a given activity
Opportunities	Constantly vigilant towards identifying new opportunities to be pursued, and awareness that opportunities have a limited life. Thus, the importance of acting quickly in order to optimize them
Participants	Values the contribution of participants in the process of entrepreneurship. Entrepreneurial teams are linked to a set of commonly held values. The firm has the ability to manage effectively the relationships involved
Resources	Ingenious mobilization of resources enables the pursuit and realization of opportunities without regard for the resources a firm actually controls
Risk and uncertainty	Evaluates the risks and uncertainty associated with projects, but does not suffer from analysis/paralysis in that it has the confidence to assume a certain degree of risk and is willing to learn from mistakes
Vision and strategy	Has the power to discern future prospects of success, and the ambition and strategies to progress towards achieving them. Clear vision and directions for the future are forces which bind the firm

expect a firm to be able to effectively, and continuously, implement all the key elements of entrepreneurship as presented in Table 1.3? In this respect, Goffee and Scase (1995, p. 20) warn:

> Traditional entrepreneurial enterprises are precarious with their viability dependent not only upon changes in market conditions and customer preferences, but also on the talents and energies of the proprietors. By nurturing cultures and structures which sustain their own indispensability these business owners sow the seeds not only for successful short-term growth but also – paradoxically – for their potential failure.

Thus, the more current way of thinking which recommends team entrepreneurship has the potential to address some of the vulnerabilities generally associated with traditional entrepreneurial enterprises, while retaining the very necessary qualities found in the talent and energies of the founding entrepreneur(s).

Summary

In management terms, the hospitality, tourism and leisure industries are well along the continuum from a managerial approach to one that embraces the qualities of entrepreneurship. Central to this is the role of personal initiative, whether in terms of the founder of a new venture, or within existing organizations. In the current environment this initiative may be a function of choice, or be in part coerced owing to the lack of alternative income-generation opportunities in more traditional employment.

In this chapter, the definition of entrepreneurship has been exploded to include intrapreneurship, and team entrepreneurship, which may take place to varying degrees in a wide range of business and societal contexts. This recognizes the dynamism of the process of entrepreneurship. In particular, the advantages of a team have been emphasized in addressing some of the vulnerabilities associated with independent entrepreneurship. Furthermore, it is recognized that in order to be effective, entrepreneurship requires the marshalling of all the various participants in the process through the development of formal and informal networks.

From analysis of the industry-specific illustrations, it is possible to identify positive outcomes of the process of entrepreneurship. Specifically, new concepts emerge which have the potential to revolutionize an industry sector and stimulate the competitive environment. These add vitality and can rejuvenate sectors through the introduction of fresh approaches to traditional activities. Furthermore, enlightened employee practices, or at the least effective employee management, can help achieve competitive advantage for new ventures. Through innovation and organizational renewal new markets and jobs are created. In turn these impact on the fabric of social and economic systems of industry sectors, geographic regions, and the nation, in a way that brings about wealth creation.

Reflective questions

1 Relative to your own locality, consider in what ways hospitality, tourism and/or leisure operators contribute to regional economic regeneration through participating in the process of entrepreneurship.

2 Discuss and debate the extent to which the definition of entrepreneurship is embedded in the ownership structure, size and life-cycle of a business.

3 Identify the range of participants which generally comprise entrepreneurs' informal and formal networks and discuss the degree to which they have the potential to contribute to the process of entrepreneurship.

4 With reference to the range of elements and features identified as associated with entrepreneurship in this chapter, select a major hospitality, tourism or leisure industry business and assess the degree to which it could be called entrepreneurial.

5 Consider the advantages and disadvantages associated with entrepreneurship in the context of the hospitality, tourism and leisure industries.

References

Afiya, A. (1996) Stars in his eyes, *Caterer and Hotelkeeper*, 15 February.

Anderson, J. (1995) *Local Heroes*, Scottish Enterprise, Glasgow.

Armstrong, N. (1996) Planet Hollywood boss richest man in leisure, *Leisure Week*, April.

Arnot, C. (1996) Blue chips at Harry Ramsden's, *Independent on Sunday*, 4 February.

Bernoth, A. (1996) Sanctuary pampers men, *Sunday Times*, 28 July.

Cantillon, R. (1755) *Essai sur la nature du commerce en general*, Imprint 1931.

Carson, D., Cromie, S., McGowan, P. and Hill, J. (1995) *Marketing and Entrepreneurship in SMEs: An Innovative Approach*, Prentice-Hall, London.

Cramer, J. (1996) The regeneration game, *Leisure Management*, June.

Chell, E. and Pittaway, L. (1997). *A study of entrepreneurship in the restaurant and café industry: exploratory work using the critical incident technique as a methodology*. Proceedings of Eurochrie, IAHMS conference (M. Rimmington and K. Nield, eds.). Sheffield Hallam University, pp. 271–277

Curran, J. and Burrows, R. (1986) The sociology of petit capitalism: a trend report, *Sociology*, **20**, No. 2.

Dale, A. (1991) Self-employment and entrepreneurship. In *Deciphering the Enterprise Culture* (ed. R. Burrows), Routledge, London.

Daneshkhu, S. (1996) Macdonald float to raise £23.8m, *Financial Times*, 13 February, p. 11.

Davis, G. (1996a) A family affair, *Caterer and Hotelkeeper*, 25 July, pp. 60–61.

Davis, G. (1996b) Filling stations, *Caterer and Hotelkeeper*, 30 May, pp. 46–47.

Deakins, D. (1996) *Entrepreneurs and Small Firms*, McGraw-Hill, London.

DfEE (1996) *Labour Market and Skills Trends*, Department for Education and Employment, Nottingham.

Dixon, S. (1996) Tableware tourists, *Hospitality*, August/September, p. 9.

Drucker, P. (1986) *Innovation and Entrepreneurship*, Butterworth-Heinemann, Oxford.

European Foundation for Entrepreneurship Research (1996) *Europe's 500: Dynamic Entrepreneurs The Job Creators*, EFER, Brussels.

Fass, M. and Scothorne, R. (1990) *The Vital Economy*, Abbeystrand Publishing, Edinburgh.

Fox, L. (1996) Ten out of ten, *Caterer and Hotelkeeper*, 20 June, pp. 60–61.

Gilder, G. (1971) *The Spirit of Enterprise*, Simon and Schuster, New York.

Goffee, R. and Scase, R. (1996) *Corporate Realities: The Dynamics of Large and Small Organizations*, Routledge, London.

Guild, S. (1996) Wizard wheeze, *Caterer and Hotelkeeper*, 11 July, pp. 52–53.

Hardcastle, S. (1996) Capital venture, *Caterer and Hotelkeeper*, 2 May, pp. 60–63.

Hyman, J. (1996) Pirate's bounty, *Caterer and Hotelkeeper*, 13 June, pp. 86–70.

Kirzner, I. (1979) *Perception, Opportunity and Profit Studies in the Theory of Entrepreneurship*, University of Chicago Press, Chicago.

Kirzner, I. (1980) The primacy of entrepreneurial discovery. In *The Prime Mover of Progress: The Entrepreneur in Capitalism and Socialism* (A. Seldon, ed.), Institute of Economic Affairs, London.

Lyons, V. (1994) Leeds united, *Interiors*, May, p. 8.

McCrimmon, M. (1995) *Unleashing the Entrepreneur Within*, Pitman, London.

Murray, A. (1996) Jarvis float includes £60m to fund further purchases, *Times*, 6 June, p. 24.

Naisbitt, J. (1982) *Megatrends*, Warner Books, New York.

Reich, R. (1994) Entrepreneurship reconsidered: the team as hero. In *Managing Innovation* (eds. J. Henry and D. Walker), Sage Publications, London.

Reid, G. and Jacobsen, L. (1988) *The Small Entrepreneurial Firm*. Aberdeen University Press, Aberdeen.

Say, J. (1800) *A treatise on political economy, or, the production, distribution and consumption of wealth*, Imprint 1964.

Terry, L. (1988) Bob Payton: Enthusiast and entrepreneur, *Leisure Management*, March, p. 12.

Timmons, J. (1994) *New Venture Creation*, Irwin, Boston.

Wolff, C. (1994) Checking into Wilson's world, *Lodging Hospitality*, November, p. 17.

2 Entrepreneurs

The objective of this chapter is to develop an understanding of the nature and characteristics of entrepreneurs and their central role in the process of entrepreneurship. The focus is on those attitudes and behaviours generally associated with entrepreneurs which contribute to entrepreneurial outcomes. Thus, the emphasis is not primarily on who they are, so much as what qualities they possess and what they actually do. The research literature contains many contradictions and there is no fixed formula for an entrepreneurial blueprint. During the course of this chapter we will:

- introduce historical and current thinking relative to entrepreneurs;
- consider definitions of entrepreneurs and entrepreneurial behaviour;
- explore different typologies of entrepreneurs;
- evaluate the range of research approaches adopted by academics;
- identify key characteristics associated with entrepreneurs within the hospitality, tourism and leisure industries.

Introduction

In generations gone by, the term **entrepreneur** was often used as a form of abuse, to describe individuals who had profited from a situation at the expense of others. It was associated with lower levels of society, the dealer, a **chancer**, someone out to make a **killing** financially, often within the 'black' unofficial economy. Consequently, it was seen to be the province of the exceptional, often obsessed individual, perceived as being eccentric, and frequently deviant from social norms. For example, in the 1970s Sir Freddie Laker, through his airline business, obtained great wealth in a style that was dashing and rather eccentric. Hobbs (1991) described such persons as **aggressively proletarian** in methodology and presentation! Furthermore, they were the very antithesis of the pinstriped paragons of decorum which tended to dominate established corporations of the time.

Thus, while it is a historical fact that there have always been entrepreneurs in society, what is different today is the higher esteem in which they are generally held. Culturally, in most countries being an entrepreneur has become socially and economically legitimate. Furthermore, entrepreneurs are held as role models worthy of emulation, and are associated with positive connotations such as spirit, zeal, and creativity. Burns (1991) goes as far as commenting that it would appear that the whole of the Western World is in the middle of a **love affair** with entrepreneurs. Moreover, entrepreneurs are presented as **economic heroes** (Cannon, 1991), combining the ability to innovate and challenge the established equilibrium of economy and society whilst in the process of recreating it.

However, it is also important to emphasize the central dynamic of entrepreneurship which involves both success and failure. The existence of a darker side has to be acknowledged. For example, in 1996 in the hotel industry, approximately eight companies per month were entering into a receivership or an administration order appointment. This is in addition to individual bankruptcies where entrepreneurs were legally set up as sole traders or partnerships. Chell and Pittaway (1997) reported that 80 per cent of restaurants and cafés started in Newcastle had failed within three years. The consequences of business failure have a ripple effect. They may include the loss of entrepreneurs' and creditors' capital and credibility, injurious psychological effects particularly relative to self-esteem, and social and economic losses including jobs and value to the local economy and community (Longnecker and Moore, 1991).

Different nations and communities have varying tolerance of failure relative to their cultural values. For instance, in the USA, having started a business and failed is almost seen as a **badge of honour**. In Ireland, there is a social stigma attached to it, it is like a **tattoo** on the failed entrepreneur's forehead (Prone, 1993). Currently, in the UK, banks and business advisers view failure reasonably positively. In their view, someone who has built up a business once can, even if it failed, have learned much from the experience. Consequently, their chances of success second time around are much improved. In this way, failure is seen as the key to future success.

It is important not to lose sight of the fact that, without failure, there is no success. For every successful **economic hero** there are many more who have sadly failed the entrepreneurial challenge. They and their families are living with the consequences. In this respect, Gilder (1971) asserts that entrepreneurs need a willingness to accept failure, learn from it, and act boldly in the shadows of doubt. What is evidenced is an extreme resilience and ability to bounce back from catastrophic situations. A prime example is provided by Lord Jeffrey Archer discussing his financial collapse (quoted in Jennings *et al.*, 1994, p. 28)

> … they got away with £8 million … I couldn't give a damn, entrepreneurs don't give a damn … (you have to) stand up and say, 'You have made a bloody fool of yourself, now forget it, and get on with it.

Definition

The term **entrepreneur** is not a recent invention, in fact, Cantillon (1755) has the much-quoted historic honour of coining the term in economic literature. The word is defined by the Oxford English Dictionary as:

> … a person who attempts to profit by risk and initiative.

A descriptive approach towards definition, pointing out the historical importance of entrepreneurs, is presented by Richard Branson, Virgin Management Limited (Anderson, 1995, p. 3) as:

> I am often asked what it is to be an 'entrepreneur' and there is no simple answer. It is clear that successful entrepreneurs are vital for a healthy, vibrant and competitive economy. If you look around you, most of Britain's largest companies have their foundations in one or two individuals who have the determination to turn a vision into reality. A lot of people tend to forget that some of the blue chip names of the late twentieth century such as Marks and Spencer's, Sainsbury's, Ford, Tate & Lyle were the sole traders of the late 19th century.

Further, Milne and Thompson (1988, p. 5) summarize the role of the entrepreneur in a very practical manner:

> … it takes a lot to become an entrepreneur. It demands the dedication to work long hours, and to persuade others to work long hours, at a kaleidoscope of tasks, ranging from immediate response to operational emergency, through to cool appraisal of planning and development for the future.

Summarizing this range of definitions we can see that many of today's dominant corporations, such as Virgin, Whitbread, and Forte (now part of Granada), have been spawned by individuals with vision and, importantly, the commitment to turn that vision into a reality. What they have in common is that they saw an opportunity, commercialized it, and in the process created wealth and jobs which benefit the rest of society. Such entrepreneurs are people who have the courage to go it alone. Furthermore, being an entrepreneur is not a soft option. It is hard work in operational, management and strategic terms.

Table 2.1 consolidates some of the characteristics and properties generally associated with being an entrepreneur. These can be divided into the **inputs** that are needed from the entrepreneurs to animate and direct resources, the **outputs** or **profit** of their actions. These outputs, in turn, reinforce the inputs, either negatively or positively. Furthermore, it can be observed that **profit** has a wider meaning than purely financial. The characteristics of an entrepreneur are returned to later in this chapter for a more comprehensive investigation and discussion.

A general conclusion from the review of entrepreneurship literature is that there are as many definitions as there are entrepreneurs! These tend to polarize around definitions which specify that specific action must take place, e.g. business start-up, and those which favour a definition based around enterprising traits and qualities. As such, it is considered a futile pastime to attempt to fashion a clear-cut definition of what an entrepreneur is. Perhaps, Pearce (1980) is astute in utilizing a metaphor comparing entrepreneurs with bees to describe what they do. He believes that, in most respects, entrepreneurs are ordinary human beings, seeking to do good for themselves in terms of material gain and social status. In the process they are unwitting catalysts, as with bees whose strictly private activities are the first cause of almost everything else. Their honey-seeking serves also to pollinate. Thus, entrepreneurs can be regarded as first among equals in the

Table 2.1 Entrepreneur characteristics and properties

Inputs	• Ambition
	• Creativity
	• Dedication
	• Initiative
	• Innovation
	• Management capabilities
	• Risk-taking propensity
	• Positive state of mind
	• Vision
Outputs	• Fun/pain
	• Rewards/losses
	• Success/failure
	• Satisfaction/unworthiness

process of wealth creation. In creating their own wealth, entrepreneurs also create wealth for others and bring about social consequences in the wider society.

Typologies and categorization

The admission that there is no universally acceptable definition contributes to the elusive nature of an entrepreneur. Furthermore, the imagery used in the popular press with the entrepreneur as a **hero** tends to result in an eulogistic aura which obscures understanding. In order to clarify the issue, a number of researchers have developed typologies aiming to distinguish entrepreneurs from the remainder of the population. These have been approached from the following seven key stances:

* Managerial orientation and vocational attachment, i.e. traditional, technocentric, marketeers, isolationist (Goss, 1991);
* Business format, i.e. craftsman, self-employed, small business, growth, corporate venture (Smith, 1967);
* Management-style behaviour, i.e. entrepreneur, quasi-entrepreneur, administrator, caretaker (Stevenson *et al.*, 1989);
* Stage model relative to the stage of development of the business, i.e. start-up, post-start-up, established, professionally managed (Chell *et al.*, 1991);
* Growth orientation, i.e. declining, plateauing, rejuvenating, expanding (Chell *et al.*, 1991);
* Social variables, i.e. first generation, descendant of founder, social class, minority group, female (Stanworth and Gray, 1991);
* Degree of dependence on other firms, i.e. dependent, competitive dependent, old dependent, new independent, franchise (Rainnie, 1989).

Typologies are useful in that they draw attention to the essential heterogeneity of entrepreneurs. Different motives, aspirations, characteristics and activities co-exist beneath a common banner. The danger is that the associated labelling and terminology may be misleading, or lead to attempts to pigeon-hole hypothetical stereo-typical entrepreneurs who do not exist in reality. Thus, while the limitations of typologies are recognized, the following typologies, presented in Figure 2.1 are presented as being useful in highlighting different entrepreneurial sub-groups. The model is based on the variables of growth orientation, and organizational context which recognizes both entrepreneurship and intrapreneurship. Its presentation is justified as it provides a starting point from which to structure meaningful discussion, relative to developing a comprehensive understanding of entrepreneurs throughout the remainder of this chapter.

Each of these sub-sets of entrepreneurs and intrapreneurs are products of a social development process. Their origins and life experiences may be different or the same, but their careers are markedly different. Furthermore, the

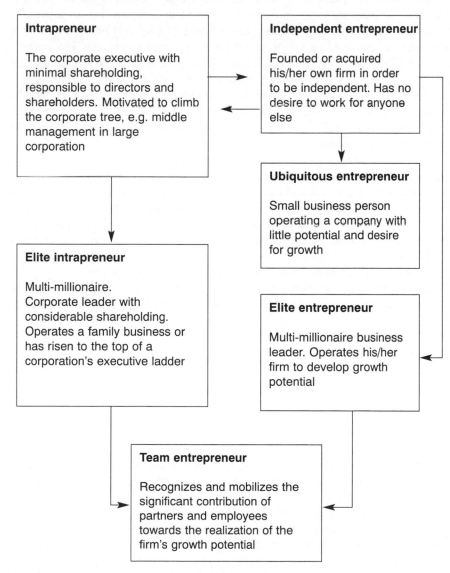

Figure 2.1 Entrepreneurial and intrapreneurial types
Source: Adapted from Jennings et al, 1994, p. 4

distinction between entrepreneur and intrapreneur reflects a difference in both attitude of mind, and ability between individuals. However, it would be misleading to suggest that once identified as an entrepreneur or an intrapreneur a person remains playing the respective role of the type. Indeed, as indicated in Figure 2.1 there may well be a cross-over in typologies given a certain set of circumstances. Each of the entrepreneurial and intrapreneurial types are now discussed, and it should be noted that the topic of intrapreneurship is returned to in Chapters 3 and 8.

Intrapreneur

Intrapreneurs envision something new and make it work. They do not start businesses, but improve existing organizations. Being an intrapreneur equates to being a change master (Moss Kanter, 1994). It is more challenging and requires more of an employee than the normal work role. However, it also has the potential to generate great self-satisfaction. Three key challenges faced by intrapreneurs are to: formulate and sell a vision; find power to advance the vision; and maintain the momentum once the vision is **bought**. Achievement requires highly effective skills of both a personal and interpersonal nature. Generally, such motivated persons will be found in middle-management positions.

Intrapreneurship appears to be unconnected with the length of time an organization has been established. Thomas Cook, the international travel company, can be considered to be intrapreneurial despite the fact that it has been established since 1841. Within this corporation change is achieved through a policy of encouraging staff to act intrapreneurially, and by investing in appropriate staff development to support the policy. The consequence is that employees actively contribute to continuous improvement of processes to the ultimate benefit of the company's profitability.

Furthermore, recent years have also seen very active intrapreneurs in public-sector organizations. Such intrapreneurs are often not motivated by profit, but by the creative buzz of developing new amenities which can impact considerably on an area's social and cultural amenities. Grant availability through regeneration funds and the UK lottery has made such activity much more feasible and a new type of intrapreneur has come forward to take advantage of the opportunity.

Elite intrapreneur

The elite intrapreneurs have risen to their positions as CEOs by working up through the corporate structure of major and highly successful corporations. While instrumental to the development and expansion of the organization, they did not financially contribute to its foundation. Essentially, the elite intrapreneurs are high-level, high-profile employees of the organization. For example, Michael Guthrie, former chairman of Mecca PLC and CEO of Bright Reasons PLC (now involved in his own new company operating roadside catering and services), and John Barnes, chairman of Harry Ramsden's.

Independent entrepreneur

Independent entrepreneurs have founded, or acquired, their own business organization. Typically, they have no desire to work for anyone else. The business is an integral part of them and reflects a desire to be alone. According to Bruce (1978) independent entrepreneurship is an act of revolution, but not in the sense of political upheaval. It enables the entrepreneurial individuals to give concrete expression to their desires and dissatisfactions. It does so in a way that brings material benefit to society. Achievement and growth is driven by the energies and vision of the solo entrepreneur. In this way, independent entrepreneurship provides a safety valve in our society. This typology refers to a multitude of self-employed persons within the hospitality, tourism and leisure industries.

Ubiquitous entrepreneur

The ubiquitous entrepreneur desires independence and achieves it through private enterprise. The firm starts small and remains small, as such it poses no threat to the established order. Even if the firm had the capacity for growth, once it had taken the growth path it would outstrip the entrepreneur's capacity to run it. Such entrepreneurs are generally moving away from a structured authoritarian situation and are motivated by a desire not to be controlled (Jennings *et al.*, 1994). This typology of a status quo, steady-state business represents the majority of firms within the UK. Examples of ubiquitous entrepreneurs are bed and breakfast operations, small specialized tour and activity firms, cafés and snack bars. As noted in Chapter 1, some academics consider that such individuals should be classed as small business operators, since their behaviour cannot be regarded as sufficiently entrepreneurial. Certainly such people were entrepreneurial at the outset of their ventures, but have since settled into the situation where they are content with their lot and are operating life-style businesses. Alternatively they may not have the necessary vision, drive or expertise to take their businesses further.

Elite entrepreneur

The elite entrepreneur represents the most successful category of independent entrepreneur. Initially, according to Jennings *et al.*'s (1994) rather critical view, those who fall into this category were searching for an unstructured situation which could be personally controlled. Later they have come to terms with authority, which they tend to manipulate to their own ends through a form of Machiavellian management. Moreover, they may often see themselves in superior roles relative to other participants in the society and economy. This is perhaps unsurprising, since they have demonstrably achieved huge success by their own efforts. Certainly, whatever their motivations and management styles, such entrepreneurs have been wonderfully creative. This type of entrepreneur is represented by individuals who have started their own companies, building them into very large corporations, for example, Charles Forte, Conrad Hilton, and Walt Disney.

Team entrepreneur

If an entrepreneur's aspirations include growing a business large and profitable enough to realize a capital gain, then perhaps they need to think in terms of an entrepreneurial team. Research (Timmons, 1994) confirms that, while there are exceptions, a team grows a business, while a solo entrepreneur makes a living. Many of the high-profile elite individual entrepreneurs are actually very proficient at building and motivating a team of specialists around them. (A more positive view than that presented by Jennings *et al*.) In this way, entrepreneurs compete by drawing on the talent and creativity of employees and partners. Thus, to compete effectively in today's world we must begin to celebrate collective entrepreneurship more, and the maverick entrepreneurs less. Entrepreneurs who have admitted the significant role of the team in the achievement of success are Prue Leith of Leith Catering, Ken McCulloch of One Devonshire Gardens, David Lloyd of David Lloyd Leisure, and Ricci Obertelli, ex-General Manager of the Dorchester Hotel.

In the interests of simplicity, the term entrepreneur as used throughout the remainder of this chapter refers to all types, unless stated otherwise.

Entrepreneurial transition

Analysis of entrepreneurs and intrapreneurs into independent, elite, ubiquitous and team typologies does not mean that a particular individual will forever remain of one type. Depending upon the individual's attributes, experience and particular circumstances they may make the transition between types, reacting appropriately to changed circumstances. Harrell (1994) refers to four transitional phases relative to entrepreneurs' careers as they develop and grow a successful business. The first category is the **entrepreneurial genius**. This is the dreamer with an idea, full of excitement, energy, and optimism. Like magnets, they draw everyone towards the realization of their dream. Second is the **benevolent dictator**, who believes completely in themself, controlling every aspect of the business, a suffocating domination of everything and everybody. In this stage, the entrepreneur think of themself as the parent teaching the children what to do. The third phase is the **disassociated director**. This is a truly confusing and frustrating time, full of distrust, inconsistencies and erratic mood swings. As the children grow up, they revolt. The entrepreneur quickly learns the organization is not, cannot be, and does not want to be dependent on them for every decision. Employees begin to trust their peers more than the entrepreneur. If this happens it is a time for the entrepreneur to let go and delegate. Finally, the **visionary leader**, is characterized by communication, co-operation and collaboration. The entrepreneur's original dream is fulfilled. They have created, built and lead a successful corporation with the ability to sustain itself.

Harrell believes that phases one and two are the stages at which most entrepreneurs excel. Phase three is a test to determine whether an individual is willing to give up the **fun element** often associated with being an entrepreneur, to become a business leader. Most entrepreneurs fail to make it through this transition, finding themselves trapped in the first two phases, destined to repeat them over and over again. These can be described as classic serial entrepreneurs. Clearly, nothing remains static. Both the entrepreneur and the business will change in nature throughout their respective life-cycles. The secret of success is that they make the transitions in tandem. The different phases which entrepreneurial businesses pass through as they develop and the challenges involved are explored further in Chapter 6.

Entrepreneur research approaches

Given the premium which society is placing on the role of the entrepreneur as the saviour of economic and social systems, it is understandable that researchers are consumed with the desire to identify what makes or moulds this precious resource. As a result, they are continuously seeking to explore the forces which shape the values, attitudes and approaches to life which lead certain people to take on the challenges of initiating, organizing, or developing activities associated with the process of entrepreneurship.

Debate tends to focus on four key questions which set the agenda for the following discussion. These ask whether entrepreneurs are:

- Purely agents central to economic development?
- A breed of individuals which are born, not made?
- Formed through exposure to social influence?
- A combination of economic agent, born and made?

Each of these questions is now addressed in turn.

Economic agents?

Key contemporary economic writers who have contributed to the development of views on the role and concept of the entrepreneur have been identified by Deakin (1996) as Say, Kirzner, Schumpeter, Knight, Shackle, and Casson. Each approach the issue from different traditions, which results in inconsistent treatment of the role of the entrepreneur. Their initial preoccupation, which has since been questioned, was with risk-taking and decision-making in conditions of uncertainty, as being fundamental to entrepreneurial behaviour. From their work Chell *et al.* (1991) concluded that there has been a gradual increase in awareness of the role of the entrepreneur in economic growth, with various approaches being used to explain motivation. However, there was no agreement as to whether entrepreneurs serve an economic equilibrium or disruptive function. Perhaps in the hospitality, tourism and leisure industries we can argue that they achieve both at the same time. Through a process of constant change (disruption) and shake out, the market for these sectors continues to keep broadly in pace with a growing and more sophisticated demand.

It can also be argued that one of the features of the hospitality, tourism and leisure industries is that, owing to the dynamic nature of their and their customers' expectations and the speed at which new supply is brought on stream, equilibrium can only ever be fleetingly attained. Individual businesses are exposed to constant change in both supply and demand. There is an almost constant state of disequilibrium brought about by economic booms, recessions, and change in market situations.

It seems rather limiting to consider entrepreneurs as either economically disruptive or agents of economic equilibrium. They certainly bring about change and have a far wider impact than simply economic. In providing new opportunities and experiences for people, they help shape our society in all kinds of ways and are hugely influential.

Born not made?

Are we to sit around powerless until some mother gives birth to the next Charles Forte, Conrad Hilton, or Walt Disney? This was certainly the perspective adopted in early studies of the origins of the entrepreneur, which concentrated almost entirely on emphasizing in-born personalities and motivations. This approach assumed that the entrepreneurial flair, the ability to take risks, and the desire to create a business were inherent in the individual – that he or she was born with these characteristics in place. This would be exhibited in the form of personality traits. Such a trait model of behaviour argues that there exists a single trait, or group of traits, in the personality of the entrepreneur which differentiates him or her from others. (A trait being a persisting dimension or characteristic of the personality.)

Whilst some of these traits may be genetically bound or influenced, they are certainly also influenced by society and learned behaviour. Each individual has a unique mix of genetic, societal and other influences which help bring about their particular traits.

Examples of traits generally associated with entrepreneurs are presented by various authors, as summarized in Table 2.2.

Whether a clearly definable entrepreneurial personality actually exists remains the subject of controversy. Many of the identified entrepreneurial characteristics are the same abilities and skills that could be applied to most successful people (Chell *et al.*, 1991), such as Olympic athletes, Premier Division football players, or leading politicians. It just so happens that the individual has chosen the arena of business as a means of self-satisfaction. McClelland (1961), a leading academic in this field, rejects the **born, not made** model. Furthermore, Deakin (1996) identifies problems associated with attempting to *measure* personality characteristics. Even if traits exist there is also the issue of to what extent they exist. Some of the problems Deakins identifies are:

* traits are not stable and change over time;
* judgements are generally subjective;
* measurement ignores cultural and environmental influences and the particular context;
* the role of education, learning and training in the entrepreneurial process is overlooked;
* issues such as gender, age, social class and education, which can have a bearing on the propensity of an individual to enter entrepreneurship, are ignored.

Table 2.2 Entrepreneurial traits generally associated with entrepreneurs

Alert to opportunities
Anxiety/neuroticism
Creativity
Decisiveness
Easily bored
Independent nature
Inner locus of control
Innovatory tendency
Leadership aspirations
Need to achieve
Risk-taking propensity
Self-confidence
Self-motivation
Versatility
Flair and vision
Self-realization through action

Sources: Schumpeter (1934); McClelland (1961); Baty (1990); Chell *et al.* (1991)

Thus, while it is clear that a number of the identified traits can generally be associated with entrepreneurial behaviour, it is extremely difficult to measure the extent to which they are present. Also this does not explain why the individual chooses to apply them within an entrepreneurial business context, rather than in some other sphere of life.

Formed through exposure to social influences?

This approach does not ignore the genetic influence on personality traits, but advances discussion through linking them to the social context of the individual. This represents a social psychological perspective which is interested in relationships between the individual and society in general. Approaches adopted to research from this perspective focus on the formative role of social influence in developing entrepreneurial tendencies.

Furthermore, it has been suggested (Carter and Cachon, 1988) that entrepreneurs often share common features and experiences of social context which distinguish them from other individuals. Examples of this were presented in Chapter 1 relative to, for instance, ethnic minority groups, family businesses, and female self-employed. These are termed as **antecedent influences** and this thinking contributes to a model of social development of the entrepreneur. This is considered to be useful in that it situates individuals within their social contexts, working through personal transitions to satisfy their changing goals, needs, and ambitions at particular points in the life-cycle. In this way we seek to understand the persistence of entrepreneurial action over time in some people, and how such action may be switched on and off as the entrepreneur moves in and out of their various **comfort or crisis zones** during their life-cycle.

Table 2.3 summarizes the features which are generally associated with the social development model of entrepreneurial behaviour.

Kets de Vries offers an extreme generalization regarding the social development of entrepreneurs. A persistently controversial author, he is quoted as follows (1977, p. 49):

> Thus, due to the frustrations and perceived deprivations experienced in the early stages of life, a prominent pattern among entrepreneurs appears to be a sense of impulsivity, a persistent feeling of dissatisfaction, rejection and pointlessness, forces which contribute to an impairment and depreciation of his sense of self-esteem and affect cognitive processes. The entrepreneur is a man under great stress, continuously badgered by his past, a past which is experienced and re-experienced in fantasies, daydreams, and dreams. These dreams and fantasies often have a threatening content due to the recurrence of feelings of anxiety and guilt which mainly revolve around hostile wishes against parental figures, or more generally, all individuals in a position of authority …

So there we have it! According to Kets de Vries it is the formative role of family background and other deprivations which shape, what he describes as, the somewhat deviant personality to be found in entrepreneurs! In his opinion, it is a personality which is insecure and unable to operate effectively in an imposed and structured environment.

Table 2.3 Social influences on entrepreneurial behaviour

Availability appropriate role models
Career experience over life-cycle
Deprived social upbringing
Family background
Family position
Inheritance of entrepreneurial tradition
Level of educational attainment
Negative/positive peer influence
Social marginality
Uncomfortable with large bureaucratic organizations

Sources: Collins and Moore (1964); Kets de Vries (1977); Chell *et al.* (1991); Timmons (1994); Deakin (1996)

Kets de Vries' perspective represents an extreme interpretation which is unlikely to fit entrepreneurs in general. Academics are generally uncomfortable with this model, as it reduces our understanding of the entrepreneur to a deviant, who is a misfit in conventional organizational life. Chell *et al.* (1991) emphasize that deviant or marginal characters exist in the population at large in the form of, for example, pop stars, tramps, and drop-outs. Thus, this certainly can not be regarded as a sufficient explanation for the development of entrepreneurs. Furthermore, successful entrepreneurs are capable of succeeding within the existing framework of society. This presupposes that their behaviour is innovatory rather than deviant. Viewed from this perspective, the entrepreneur has high energy and can be a productive member of society. Conversely according to Jennings *et al.* (1994, p. 144) entrepreneurs are:

> ... truly well adjusted individuals, in harmony with the environment and community, do not need to achieve great things but simply their own ambitions.

However, it is accepted that entrepreneurs can never form a social class owing to their mobility as they clamber up and down the social ladder, sometimes falling off either at the top or the bottom! However, that is not to say that they are exiled to the margins of society.

Human nature is such that we can rarely remain untouched by daily exposure to a range of values, situations and experiences. Every day individuals are meeting people and dealing with experiences which will influence their behaviour, attitudes and values. People live in the real world, not in a vacuum. Each person has their own life story to tell, of the experiences which have shaped, inspired and deflated them at different points in time. What is important then, is not to generalize that entrepreneurs can be categorized as resulting from being processed through a specific social development model. Life is not that simple. It can be concluded that the factors identified in Table 2.3 will surely have had an influence in the development of entrepreneurial behaviour, as they will in having developed a whole range of other behaviours exhibited by human beings.

Economic agent, born and made?

From the foregoing it is clear that the entrepreneur as an economic agent, both born **and** made, represents a more useful perspective. Cooper (1966) assists in this consolidation, bringing together the various factors which have been identified as contributory to entrepreneurial behaviour. He classifies them into three distinct groups, which are now described and illustrated in Table 2.4. (See page 40)

Table 2.4 Factors contributing to entrepreneurial behaviour

Category	Factors
Antecedent	• Genetic • Family influences • Educational choices • Previous career experience
Incubator organization	• Geographic location • Nature of skills and knowledge acquired • Contact with possible fellow founders • Experience within a 'small business' setting
Environment factors	• Economic conditions • Accessibility and availability venture capital • Examples of entrepreneurial action • Opportunities for interim consulting • Availability of personnel, supporting services, and accessibility of customers

Source: Cooper (1966)

Illustration: Alison Price, career and social influences

Few in the UK catering industry command Alison Price's reputation for bespoke upmarket catering. Her client list now includes some of the UK's leading companies and financial institutions. She caters for them at London venues such as the Tate and National Galleries. Price is also a leading restaurant consultant, creating chic and fashionable restaurants in London, including L'Express, Joe's Café, and Nicole's. She began her career as a nurse before going on to be an air stewardess for BOAC. Two very contrasting career influences on her subsequent entrepreneurial development. At 22, she married and had to stop flying in accordance with the then company policy. 'It was a good insight into organizational skills and in those days it was all silver service and napkins', she says. Price describes herself as tough, in the sense that she is a stickler for detail and pays a great deal of attention to every aspect of her business. 'If something is not up to scratch I won't let it go out. It is as simple as that', she says.
Source: Moody, 1996

Antecedent influences

Antecendent influences include many aspects of the entrepreneur's background which affect motivations and perceptions, as well as skills and knowledge.

It is clear that Price's motivations, perceptions, skills and knowledge have been significantly influenced by her previous career background and social circumstances. These factors combine with a personality which is determined to succeed, through attention to detail, in the achievement of success.

Incubator organizations

Businesses and other organizations in which the entrepreneur has previously been working may be extremely influential in entrepreneurial activity. Their characteristics can influence the location and the nature of new firms, as well as the likelihood of further spin-off effects. This represents the concept of apprenticeship (Timmons, 1994), and can be an integral part in the process of shaping an entrepreneurial career. Thus, the part played by incubator organizations, and entrepreneur role models is significant.

Illustration: Michael Gottlieb, incubator organizations

Dissatisfied with his career in the travel industry, Michael Gottlieb spotted an advertisement in the Daily Telegraph for the position of general manager with the Chicago Pizza Pie Factory. He went to see the guy behind it, Bob Payton, and the two hit it off, so Gottlieb soon found himself ensconced in the business. Payton handed him the keys and promptly went on holiday. That was to prove Gottlieb's baptism by fire into the restaurant business. 'I enjoyed it and found I was good at it. It was a very personal business and different from the traditional executive position I had been used to.' Eventually, Gottlieb became a minority shareholder. Five years later came a parting of the ways. 'I wanted to work on my own', he said. Because the City recognized him as the key man who had helped to build up the Chicago Pizza Pie Factory he had no problems in raising finance. Gottlieb himself put his life savings of £40 000 into the venture: 'I put everything on the line – personal guarantees and all that'. So Smollensky's restaurant opened its doors in Mayfair, London in 1986. **Source**: Sall, 1996

The Chicago Pizza Pie Factory acted as an incubator organization in which Gottlieb served his apprenticeship. It nurtured his skills, inspired him, and gave him the confidence to go it alone. Moreover, Bob Payton served as a role model worthy of emulation. Not all entrepreneurs have served an apprenticeship of this nature. Certainly, as we will learn in Chapter 5, providers of funds prefer this kind of preparation for entrepreneurship. However, as is often the case with entrepreneurship theory, there are so many exceptions that it is difficult to identify the rule.

Environmental factors

Entrepreneurship does not take place in a vacuum and factors external to the individual and his/her organization may make the climate more or less favourable to the birth of a new venture.

Clearly factors at work in the environment external to the firm, such as unemployment, the state of the economy and financial influences such as interest and exchange rates, will impact in terms of the available volume of opportunities and resources, and the nature of consumer demand. These combine to influence entrepreneurial activities and degrees of success achievable within certain markets.

The debate regarding the supremacy of different approaches to the development of entrepreneurs continues, and each has its individual champion.

Illustration: external influences

Vulnerability to unemployment and a perceived reduction in government aid to the individual are negatively affecting consumer confidence. As a result, a growing proportion of people's incomes will be spent on the private provision of welfare services, thus constraining true discretionary spending power. Consequently, consumers in the UK will remain cautious and the hospitality industry will have to work harder at persuading them to part with their money.
Source: Henley Centre, 1996

All contribute significantly in their own way to enhancing understanding about who the entrepreneur is and what he/she does. Cooper's approach is in itself limiting, but does provide the insight that it is different factors working together which contribute to entrepreneurial behaviour. No one approach has the definite answer but together they bring us close to some degree of understanding (Carson *et al.*, 1995). It is clear that any approach to defining what shapes an entrepreneur must work from a consolidation of understanding relative to a wide range of factors at work in society, social and family background, and the wider economy which all influence entrepreneurial behaviour (Morrison, 1998). In this way a constructive, holistic perspective can be developed, rather than attempting to categorize it according to one specific academic discipline.

Characteristics, features, attitudes, and behaviours

Each of these approaches to studying the nature and development of entrepreneurs has spawned the identification of a vast array of characteristics, features, attitudes and behaviours which are generally associated with defining who entrepreneurs are, and what they do. Timmons (1994) assists understanding in the production of a consensus around six dominant themes, which he calls **desirable and acquirable**. These are presented in Table 2.5.

Timmons' approach represents an evolving view which is that variables might be more usefully studied in clusters or constellations. Other desirable but not so acquirable attitudes and behaviours are recognized by him as:

- energy, health and emotional stability;
- intelligence;
- capacity to inspire;
- personal and ethical values.

An approach such as this, which works on the principle of a critical mass of attitudes, behaviours and features, recognizes that such a critical mass can take many different forms. Effective entrepreneurs come in very different combinations of qualities which work for them in a particular context. This approach, moreover, allows more people to be identified as potential entrepreneurs and supports the stance adopted throughout this text. Some entrepreneurs will have strengths in some dimensions which offset weaknesses in others. However, it is vital to recognize that each entrepreneur will develop these characteristics in association with the particular influences which have shaped, and continue to shape, their social development process as set out in Table 2.3. Furthermore, it has been established that these influences are not static, but dynamic in nature as the human being continually evolves.

Table 2.5 Desirable and acquirable attitudes and behaviours

Theme	Attitude or behaviour
Commitment and determination	• Tenacity and decisiveness, able to decommit/commit quickly • Discipline • Persistence in solving problems • Willingness to undertake personal sacrifice • Total immersion
Leadership	• Self-starter; high standards but not perfectionist • Team builder and hero maker; inspires others • Treat others as you want to be treated • Share the wealth with all the people who helped to create it • Integrity and reliability; builder of trust; practices fairness • Not a lone wolf • Superior learner and teacher • Patience and urgency
Opportunity obsession	• Having intimate knowledge of customers' needs • Market driven • Obsessed with value creation and enhancement
Tolerance of risk, ambiguity, and uncertainty	• Calculated risk-taker • Risk minimizer • Risk sharer • Manages paradoxes and contradictions • Tolerance of uncertainty and lack of structure • Tolerance of stress and conflict • Ability to resolve problems and integrate solutions
Creativity, self-reliance, and ability to adapt	• Non-conventional, open-minded, lateral thinker • Restlessness with status quo • Ability to adapt and change; creative problem-solver • Ability to learn quickly • Lack of fear of failure • Ability to conceptualize
Motivation to excel	• Goal-and-results orientation; high but realistic goals • Drive to achieve and grow • Low need for status and power • Interpersonally supporting • Aware of weaknesses and strengths • Having perspective and sense of humour

Source: Timmons (1994, p. 191)

Adopting Timmons' themes as a framework, each is now discussed and industry illustrations presented. This serves to enliven and inform the discussion and clearly illustrate the associated attitudes and behaviours.

Commitment and determination

Entrepreneurs are generally committed and determined characters, they need these qualities to survive. This represents a positive approach to life, in part resulting from their high level of self-confidence. Commitment is demonstrated relative to high dedication to the job. They work long hours and regard their firm as by far the most important element of their lives, with the possible exception of their families. Clearly, much of their personal fulfilment, and confirmation of their worth as successful individuals, comes from their dedication to the work ethic. A day in the life of Michael Gottlieb illustrates this high level of commitment and determination.

Illustration: Michael Gottlieb, commitment and determination

Earlier we described the way in which Michael Gottlieb came to operate his own business. He is now a restaurateur owning three restaurants in London's West End. In addition, he was chairman of the Restaurateurs Association of Great Britain (RAGB) in 1996, and writes regularly for the *Caterer and Hotelkeeper*. Such high energy output requires total commitment He has been described as brash, controversial, loud, a survivor – a ducker and diver. On a typical day he will get up at 5.30 a.m. for a run. This is followed by a 45-minute workout and breakfast. Then it is down to the office to look at the previous day's figures. The rest of the day will involve flitting between the restaurants, his duties as RAGB chairman, and sometimes interviews with the media. It will be 9 p.m. before he leaves for home.
Source: Sall, 1996

Leadership

Leaders, by definition, achieve their organizational objectives through other people. It follows that, to be successful, they must have a high degree of interpersonal skills. The leadership style will reflect the personality of the lead entrepreneur. Consequently, it can range from authoritarian to participative, however the skills required are the same. These include the ability to select appropriate team members, communication, mediation, negotiation, and persuasion skills. Furthermore, motivation and empowerment of, and the sharing of credit for achievement with, team members and/or employees is crucial. In this way, entrepreneurs appreciate their own strengths and weaknesses when it comes to managing the business. Moreover, they understand that its future prospects depend on addressing existing skills and knowledge deficits through entrepreneurial teams and external networks. Building and developing relationships to sustain an effective internal team requires strong leadership and vision. The approach adopted by Prue Leith provides an illustration of success achieved through the combination of benevolent leadership and creative teams.

Illustration: Prue Leith, leadership

In 1994 Prue Leith sold her £17-million catering enterprise to French multinational Eurest. She asserts that she could not have grown her empire, over a 25-year period, if it had not been for the support of creative teams. These enabled quality to be maintained, costs to be controlled, and profits to be maximized. One adjective keeps cropping up when colleagues, competitors, or former employees describe Ms. Leith: 'nice'. Niceness is not a quality usually associated with successful entrepreneurs, but it seems to be a major ingredient in her recipe for success. She is equally relaxed with the kitchen porter as with the chief executive of a major organization. Ms. Leith allows people to think for themselves, even if they make mistakes, and in return her staff give her loyalty, tremendous commitment, and hard work.
Source: Finn, 1995

Opportunity obsession

The entrepreneur is market-driven, continuously seeking that one idea on which the window of opportunity is opening and which offers the prospects of a worthwhile return on effort and resources, for some time to come. The entrepreneur is steeped in the market and sensitive to the challenges the market place is likely to present to the fulfilment of ambitions. Jennings *et al.* (1994) propose that while intrapreneurs also search for the next opportunity, their approach is more moderate and cautious than that of independent entrepreneurs. This may be due to seeing their role within an organization as that of a **steward**, rather than an opportunist. This may hold true in general, however there are examples of the converse being true. Both intrapreneurs and entrepreneurs understand that a systematic progression of steps is required to achieve identified opportunities. High motivation and knowledge from his previous career as an international tennis player resulted in David Lloyd being acutely sensitive to the market place. Consequently, he **exploded** with ideas for new opportunities.

Illustration: David Lloyd, opportunity obsession

Started in 1989, by 1996 David Lloyd Leisure was the biggest operator of health clubs which include tennis. By then it was owned and backed by the financial muscle of brewing giant Whitbread. Lloyd had become one of Britain's most successful sports business entrepreneurs, one of the few to make a successful transition from sports star to successful businessman. When asked in 1989 if he had any plans to diversify the company a whole list of potential opportunities flowed, including: clubs abroad; mail-order catalogue of top-quality merchandise; computer program membership card; designing and building tennis centres; and management of youth tennis training schemes. In order to realize these he recognized that the management structure of the company needs to be: 'Flexible and upgraded. You have to be ready for the explosion (of opportunities)', he said.
Source: Anonymous, 1989

Tolerance of risk, ambiguity, and uncertainty

The environment of the entrepreneur is characterized by ambiguity, inconsistencies and in substantial knowledge. For many, such an environment would be unacceptable and debilitating. For the entrepreneur, in such dynamic change lies opportunity from which the potential degree of risk is evaluated. Risk takes the form of financial and damage to personal standing and reputation. This is not only in the entrepreneur's own eyes but also in those of social peers. This results in a level of caution and measured calculation of the risk element involved in entrepreneurial decision-making. Thus, it is helpful to regard the entrepreneur as a risk-manager, rather than a risk-taker. In this role they deal with uncertainty by identifying, assessing, evaluating, managing, and transferring risk. It is a systematic process, not a function left solely to chance and luck. This represents a critical entrepreneurial skill. Despite what friends and colleagues say, George Finnegan is quite sane! As can be seen from the following illustration, he identified and evaluated a business opportunity in a rational manner. Although he is powerless to control unforeseen challenges arising from the external environment, he has the personal capability to respond positively to uncertainties.

Illustration: George Finnegan, tolerance of risk, ambiguity and uncertainty

George Finnegan had a vision of the hotel he wished to create in Dublin. It would have a country house atmosphere, located in the heart of the city. For sophisticated markets, the idea is not new. But for Dublin, where most developments were rooted in the three-star market, the move represented a departure. 'Friends and colleagues thought I was out of my mind', recalls Finnegan. He approached the venture with extensive industry-sector knowledge and expertise, and quickly built a network of professionals around him. Finnegan used their strengths to evaluate, manage and minimize the risk element. His project got underway in 1996 at a time when the IRA campaign of violence had been renewed. This is of particular significance as recent tourism marketing activity had focused on promoting the island of Ireland as one. Now tourists found it difficult to differentiate between North and South. This was out of Finnegan's control. However, he remained confident and believed that the quality of the product and effective marketing would overcome this challenge.
Source: Webster, 1996

Creativity, self-reliance, and ability to adapt

Entrepreneurs are creative and innovative. They are not constrained by existing systems, and challenge established procedures and assumptions. Thus, they often produce something new rather than just modifying what currently exists. Entrepreneurs combine these creative and innovative skills with the ability to analyse a problem and quickly reach an effective solution. Such problem-solving is seen as a fundamental skill, often not highly intellectual or rational, but more intuitive in nature. Central to this theme is an entrepreneurial learning curve which involves an experiential iterative process. It is highly personal, established from observation and confirmation of both a positive and negative nature. Thus, the entrepreneur tends to act first and learn later from experiences of his/her actions. Prior to taking over the family business, the following illustration tells how Mohammed Aslam was a bus driver with no experience in the catering sector. Through a concentrated effort of personal learning and development, combined with innovation and creativity, he responded to the requirements of the business and excelled in the role.

Illustration: Mohammed Aslam, creativity, self-reliance and ability to adapt

The Yorkshire chain of Aagrah Restaurants grew under the direction of Mohammed Aslam to a combined turnover of £1.78 million in the period 1994/1995. He took over the one-restaurant family business in 1981, when he was a bus driver with no catering expertise. Remarkably, by 1996 he was voted International Indian Chef, and won the Booker Award for Excellence as Best Entrepreneur. Vital to his success has been the focus on food that the Kashmiri Aslam would expect to eat in a Pakistani home, coupled with the creativity to go beyond standard Indian dishes. Aslam taught himself to prepare and marinate the food by carefully observing the restaurant's chef. 'I realized if you are not a chef you do not exist in the restaurant trade. So I learnt', says Aslam. He has now reached his mid-forties, and asked if he wished to slow down he smiled slowly. 'Every time we open a new restaurant, I say that is it. But then I begin to think, what can I do now? It is beyond my control to stop expanding!'
Source: Guild, 1996

Motivation to excel

Entrepreneurs and intrapreneurs are ambitious individuals with a strong passion to achieve. They are highly proactive and respond to challenges with enthusiasm, self-confidence, and the determination that they have the potential to excel. This motivation is driven by a need to achieve a combination of personal and economic goals. Thus, in addition to business profitability, many measure their success by the degree to which an inner sense of achievement has been satisfied. While entrepreneurs, perhaps more so than intrapreneurs, seem to be motivated by a self-belief that they can succeed, that does not imply a complete lack of the **fear of failure**. As business persons, entrepreneurs are both goal- and result-oriented, setting ambitious but realistically **do-able** goals. In the following illustration Ken McCulloch consolidates all of Timmons' themes in Table 2.5 to achieve excellence at One Devonshire Gardens.

Illustration: Ken McCulloch, motivation to excel

Ken McCulloch created One Devonshire Gardens in the West End of Glasgow in 1986 with a rashness he and his bankers knew was only too characteristic of the man. Everyone from the money men to Davie the painter and decorator was saying: 'Do you really think this is a good idea?'. McCulloch had the faith in creating a small,

top-of-the-range hotel in a Victorian terrace house. Conventionality is not the name of his game at One Devonshire Gardens. This can even be seen in the name itself, with no mention of the word hotel to explain the business in hand. He did not want a hotel, but a house where people could feel comfortable. McCulloch is not so arrogant as to believe the ten years have been good solely because of his entrepreneurial skills, or the sex appeal of the hotel. He takes pride in individually naming chefs, interior designers, managers, and the staff in general as all enthusiastic contributors to the excellence achieved by One Devonshire Gardens. McCulloch says: 'I don't think we are in the hotel business, we are in the amazing business. I want people to be amazed by Devonshire'.
Source: Pallister, 1996

Strong evidence that many entrepreneurs are motivated by achievement rather than simply monetary reward is shown by the existence of serial entrepreneurs. Those who, having built up one organization and achieved great personal wealth, start all over again!

Illustration: Albert Gubay and Sir Rocco Forte, serial entrepreneurship

Albert Gubay is a multi-millionaire, said to be worth around £250 million, who made his very considerable fortune from building up the Kwik Save chain of supermarkets. At the age of 70, he could be excused for taking life easy, but instead he has invested £14 million in two health and leisure clubs in Dublin. He is personally involved in their management and works between 60 and 70 hours a week! He has lots of plans for the future expansion of his leisure business, including the establishment of a sports science institute and athletes training centre alongside a further leisure club.

Sir Rocco Forte could also have been excused if he had lost his entrepreneurial appetite following the take-over of Forte by Granada. It would have been easy to feel that enough was enough, having seen the company which he had helped to build transfer into other hands following its enforced take-over. However, within weeks Sir Rocco had formed a new company, RF Hotels. The company already owns a five-star hotel in Edinburgh, has a site in Cambridge, and is developing a 120-bed hotel as part of the Cardiff Bay development. The company has also been exploring the potential for expansion into Russia.
Source: authors

Serial entrepreneurs, such as Albert Gubay and Sir Rocco Forte, are certainly motivated by much more than financial gain. Yet they do own their entrepreneurial vehicles and will profit from their development and their achievements. The advent of the National Lottery and the possibility of securing substantial funding for ambitious new projects which benefit communities and wider society has seen the emergence of a new class of entrepreneurs motivated by their passion for what they are creating. Since the organizational vehicle for such developments is a non-profit one, such as a Trust, there is no question that the people behind such ventures are in it for monetary gain. The motivation is centred purely around the desire to excel and to create something in which they strongly believe.

Lottery funding has therefore seen the emergence of a new class of entrepreneur driven by a desire to help shape society, rather than by personal gain. As we have discussed, entrepreneurs acting on their own behalf may also be driven by the desire to achieve as well as by economic considerations. However, the new altruistic entrepreneurs are an unusual new phenomenon since personal monetary gain is completely out of the equation.

Illustration: altruistic entrepreneurship

Tim Strickland and Stuart Rogers are the driving forces behind the National Centre for Popular Music in Sheffield. The Centre is to be a celebration of the nation's musical culture and an educational experience which aims to communicate the joy of music to a wide range of visitors. The £15 million Centre is primarily being funded by Lottery money and Tim and Stuart had to put immense effort and commitment behind the project for a prolonged period during which its future was by no means certain. The Centre is being developed by the Musical Heritage Trust and the satisfaction for the originators will be in seeing their passion for music bring about an exciting and ambitious new educational centre and visitor attraction.

Similar passion and dedicated commitment was also displayed by Jonathon Smales during the eight years which it took for him to see his Earth Centre vision realized. Jonathon was previously a Director of Greenpeace and is driven by a passionate belief in sustainable development and the need to provide a showcase for the way in which environmental problems can be successfully tackled, given the will and the imagination. For the first two years during which he was working on the Earth Centre concept, Jonathon was unpaid. He eventually gained a £50 million Millennium Commission award to construct the Earth Centre on a disused colliery site at Conisbrough near Doncaster. His passion for the project continues in his role as its Chief Executive and he is now engaging with the challenges of making it work, as well as getting it built.

Source: authors and Swift, 1997

Summary

While it has not always been the case, it is now socially and economically legitimate for individuals in society to opt for an entrepreneurial career. Today, entrepreneurs are generally associated with positive terminology such as spirit, zeal and creativity. However, it is also recognized that there is the darker side in the intrinsic possibility of failure. This can have a significant negative ripple effect throughout the affected families and communities.

In this chapter, the term entrepreneur has been deconstructed to include intrapreneur, elite intrapreneur, independent entrepreneur, ubiquitous entrepreneur, and team entrepreneur. This supports the stance adopted in Chapter 1, and again reinforces the dynamism of the entrepreneur and the different contexts which host entrepreneurial behaviour. Furthermore, dynamism has been evidenced relative to entrepreneurial transition which recognizes that entrepreneurs and their businesses are in a state of constant momentum as they change and adapt to the demands of their respective life-cycles. Providing the entrepreneur and business can evolve in tandem, success is possible. However, if there is a mismatch then the entrepreneur may become divorced from the venture he/she has created, or even be instrumental in its demise.

Whilst attempts to formalize one clear-cut definition of an entrepreneur were abandoned, it was generalized that he/she is first-among-equals in the process of wealth creation and also helps bring about wider social change. Furthermore, it has become evident that it is not constructive to study the person who is the entrepreneur in isolation. What is important is to consider how the entrepreneurial personality interacts within the social structure and external environment in which they are located. This provides a perspective of the factors which combine to promote and/or inhibit entrepreneurial behaviour.

Our understanding of entrepreneurial behaviour and attitudes was progressed through the application of Timmons' cluster themes to hospitality, tourism and leisure industries examples. Whilst it was fairly straightforward to find appropriate examples for each cluster theme, it has to be questioned whether there exists some exceptional person who exhibits all these themes simultaneously. For example, many entrepreneurs are independently minded, committed to pursuit of personal goals, and have the tendency to ignore the advice of others. As such, they may exhibit strengths such as rapid decision-making, adaptation to market opportunities and fluctuating trading capacities. They may even practice good employee relations and tight cost control! Such strengths may also be overshadowed by weaknesses in the entrepreneur's management capability. Clearly, the increasing support for teams of entrepreneurs is evidence of one way of addressing these vulnerabilities. The entrepreneurial team can harness the positive qualities of entrepreneurs whilst minimizing the weaknesses.

Finally, it can be observed that the rewards of entrepreneurial success are usually a mixture of monetary and psychological. Financial achievement is important to many, though not all. However, so are additional rewards such as status and respect achieved within a community; satisfaction of having achieved success as a direct outcome of personal endeavour; social benefits of flexible work patterns; and the opportunity to create wealth, employ others, and contribute to society. As we have illustrated, a new breed of altruistic entrepreneurs appears to be driven totally by such non-financial factors. On success, Richard Branson emphasizes that it is open to anyone (Anderson, 1995, p. 3):

> Entrepreneurial success shows no respect for age, background, sex, race or class. It is open to anyone, all you need is the drive and personal ambition and a refusal to listen to those who do not share your vision.

In today's world, success belongs to those committed, self-reliant, individuals who work from the heart and invest themselves passionately in their jobs. These qualities are equally relevant to both entrepreneurs and intrapreneurs.

Reflective questions

1 In society today, entrepreneurs deserve hero status. Argue either for or against this statement, and provide justification for your arguments.
2 Formulate your own definition of what constitutes an entrepreneur and entrepreneurial behaviour.
3 Select one from the range of typologies presented in this chapter. Research it and present a synopsis of your findings relative to its use in increasing understanding of the subject area.
4 An entrepreneur behaves in the same manner as any individual who is strongly motivated to be a successful sportsperson. Discuss.
5 Identify an entrepreneur within the hospitality, tourism and leisure industries and evaluate the range of entrepreneurial characteristics which they exhibit.

References

Anderson, J. (1995) *Local Heroes*, Scottish Enterprise, Glasgow.
Anonymous (1989) David Lloyd as sportsman turned leisure entrepreneur, *Leisure Week*, 27 October, pp. 11–12.
Baty, G. (1990) *Entrepreneurship for the Nineties*, Prentice Hall, Englewood Cliffs, New Jersey.
Bruce, R. (1978) *The Entrepreneurs*, Libertarian Books, Bedford.
Burns, P. (1991) *Small Business and Entrepreneurship*, Macmillan Education, London.
Cannon, T. (1991) *Enterprise: Creation, Development and Growth*, Butterworth-Heinemann, Oxford.
Cantillon, R. (1755) *Essai sur la nature du commerce en general*, Imprint 1931.
Carson, D., Cromie, S., McGowan, P. and Hill, J. (1995) *Marketing and Entrepreneurship in SMEs: An Innovative Approach*, Prentice-Hall, London.
Carter, S. and Cachon, J. (1988) *The Sociology of Entrepreneurship*, Stirling University, Stirling.
Chell, E., Haworth, J. and Brearley, S. (1991) *The Entrepreneurial Personality*, Routledge, London.
Collins, O. and Moore, D. (1964) *The Enterprising Man*, Michigan State University, Michigan.
Cooper, A. (1966) *Small Business Management: A Casebook*, Irwin, Homewood, Illinois.
Deakins, D. (1996) *Entrepreneurs and Small Firms*, McGraw-Hill, London.
Finn, W. (1995) Management a la carte, *Human Resources*, January/February.
Gilder, G. (1971) *The Spirit of Enterprise*, Simon and Schuster, New York.
Goss, D. (1991) *Small Business and Society*, Routledge, London.
Guild, S. (1996) Family man, *Caterer and Hotelkeeper*, 27 June, pp. 60–61.
Harrell, W. (1994) *For Entrepreneurs Only*, Career Press, Englewood Cliffs, New Jersey.
Henley Centre (1996) *Hospitality into the 21st Century: A Vision for the Future*, Henley Centre, London.

Hobbs, D. (1991) Business as a master metaphor: working class entrepreneurship and business-like policy. In *Deciphering the Enterprise Culture* (ed. R. Burrows), Routledge, London.

Jennings, R., Cox, C. and Cooper, C. (1994) *Business Elites*, Routledge, London.

Kets de Vries, M. (1977) The entrepreneurial personality: a person at the cross-roads, *Journal of Management Studies*, February, **14**, No. 1,pp. 34–37.

Kirzner, I. (1979) *Perception, Opportunity and Profit Studies in the Theory of Entrepreneurship*, London University of Chicago Press, Chicago.

Longnecker, J. and Moore, C. (1991) *Small Business Management: An Entrepreneurial Emphasis*, South-Western Publishing, Cleveland, Ohio.

McClelland, D. (1961) *The Achieving Society*, Van Nostrand, New York.

Milne, T. and Thompson, M. (1988) *Patterns of Successful Business Start-up*, Stirling University, Stirling.

Moody, A. (1996) Queen of banquets, *Caterer and Hotelkeeper*, 22 February, p. 93.

Morrison, A. (1998). *Entrepreneurship: an international perspective.* Butterworth-Heinemann, Oxford.

Moss Kanter, R. (1994) Change-master skills: what it takes to be creative. In *Managing Innovation* (eds. J. Henry and D. Walker), Sage Publications, London.

Pallister, M. (1996) Bringing it all back home, *The Herald*, 3 August, p. 11.

Pearce (1980) Reforms for entrepreneurs to serve public policy. In *The Prime Mover of Progress: The Entrepreneur in Capitalism and Socialism* (A. Seldon, ed.) The Institute of Economic Affairs, London.

Prone, T. (1993) *Be Your Own Boss*, Business Poolbeg, Dublin.

Rainnie, A. (1989) *Industrial Relations in Small Firms: Small Isn't Beautiful*, Routledge, London.

Sall, B. (1996) Controversial – perhaps, but still a survivor, *Hospitality*, February/March, p. 11.

Schumpeter, J. (1934) *History of Economic Analysis*, Oxford University Press, New York.

Smith, N. (1967) *The Entrepreneur and His Firm: The Relationship Between Type of Man and Type of Company*, Michigan State University Press, East Lansing, Michigan.

Stanworth, J. and Gray, C. (1991) *Bolton 20 Years On*, Paul Chapman, London.

Stevenson, H., Roberts, M. and Grousbeck, H. (1989) *New Business Ventures and the Entrepreneur*, Irwin, Boston.

Swift, M. (1997) Earth control, *Leisure Week*, 24 October, p. 4.

Timmons, J. (1994) *New Venture Creation*, Irwin, Boston.

Webster, J. (1996) A grand entrance, *Caterer and Hotelkeeper*, 4 July, pp. 48–49.

3   Corporate entrepreneurship

This chapter considers the concepts and conditions associated with corporate entrepreneurship. This progresses the stance adopted through Chapters 1 and 2 which recognizes that the principles of entrepreneurship can be employed effectively within established organizations. Thus, the ideas within this chapter are considered to be equally applicable to profit-making organizations and those within the not-for-profit sector. The chapter describes and evaluates a number of approaches through which organizations can effect an entrepreneurial approach towards their operating environment. More specifically, the chapter will consider:

- the entrepreneurial challenge for established organizations;
- conditions which impede and encourage entrepreneurial behaviour within organizations;
- intrapreneurs and intrapreneurship;
- the relevance of corporate entrepreneurship to hospitality, tourism and leisure businesses.

Introduction

The challenge facing established organizations is that they have often reached a stage of development where they may find that transformation is necessarily constrained by numerous mechanistic and bureaucratic controls. Along with a degree of centralization, these are embedded in the corporate culture as a result of the need to control ongoing operations. There is a basic tension between the organizational paradigm most suited to doing successfully what is already being done and that needed to do something different. Moss Kanter (1989) describes it as the challenge of creating a **newstream** whilst at the same time keeping up with the **mainstream**. This challenge applies whether the **something different** is a modification to existing services or procedures or whether it is a completely newstream initiative. The point is that the required organizational mind-set is different and there is tension in trying to run with both models simultaneously. The strategic implications of this tension between what Stacey (1996) terms **ordinary** and **extraordinary** management are explored further in Chapter 8, in terms of specific strategies available. Meanwhile, this chapter focuses on approaches and processes which organizations can adopt in order to become more entrepreneurial.

Intrapeneurship

What is it?

The majority of the literature on corporate entrepreneurship is concerned with intrapreneurship. Confusion abounds over what is meant by the term. For example, Shatzer and Schwarz (1991) use it to refer to what others term **corporate venturing** (the buying of small businesses to grow) as well as the building of businesses created within the organization. The definition most often adopted is that of Pinchot (1985, preface) who originated the term to describe

> Any of the dreamers who do. Those who take hands on responsibility for creat-
> ing innovation within an organization. The creator may be the creator or inven-
> tor but is always the dreamer who figures out how to turn an idea into a
> profitable reality.

As envisaged by Pinchot, this involved individuals championing new business ideas from development through to profitable reality. This is similar to the approach taken by Schollhammer (1982) in his earlier work describing **internal corporate entrepreneurs**. Schollhammer proposed that internal entrepreneurship should be used to describe formalized entrepreneurial activities within existing organizations. Such formal activities were defined as those requiring explicit organizational sanction and resource commitment.

The illustration on the following page provides examples of entrepreneurship and intrapreneurship. In essence, it is difficult to differentiate between the entrepreneurial impact of the two organizations. Both have been developed from a single unit and have become significant businesses in their own right. Thus, the question which has to be asked is, is intrapreneurship that much different from entrepreneurship?

Subsequent to Pinchot's contribution, the scope of the activities inferred by the term intrapreneurship has been widened. Geisler (1993, p. 57) refers to the internal corporate entrepreneurship activity of middle managers and the outcome of their efforts being not new ventures, 'but innovative solutions to traditional problems and new and imaginative means to deal with changes in their environment'. Geisler and others therefore extend the concept to incorporate not just the setting up of new activities but also the continuous improvement of existing ones.

This approach was also adopted by Ferguson *et al.* (1987) who discussed intrapreneuring in hospitality organizations. Good ideas, creativity, and innovation were described as being outcomes of intrapreneurship within a hotel group and a hospitality consulting company. Clearly, this concept of intrapreneurship is inclusive of a wider range of creative activity. It incorporates all kinds of employee-initiated minor-scale improvements. These can be incremental improvements to existing activities, rather than the creation and development of major new areas of business. In this respect the more encompassing view of intrapreneurship has overlapped with approaches to employee empowerment. Both intrapreneurship, in this view, and empowerment envisage a situation in which employees are encouraged to take

---

Illustration: Pret a Manger and All Bar One: entrepreneurship versus intrapreneurship

Pret a Manger was started by two former property men, Julian Metcalfe and Sinclair Beecham. As office workers in the West End of London they had been dissatisfied when they could not find a quick, tasty take-away lunch. Although not experienced in catering, they decided to remedy this. Pret a Manger was the result. Its uncompromising commitment to high standards in respect of its freshly prepared food, service and surroundings has brought tremendous success. Since its opening as a single unit in 1986, the company has now expanded to around forty outlets with a turnover of around £30 million. By any yardstick Pret a Manger has been a tremendous success story. Metcalfe and Beecham are archetypal successful entrepreneurs who have built a multi-million-pound business from modest beginnings.

Jeremy Spencer is Managing Director of All Bar One, an innovatory café bar .concept. All Bar One features light airy female friendly premises, contemporary fresh food and a great range of wines. With the opening of its first unit in Sutton in 1995, All Bar One also broke the mould by bringing new standards into an established market. It was a tremendous success, generating extremely high levels of business and delivering very high returns on capital. As with Pret a Manger, All Bar One is also being rolled out at pace and currently has a similar level of turnover.

The Metcalfe/Beecham partnership and Spencer both introduced innovatory concepts and have had the vision, energy and acumen to successfully grow the business. The difference between them is that Pret a Manger is independent, All Bar One is a subsidiary of Bass. Metcalfe and Beecham are entrepreneurs, they can make their own decisions and implement them. Spencer is an intrapreneur. He has to operate within the constraints and policies of a major PLC. Inevitably this means that, on occasions, he must necessarily compromise and do things differently than he would choose to do were All Bar One his own business. For example, Bass as a company is committed to NVQ's, a development which would not normally be seen as high priority in a business at All Bar One's stage of development. He also has to spend time representing All Bar One in its relations with the wider company. He will be expected to reach agreed growth and profit targets and negotiate capital requirements with the Company rather than with venture capital providers.

Source: authors

---

responsibility, view things critically and come up with variations on the **normal** ways of doing things, in order to deliver customer satisfaction. With empowerment, Lashley (1995) has demonstrated that the scope for discretion is bounded by carefully prescribed limits to action. Later in this chapter, we propose that that should also be the case with intrapreneurial behaviour.

In considering intrapreneurs, we are therefore concerned with people who undertake what can **loosely** be described as **entrepreneurial activity within organizations**. Are there therefore any significant differences between intrapreneurship and entrepreneurship? The consensus in the literature seems to be that the constructs of the entrepreneur and intrapreneur do overlap, as was identified in Chapter 2, but that there are also significant differences in context. Intrapreneurs have to work within the established dynamics of an existing organization. They are affected by organizational variables such as structure, processes, procedures, and culture. Geisler (1993) claims that, owing to the fact that they work within established organizational frameworks, intrapreneurs have to place more emphasis on integration and co-ordination than do entrepreneurs. Since intrapreneurs can have many different formal positions within organizations, they can also be difficult to identify. Furthermore, sometimes such individuals do not gain credit for developments that they have initiated.

Ferguson *et al.* (1987) claim that intrapreneurs do not have the temperament or desire to take their entrepreneurial instincts onto the open market. They may be averse to the personal economic risks of entrepreneurship and prefer to work in established organizations, within recognized boundaries, but with a degree of flexibility and freedom. Certainly the absence of direct personal economic risk is a significant difference between individual and organizational entrepreneurs. However, successful intrapreneurs do possess the entrepreneur's ability to take action-oriented decisions and implement them. They therefore share many of the personal characteristics and behaviours identified in Chapter 2 which are associated with successful entrepreneurs. Indeed, the characteristics and behaviours, though developed to illustrate entrepreneurship, seem to generally apply equally as well to intrapreneurship and intrapreneurs. In many respects, it is the context and setting which are different, rather than the individual and what they do.

A further issue is the degree of determinism with which the organization approaches intrapreneurship. With the more encompassing notion of intrapreneurship, there is the prospect of employees acting on their own initiative. Minor-scale innovations are devised and perhaps implemented by the employee. If the formal organization has a role, it is a reactive one to do with retrospective approval and support. However, if the initiative is more major, involving some new business activity, then there are likely to be more substantial implications for the deployment of organizational resources. It is possible that this kind of new project will require the investment of capital, rather than simply being limited to changes involving procedures or ones which lead to increased operating cost. If the investment of capital is substantial, then the project will be subject to the organization's formal capital investment approval procedures. In this situation, the organization is involved far more explicitly in determining which new initiatives will proceed. It will also probably be selecting from amongst different alternative proposals. Capital, strategic, and managerial capability constraints will inevitably mean that not every good new entrepreneurial business idea can be pursued.

Organization for intrapreneurship

In order to better separate new initiatives from the ongoing management of existing business, some organizations concentrate their more substantial intrapreneurship activities in specially designated areas of the organization. This enables clearer differentiation between ongoing management of existing operations and the development of new areas of business activity. This is the service industry's equivalent of the manufacturing and pharmaceutical industries' research and development departments. In the service industries with which we are concerned, the emphasis is often not so much on technical breakthrough, but on innovative and creative ways of satisfying customers. Once a concept is worked up and justified by initial market research, the laboratory is more likely to be a pilot unit than a behind-the-scenes simulation. Potentially, separation of new developments gives advantages in terms of better managerial focus in both new and existing business areas. A possible disadvantage is that major entrepreneurial initiatives are limited to particular individuals and areas of the organization. Those concerned with ongoing operations are expected to stick to the knitting and a control and bureaucratic culture can result. (This need not necessarily be inevitable as we will discuss.) Such separation strategies are one way in which large organizations can both have their cake and eat it

A separate area of the organization can receive special attention. At the same time, the area can establish a climate and culture which can be radically different from that in place in the ongoing mainstream business. Separateness can provide insulation from the dominant organizational values and norms. Such strategies can prove very successful and enable larger organizations to be more innovatory than their smaller counterparts. Large organizations generally have substantial funds available. Since the occasional failure of a new venture may not be significant in terms of the overall organizational assets, this means that they can better afford to take a risk than their smaller counterparts. They can also afford to attract and retain well-qualified entrepreneurial individuals, perhaps a number of them to reflect the range of expertise required in the team. If such individuals are given the necessary space and resources, then they have tremendous potential to deliver, as shown by the illustration on the following page.

Intrapreneurship can therefore be the result of new ideas conceived, tested, and implemented as a result of deliberate organizational policy and procedures. Alternatively it can occur as a bottom-up activity through the actions of entrepreneurial individuals, perhaps acting outside of their formal responsibilities. In the latter case, if the innovation is major in scope, the organization will ultimately need to respond in a supportive way and commit capital and managerial resource. Burgleman (1983) recognized these different processes by which innovation occurs, referring to **induced** behaviour as being the outcome of deliberate strategy, whilst **autonomous** innovation results from operational-level participants seeing opportunities that exceed the opportunity set proffered by top management.

Pearson (1989, p. 90) believes that in these turbulent times flexibility and responsiveness are vital. He proposes that wide participation in innovation is desirable and that organization-wide intrapreneurship should be encouraged.

> It needs to be built in as part of the entire organization, not permitted to take place in some culturally deviant sub organization. It is no longer sufficient to get round an organizational structure which cannot innovate, in today's environment such organizations need to be eliminated and replaced.

We are not convinced. Service industries are very difficult businesses to control, involving as they do the bringing together of resources and customers in a dynamic process of service provision and delivery. Particularly with the increasing emergence of brands, there seem to be compelling reasons for saying that consistency of service delivery, at least in respect of

Illustration: Whitbread, organization for innovation

Whitbread is widely considered to be a highly professional and innovatory retailer. It has successfully moved away from a product-oriented brewing culture to a customer-oriented marketing culture. In the fast-moving areas of food service, liquor and leisure retailing, constant innovation in both existing and new areas of business is required. Whitbread have a New Product Development Manager (at the time of writing this is Paul Kemp) responsible for new concept development in the restaurant area of their business. Such an organizational commitment enables the development of a number of prototype businesses, the most successful of which can then be rolled out to additional sites. Examples of prototypes developed in this way include the **Twenty Two Degrees South** Latin American restaurant concept and the **Menu Market** up-market food take-away concept. Whitbread's size means that it can try out a number of promising concepts and be adventurous and aggressive. At the same time, if a concept does not deliver the required returns on capital or the required degree of organizational fit, it will be discontinued. The company's financial resources are such that it can be relatively relaxed about the fact that some ideas will work and some will not. Indeed it can be argued that unless some concepts fail it is not being sufficiently adventurous.

Innovation is not limited to organic growth, the company's Special Projects Department can also investigate possible acquisitions. In December 1966, Whitbread bought the **Bright Reasons** restaurant business. The Special Projects Director was also responsible for rolling out Bright Reason's **Bella Pasta** chain and its operation during the roll-out phase. This illustrates that the boundary between new project innovations and operational responsibility need not be absolute. In fact it can be argued that the discipline of initial operational responsibility is desirable for those involved in development. Of course, the potential danger is that the demands of operational responsibility deflect management attention away from further innovation.

Source: *Caterer and Hotelkeeper*, 8 January 1997; *Financial Times*, 11 December 1996

its key and differentiating features, is both very important and also sufficiently difficult to achieve without attempting to innovate at the same time. Innovation is important, but it needs to be achieved other than at the expense of control. This is not to say that it should not be encouraged throughout the organization, but it is important that it should be managed in a proper way through defined systems. If not, innovation can be the vehicle for a descent into adhocracy.

As already identified, most of the larger organizations have a well-defined capital project authorization and management system. This is one outlet for employee entrepreneurship, though it focuses on achieving improvement within existing spheres of business, rather than developing completely new ones. Nevertheless, as those responsible for proposing, justifying, and implementing such new projects will testify, these initiatives do demand considerable entrepreneurial expertise. There still needs to be careful assessment as to what is required to meet market needs. For example, many of the pub retailing companies have further developed business by building accommodation units alongside existing food and beverage facilities. Such a development is at one level simply a rolling out of existing policies across the estate.

Yet decisions still need to be made regarding the number of beds required, likely occupancy and pricing levels. Once approved, liaison with surveyors, architects, suppliers and regulatory authorities will be required. The project then needs to be implemented alongside existing operational responsibilities. This is challenging. Perhaps not quite so challenging as creating a concept from new, but nevertheless a major test of entrepreneurial ability. Even with an established formula, there is risk. Few such projects come in on capital budget, or exactly meet anticipated levels of return. Variances can be as often negative as positive. It is easy to underestimate the entrepreneurial expertise required by the regional and unit operations managers involved in this process.

Neither are operating systems and business formulae static within large organizations. There are frequently defined channels for the review of existing practice with a view to continuous improvement. At the simplest level this may be via a suggestion scheme, but companies often have review groups which involve cross-sections of employees and which feed agreed changes to procedures through to relevant operational managers. Again the scope for innovation and change is channelled into improvement of the existing business. Nevertheless, it does allow an outlet for those line managers who identify better ways of doing things than provided for by the current business formula.

The challenge, therefore, is to provide sufficient available channels for employees' entrepreneurial energies that they do not need to act outside of these procedures in an autonomous way. With well-developed intrapreneurial systems and defined areas of empowered discretion, it should be possible for all employees who care about the continued success of their work organizations to contribute their ideas and expertise. Particularly creative individuals should find their niche in a **New Business Development** role. Others can find satisfaction and reward from further development and **continuous improvement** of existing business activities.

Intrapreneurship encouragement

Given that there are such different approaches to intrapreneurship, it is difficult to be specific about the conditions which support or hamper it. In any event, empirical evidence to support particular positive and negative influences is limited. Kuratko *et al.* (1990) reviewed preceding intrapreneurship research and found that it identified varied factors as being important to success. Nevertheless, some were consistently present. These factors were: the appropriate use of rewards; the availability of financial and management resources; the degree of top management support; and a willingness to take risks and a tolerance of failure. However, Kuratko *et al.* noted that much of the research underpinning these findings was based on case studies, limited surveys or anecdotal evidence. Their own empirical research, based on a limited sample within one large US company, also found support for the existence of a set of factors that need to be present if organizations wish to develop an intrapreneurial approach. These also included top management support and availability of resources, together with an organization structure and culture which facilitates intrapreneurial action. It should also be noted that this research was carried out in conjunction with a company intrapreneurship training scheme and was related to a wide participation, rather than a separatist, intrapreneurship approach.

If a decision is made that innovative efforts are to be focused in a specific area of the company, such as Whitbread's Special Projects and New Product Development Department, there is then the issue of who will be the key people in this area and how they will be supported. Wood (1988) proposes the setting up of formalized programmes to encourage what he calls **corporate entrepreneurs**. To do this it is first necessary to identify those people in the organization who are particularly aware of what is going on in the world around them, are adept at perceiving opportunities, and are action oriented – they can convert ideas into reality. Wood believes that an entrepreneurship programme should be publicized within the organization, that potential participants should then receive a briefing, and subsequently choose to apply or not. Selection is recommended to be via interview and psychological test. Successful participants are then put through an ongoing training programme covering such areas as personal development, creativity, goal- and time-management, business-plan development, networking and presentation skills. Though this may sound appealing, we know of no hospitality, tourism and leisure industry examples of such a high-profile and structured programme.

Business Development, rather than **Entrepreneurship** seems to be the name currently favoured in hospitality, tourism and leisure industries for the area of the organization entrusted with the role of innovation. Within large organizations, recruitment is normally via standard procedures. These often include psychological tests which will identify conceptual, creative and innovatory predispositions. However, despite their extensive use, psychological tests remain controversial and Blinkhorn (1991) reports that there is conflicting evidence as to their power to predict effectiveness in particular roles. Internal candidates are known and there should be an existing awareness of their backgrounds. There is much merit in the view that past behaviour is the best indicator of future performance. (In favouring this approach, it can be argued that we are supporting the activity-based definition of an entrepreneur/intrapreneur!) Those who are sufficiently action-oriented to successfully face the challenge of developing projects through from the initial perception of opportunity to feasibility, planning, piloting and launch will probably already have provided evidence of this. Of course, this presupposes that those involved in the selection and evaluation process are good judges, and are not (as can sometimes be the case) threatened by those with the capability to innovate and achieve.

Support in the literature is also given for the idea of product champions. Presumably there can also be service champions! Pinto and Slevin (1989, p. 15) describe a champion as: 'a person within the organization who uses power entrepreneurially to enhance project success'. They state that champions have four characteristics. They:

- have personal or positional power within the organization;
- are willing to use it to support a project;

- use their power non-traditionally or entrepreneurially;
- do not have to do what they do, they go well beyond their expected responsibilities.

According to Pinto and Slevin, such champions can occupy many different formal positions within organizations, but are normally fairly senior managers. They may eventually assume formal project leadership for a project, once it reaches a degree of maturity. Wood also favours the appointment of mentors to support entrepreneurs or business development managers. However, the currently favoured strategy of separating out business development into its own department means that the use of project champions or mentors is not so relevant. Within the Business Development Department there should be clear lines of responsibility and there is normally a link reporting directly to a main board director. Given these circumstances, the ability to drive projects forward is embedded in the formal structures of the business and there is less need to operate informally. Whilst the ability to operate across functional boundaries is still needed, this should be less problematic, given the clear support for selected initiatives at the highest level within the organization. Those formally responsible are effectively fulfilling the four functions of product/service champions. Whilst research by such organizational theorists as Moss Kanter (1989) has shown that the most effective organizational entrepreneurs are adroit at amassing necessary power without the support of champions, it seems to us that if an organization is setting out upon the intrapreneurial path, it should do so wholeheartedly and not rely on ad hoc, informal or unauthorized support.

It seems that achieving new development through the creation of a separate responsible department is the preferred option for larger organizations in the hospitality, tourism and leisure industries. Obstacles to development, even with this separatist strategy, have been identified by Sykes and Block (1989). They identify management practices in established organizations which, if allowed to impact on new ventures, will have an adverse effect. They state that top corporate management need to understand the inherently different management needs for new ventures compared with established organizations.

Dysfunctional management practices

Table 3.1 presents common management practices which are considered to have an entrepreneurially dysfunctional effect.

It is worthwhile considering each of these **obstacles** in relation to the issues that they raise within our service industries. In discussing them we shall also demonstrate that, whilst they potentially represent substantial impediments, in practice the industry seems adept at finding ways around many of them. The need for control also requires to be borne in mind. It is no good producing optimum conditions for new ventures without also considering that ultimately they will need to operate consistently and be embedded in the larger organization.

Table 3.1 Common management practices which are entrepreneurially dysfunctional

Practice	Effect
Enforce standard procedures to avoid mistakes	Innovative solutions blocked
Manage resources for efficiency and return on investment	Competitive lead lost, low market penetration
Control against plan	Facts ignored which should replace assumptions
Plan long term	Non-viable goals locked in, high failure cost
Manage functionally	Entrepreneur and/or venture failure
Avoid moves which risk base business	Missed opportunities
Protect base business at all costs	Venturing dumped when base threatened
Judge new steps from prior experience	Wrong decisions about competition and markets
Compensate uniformly	Low motivation and inefficient operations
Promote compatible individuals	Loss of innovators

Source: adapted from Sykes and Block (1989, p. 161)

Enforce standard procedures to avoid mistakes

In a venture's early stages the intrapreneur will need to be sensitive to new information relating to market effectiveness and operational capability. The operation will inevitably need to be modified to take account of this market feedback. However, for a venture to succeed and grow, standard operating procedures do need to be developed and adhered to. Otherwise, consistency in the product/service offering may never be achieved. Indeed, it is likely that, with a new venture, standard procedures will play a key part in differentiating and positioning the offering and bringing about success. Nevertheless, it is true that things very rarely turn out as anticipated. It is not so much a case of not enforcing procedures, but being prepared to change and modify those which are enforced.

Manage resources for efficiency and return on investment

It is certainly the case that with new ventures the main initial emphasis is likely to be on effectiveness, for instance meeting customer needs in a better way. However, without concurrent efficiency the operation will not deliver profitability and the intrapreneur will be into the **busy fool** syndrome. With a PLC considering whether to roll out a new venture, Return on Investment, as measured by Return on Capital, is likely to be vitally important, since it is so fundamental in delivering shareholder value. Indeed, enhanced levels of return are likely to be one of the major motivations for developing new concepts. Furthermore, without attention to efficiency as well as effectiveness, the true potential of a new venture will be understated.

Control against plan

Failure to meet plan in mature businesses is considered an indication of business failure. That is not to say that in service-industry sectors so heavily reliant on discretionary spending it never happens. Market conditions can change very quickly. The last recession was extremely painful for hospitality, tourism and leisure businesses. Many plans were way underachieved because they were based on extrapolations of past performance, rather than on current and future market conditions. Nevertheless, it is unthinkable that an established commercial organization would launch a new venture without a plan. It is equally unthinkable that it would not carefully monitor actual against anticipated performance, model the impact of changes, and continuously review the venture.

Planning is not confined to established organizations. Independent entrepreneurs have business plans and these are considered as an aid to development, rather than an impediment. Certainly, in the early stages of business development, plans need to be flexible and will rarely work out as anticipated in practice. Nevertheless, a plan sets out what is intended given the information currently available and at least provides an initial benchmark against which progress can be judged.

Plan long term

Sykes and Block (1989, p. 163) state that:

> ... looking beyond the current period is important to business survival. Future financing needs, personnel requirements and facility expansions must be anticipated. However for new ventures five or ten year financial and facility projections (usually to conform with some central corporate planning process) are meaningless.

We consider that this all depends on the stage of the new venture development. Certainly in the initial evaluation phase, there will be no long-term plans, simply because no decision will have been made as to whether to roll a concept out. However, a decision to roll out can involve very considerable capital expenditure and considerable impact on long-term business performance. At this stage a plan of at least three years will be required, if only to ensure that funds flow can be managed. Far from being meaningless, we would argue that long-term planning is essential if the venture is to succeed.

Manage functionally

In many kinds of business, functional specialism occurs as the business grows. The specialism that functional management brings has the potential to lead to greater effectiveness. Often lower-level management specialize from quite an early stage in their careers and may not gain multi-functional experience until they reach more senior levels. For new ventures, so this argument goes, there can be functional misjudgement if the venture team do not have the necessary mix of discipline expertise. The venture's managerial needs have outgrown the venture management team's capabilities.

We would argue that managers in the hospitality, tourism and leisure industries are far less likely to have this specialism imbalance. The dispersed decentralized structure of the industry is such that managers are very likely to gain general management responsibility at quite an early stage in their careers. Hence there should be no shortage of properly qualified employees experienced in operating across the different management specialisms, and capable of managing in a holistic way.

As a new venture grows, the scope for introducing specialist management roles will increase, but again managers in these sectors are well used to exercising general management responsibility alongside corporate functional specialists. Stephen Evans, Whitbread's Special Projects Director, had an operational background with Forte, latterly as Managing Director of the Happy Eater, Little Chef and Travelodge brands. No shortage of general management experience there! On the other hand, the importance of this background is illustrated by Pret a Manger's founders, Metcalfe and Beecham. They did not have this multi-functional experience and acknowledge that it took them two years to learn the business before they were ready to grow the brand.

Avoid risk to, and protect, the base business

The thrust of the argument is that new ventures are usually launched during the fat years of the business cycle and may be trimmed back in the lean years. Therefore, if the core business has a downturn in earnings, then it will be given priority in terms of both management attention and resources. As Sykes and Block point out, this can actually work in the opposite way. A portfolio of business activities will usually reduce risk. If a company does wish to increase its business activities, then developing them itself can be less risky than buying through take-over. Growing of new ventures organically can be more easily assimilated within an organization's existing resources than a more major take-over. Consequently financial gearing is not so likely to be stretched.

The evidence seems to be that as commercial companies grow they seek to develop a number of key business areas rather than focusing on only one. Whether they do this through organic growth or acquisition/take-over, or a mixture of both, depends on their circumstances and opportunities. The illustration opposite, again using Whitbread, provides an example of one company's approach.

Judge new steps from prior experience

The potential problem here is that if completely new initiatives are being considered, then the accumulated expertise which the organization has acquired may not be relevant and could even be detrimental. We would, in any case, argue against new ventures which are outside of the organization's core competencies (the idea of strategic fit is explored further in Chapter 8). If the new venture involves new technical expertise, then the task of the organization is to quickly acquire it. Beginning in a more modest controlled

---

Illustration: Whitbread, risk management

Certainly, a company such as Whitbread has expanded its operations both by acquisition/take-over and strong organic growth. It has moved into a number of related but different leisure-based businesses. It expanded its leisure interests, through the acquisition of the David Lloyd Leisure Centres, at the same time as growing its golfing hotels business through cherry-picking purchase of individual hotels. It has also strengthened its licensed retailing brands through the acquisition of Pelican and Café Rouge. At the same time it has continued to build its own very strong Brewers Fayre brand, broadening the brand's family appeal through the development of Charlie Chalk family fun centres. Its hotel interests are to be further developed through a tie-up with Marriott, and Pizza Hut was a joint venture with Pepsi Co. It seems that Whitbread has pursued a policy of developing a number of related leisure-based businesses. Far from retrenching into its original core brewing business, it has consistently followed this line of development during both fat and lean times. As a consequence, it is now more a leisure retailer than a brewer.

Whitbread now has several related core businesses rather than one, but it was significant that the new chief executive, David Thomas, was previously the managing director of the restaurants division. It is the retailing, rather than the previously core brewing business, that now provides the focus for the company.
Source: authors

---

way will enable the learning curve to be climbed without risk to the core business. Effectively the thorough trialling of new concepts is one way of achieving this expertise. Other solutions considered in Chapter 8 include recruiting experienced individuals, buying an existing organization, entering into a joint venture/strategic alliance, or taking on an established franchise in the business area. Such actions can short-cut the learning process.

Of course the organization has to first recognize that it is deficient in the expertise and needs to develop it. The illustration on the following page presents an approach involving trialling which, in one case provided the company with knowledge and confidence to take the next developmental steps, and in the other provided the decision-making information needed not to progress development.

Compensate uniformly

Organization-wide wages structures are common in large businesses. One advantage of these is that employees are able to more easily move about and assume different positions within the organization. Equitable earnings can be readily gauged in respect to the position to be assumed, since all management positions are graded. This is normally done according to defined criteria which should result in consistency. A salary band is then attached to the grade.

Sykes and Block (1989) consider that, since earnings level is such an important motivator, key individuals involved in new ventures should be given compensation packages which reflect the extra effort and career risk involved. It is difficult to assess the extent to which such packages are

---

Illustration: First Leisure and Blue Boar, trialling and organizational learning

First Leisure PLC is involved in a range of leisure-related businesses, including night-clubs, pubs, bowling, resorts, which include Blackpool Tower, and health and fitness. During 1995 it operated its first Snowdome in Tamworth. The Snowdome is a leisure facility which gives skiers the possibility of skiing on 'real' snow, all year round, in an indoor controlled environment. The Snowdome traded well in its first year and gave First Leisure the confidence to announce that it is to build two further domes.

This illustrates how a company will often move into a new area of activity in a fairly modest way, test out what is involved, and assess the returns which can potentially be gained. Armed with this experience, it can then decide whether to make further commitment within the area, or withdraw. First Leisure's experience with the Snowdome was sufficiently encouraging to persuade it to increase its investment.

Interestingly Blue Boar, the motorway services group, bought and for a time operated the Sheffield Ski Village (an outdoor artificial slope). However, it decided not to expand in the area. It subsequently sold the ski business to the incumbent managers and focused on its core motorway service-station business.

Both these examples illustrate how organizations can test out a new initiative in a controlled way, before entering into a significant commitment. In this way, the core business is protected whilst organizational learning takes place.
Source: authors

---

deployed at the new-venture-responsibility level within established large organizations. Certainly top management usually have in place incentives such as share options and profit-related compensation packages. It is our impression that more junior managers are more commonly motivated by the prospect of advancement, but also have performance bonuses, profit-related pay and share-option schemes. However, such share-option schemes tend to be based on overall company performance, rather than on the managers' own responsibility centres. Equity schemes more specifically linked to new ventures are difficult to administer, since the ventures are usually subsidiaries. There is the additional issue of causing resentment amongst those managers working within established businesses. It is important that they should also feel motivated and that they continue to manage existing operations well.

It is also open to debate whether earnings are such an important motivator as Sykes and Block maintain. Certainly it is our view that many managers in these service industries have a genuine passion for their work, in common with many entrepreneurs. For these managers it is the sense of achievement that is the prime motivator. Certainly earnings are important in that they are a powerful symbol and recognition of achievement. However, to be effective in this way earnings need not be directly related to the financial performance of new ventures. The following illustration provides examples of different management equity schemes.

Promote compatible individuals

This possible obstacle results from the belief that truly innovative and creative individuals are not necessarily the easiest people to work alongside.

Illustration: management equity schemes

It is more straightforward to set up equity schemes linked to the growth of new ventures when the organization is small and newly established. Such schemes can be difficult for larger organizations to compete with. At the time of deciding to roll out their Tiger Lil's restaurant concept from the existing three units to ten, Alan Lorrimer and Chris Turrell realized that they needed to further develop their operating standards and controls. They recruited Mary-Jane Brook from her position as operations director with All Bar One. What they were able to offer her compared with Bass was the prospect of considerable equity-value growth through the incorporation of share ownership in her compensation package. This effectively gives her the prospect of considerable wealth generation, providing she helps bring about Tiger Lil's success.

Within large organizations such share-equity-linked performance packages are often limited to senior directors. They are associated with the performance of the entire organization. For example, Gerry Robinson of Granada PLC has a compensation package linked to the performance of Granada shares compared with those of other companies. This motivates him to maintain Granada's earnings-per-share performance at a high level and will bring him the possibility of substantial further wealth accumulation through the granting of share options.

Sometimes the amount of wealth that can be gained causes shareholder dissension. Robinson's Granada scheme had its critics. Pension & Investments Research Consultants also accused Airtours PLC (the package holiday operators) of breaching the Greenbury code on executive pay by adopting a new long-term incentive plan for senior directors without first seeking shareholder approval. According to *The Times* (20 January 1996), the scheme is potentially worth £3.7 million to the first four Airtours directors to benefit.

A similar, though considerably more modest, scheme is enjoyed by David Michels (Chief Executive) and Neil Chisman (Finance Director) of Stakis PLC. Their share options are conditional upon them achieving growth in earnings per share over a three-year period. They will receive two-thirds of the shares if Stakis' growth in earnings per share is equal or more than the median achieved by the FT-SE 100 companies. A further third will be awarded if earnings-per-share growth meets the upper quartile performance of the FT-SE 100. Stakis also have an executive share option scheme which extends to 122 senior employees. This rewards senior managers with share options if the company's earnings-per-share growth is equal to or higher than 2 per cent above inflation. During 1996 options totalling 1 142 287 shares were granted. This gives the executive employees the right to acquire shares, during a period in the future, at a rate which should be very attractive if the company as a whole continues to make progress.

As soccer clubs rush to become PLC's there is the opportunity to link employee equity participation with success on the field. Sheffield United are reported to have offered players as well as management the opportunity to participate in share options. The value of such options will rise considerably if the club achieves promotion to the Premiership league. Other clubs seem to be limiting options to management rather than players.
Source: authors

This could be taken to correspond with the social-deviant theme identified in Chapter 2. However, we know of no existing research regarding whether innovators are incompatible individuals. Certainly they are people who question the status quo. Judging by the outcome in terms of innovation within the hospitality, tourism and leisure industries this does not seem to be a major problem.

Overall it can be seen that there **are** obstacles to intrapreneurship within established commercial organizations. Some of these apply within the hospitality, tourism and leisure industries to a greater extent than others. The structure of the industry, its highly competitive nature, and the low barriers to entry which often apply, all mean that organizations need to be entrepreneurial if they are to prosper. Consequently, as has been demonstrated, the industry has often found effective ways around such obstacles. Further specific solutions are described in Chapter 8.

Summary

The hospitality, tourism and leisure industries are widely regarded as being extremely competitive and fast moving. Given this situation, it is hardly surprising that there are so many examples of established organizations acting entrepreneurially. In a situation where all around you things are happening, it is hardly a viable option to stand still. The main thrust of this chapter is that organizations within the industries vigorously pursue different approaches in order to realize their entrepreneurial ambitions.

Certainly any form of corporate entrepreneurship represents a risk, but the structure of the industry means that such risks can often be more readily managed than in some other sectors of industry. In particular, new retail concepts can initially be developed by established organizations with very little corporate risk. Only when the performance indicators are strongly positive will the concept be rolled out and considerable organizational resources devoted to it. This is a very different scale of asset commitment than, say, investing in a new car-production line. Some companies within the industry seem to be particularly good at developing new concepts in-house.

In doing this, the challenge is to develop the newstream whilst at the same time sustaining and continually improving the mainstream. Given the perhaps conflicting requirements involved in these activities, many hospitality, tourism and leisure organizations progress newstreams in separate strategic business units. Even with this separate approach there is a danger that obstacles to intrapreneurship can spill over from the mainstream to the newstream. However we have argued that these industries seem adroit at overcoming such obstacles.

Certainly the overall picture is of a vibrant and fast-moving industry where organizations are employing a comprehensive range of entrepreneurial strategies. This is not to say that every organization within the industry is at the positive end of the entrepreneurial continuum. Certainly there are many organizations where management practices remain unprofessional. For them, there is difficulty enough in maintaining existing operations successfully, without taking on new challenges. Yet, in an industry of endless shake out, pressure on such poor performers is relentless. There now seems to be a critical mass of organizations with the entrepreneurial energy and expertise to continue to take the industry forward. As organizations seek new opportunities to create added value, customers will continue to be presented with innovatory offerings and receive the benefit in added choice and value for money.

Clearly, the organizational context of individual and corporate entrepreneurship is quite different in structure, nature and resource allocation. Consequently, corporations are enabled to apply a wider range of entrepreneurial strategies than are generally accessible to the individual entrepreneur. Such strategies are presented and discussed in Chapter 8.

Reflective questions

1 Identify the range of issues which established corporations require to address if they are to make a successful transition from a managerial to an intrapreneurial culture.
2 Describe current understanding, as evidenced in literature, relative to the definition of an intrapreneur and intrapreneurship.
3 Discuss the various organizational structures which can be put in place to encourage intrapreneurship.
4 Evaluate the approaches which have been successfully implemented in the stimulation of intrapreneurial behaviour and draw conclusions relative to the one you consider most effective.
5 Discuss the degree to which Whitbread PLC has explicitly adopted a strategy of intrapreneurship and consider the extent to which it has been successful.

References

Kuratko, D. F., Montagno R. V., and Hornsby J. S. (1990) Developing an intrapreneurial assessment instrument for an effective corporate entrepreneurial environment, Strategic Management Journal, 11, pp. 49–58.

Blinkhorn, S. (1991) Personality tests: the great debate, *Personnel Management*, September, pp. 38–42.

Ferguson, D., Berger, F. and Francese, P. (1987) Intrapreneuring in hospitality organizations, *International Journal of Hospitality Management*, **6** (1), 23–31.

Geisler. E., (1993) Middle managers as internal entrepreneurs: an unfolding agenda, *Interfaces*, **23**, Nov.–Dec., 53–63.

Kuratko, D., Montagno R. and Hornsby, J. (1990) Developing an entrepreneurial assessment instrument for an effective corporate entrepreneurial environment, *Strategic Management Journal*, **11**, 49–58.

Burgleman, R. A. (1983) Corporate entrepreneurship and strategic management: insights from a process study, Management Science, December, pp. 1349–1363.

Lashley, C. (1995) Towards an understanding of employee empowerment in hospitality services, *International Journal of Contemporary Hospitality Management*, **7** (1), 27–32.

Moss Kanter, R., (1989) *Mastering the Challenges of Strategy, Management and Careers in the 1990s,* Simon and Schuster, London.

Pearson, G. (1989) Promoting entrepreneurship in large companies, *Journal of Long Range Planning,* **22** (3), 87–97.

Pinchot, G. (1985) *Intrapreneuring: Why You Don't Have to Leave the Corporation to Become an Entrepreneur,* Harper and Row, New York.

Pinto, J.K. and Slevin, D.P. (1989) The project champion: key to implementation success, *Project Management Journal,* **20**, 15–20.

Schollhammer, H. (1982) Internal corporate entrepreneurship. In *Encyclopaedia of Entrepreneurship* (eds. A. Kent, D. Sexton and K. Vesper), pp. 209–206, Prentice Hall, London.

Shatzer, L. and Schwartz, L. (1991) Managing intrapreneurship, *Management Decision,* **29** (8), 15–18.

Stacey, R.D. (1996) *Strategic Management and Organizational Dynamics,* Pitman, London.

Sykes B. and Block, Z. (1989) Corporate venturing obstacles: sources and solutions, *Journal of Business Venturing,* **4**, 159–167.

Wood, I., (1988) Corporate entrepreneurship – a blueprint for action, *Management Decision,* **26** (4), pp. 77–84.

4   Environment for enterprise

The objective of this chapter is to consider the degree to which the social, economic, and political environment promotes or inhibits entrepreneurial behaviour in the UK. Specifically, the chapter will:

- identify the nature and role of political intervention;
- evaluate factors affecting the entrepreneur-formation phase;
- consider aspects of social structure which promote and inhibit entrepreneurship;
- evaluate government policies designed to increase entrepreneurial activity;
- consider the overall impact of the environment on entrepreneurial activities within the hospitality, tourism and leisure industries.

Introduction

It has been established in Chapter 1 that the process of entrepreneurship, whether individual or corporate, is essentially a human creative act, to which the entrepreneur is central. Furthermore, to a significant extent, entrepreneurs are products of their society. Thus, responses to events which affect them will be influenced by the value system of the society, earlier formative experiences, and their personal characteristics. Moreover, individuals may enter into entrepreneurship as a result of push and pull factors at work within their social context, such as unemployment, family tradition, need for independence, or lack of personal or financial security. Thus, this chapter explores the contributory factors which shape the degree to which the UK's socio/cultural and economic environment promotes and/or inhibits entrepreneurial behaviour.

According to Timmons (1994, p. 9), stimulation of such behaviour needs a favourable climate which combines social, political and educational attributes in the following manner:

> A culture that prizes entrepreneurship, an imperative to educate our population so that our entrepreneurial potential is second to none; and a government that generously supports pure and applied science, fosters entrepreneurship with enlightened policies, and enables schools to produce the best educated students in the world.

These attributes and the extent to which they are present within the UK will be addressed throughout the chapter, commencing with the nature and role of political intervention.

Political intervention

From when the Conservative Government was voted into power in 1979, there was a period of unprecedented political intervention aimed at the stimulation of an environment conducive to enterprise. Prior to this, economic policy had encouraged industrial, commercial, and financial mergers. Progress had been seen to lie with large technologically oriented corporations operating within a regulated economy. These goals were pursued with such enthusiasm that little attention was paid to the potentially negative psychological and social consequences. By 1979 the UK was experiencing the severest recession since the 1930s, and many large firms were making workers redundant. Consequently, politicians were searching for a fresh direction. It was believed that the creation of a new culture to stimulate enterprise, maintained by a reinvigorated small-firm sector and entrepreneurs, provided the solution. This was perceived as having the potential to enhance job creation prospects, generate a greater self-reliance by the populace, and contribute towards an ethic of self-responsibility.

So developed the ideal of entrepreneurship as a cure for the various problems in the UK. These problems were wide-ranging, from unemployment and low economic growth, to the destruction of traditional values surrounding work, family, and social responsibilities. Clearly, the appeal of a transition from a managerial to an entrepreneurial society was not solely economic but also cultural (Scase and Goffee, 1989). Moreover, if the process of political reformation was successful, it would enable the Government of the time to withdraw from hands-on, detailed economic management, and the provision of extensive personal, social, and welfare services. More responsibility would be assumed by individuals and less by Government. Thus began a far reaching programme of economic, social, and political change, initiated by the Thatcher Government.

A comprehensive documentation of public policy relating to small firms in the UK is presented by Beesley and Wilson (1984). Although now dated, it gives an account of parliamentary attention from the mid-1960s. The first formal interest exhibited was in the commission of the Bolton Committee to investigate the small firm in 1969, the report of which was published in 1971. More than twenty-five years on the Bolton Report is still widely referred to. It emphasized the characteristics which differentiated the performance and problems facing small firms from those of their large competitors, and marked the first major attempt to produce a comprehensive survey of the UK small-firm sector. The Conservative Government acted on many of the Bolton Report's recommendations. According to Goss (1991), during Margaret Thatcher's administration, the Government claimed to have introduced 108 new measures during the period 1979 to 1983 to assist the small-firm sector. This is in comparison with no specific small-firm measures during the decade of the 1960s.

The intermediate and final objectives of small-firm and entrepreneurship policy (1979–1989) are identified by Storey (1995) and presented in Table 4.1, ranked in order of priority. From this the Conservative Government perspective can be summarized as follows. As a result of an increased stock of growth-oriented firms, employment opportunities would be enhanced. These factors would combine to positively impact upon the wealth-generation potential of the UK, reflecting positively upon the policies of that Government, a tangible outcome of which would be votes gained. However, the absence of tangible targets for small-firm policies as a whole made any attempt to evaluate performance difficult. Simplistically, it can be concluded that the ultimate goal of Conservative Government policy, at that time, was wealth creation through entrepreneurship, the success of which was hoped would contribute to the retention of the Conservative party in power. However, the return to power of the Labour Party in 1997 indicates the lack of long-term success of this particular strategy.

Morris (1991) identifies that Conservative Government policy formulation, towards the creation of a more enterprising society, went through three distinct phases. This can be taken to reflect a learning curve of the policy makers. The three phases were:

- **Marxist**: external structural changes would suffice. It was felt that economic policies, designed to free the market, would be sufficient to liberate enterprise in the UK and to create the culture for enterprise. This took the form of eliminating any discriminatory policies which might disadvantage smaller firms. One example is changes to corporation tax to ensure a fairer treatment of small firms.
- **Freudian**: attempt to change 'man' himself. It was recognized that no amount of structural change could by itself affect the cultural and psychological foundations of the population. As such, Government emphasis moved towards a 'softer' approach. This involved the promotion of entrepreneurial role-models and economic heroes worthy of emulation, and information campaigns generally targeted at socially legitimizing the entrepreneurial career route.
- **Partnership and cultural engineering**: a conscious attempt to create conditions to affect a massive unprecedented cultural and psychological transformation of UK culture. The aim was to undo the damage of the

Table 4.1 Objectives of small-firm policy (1979–1989)

Ranking	Intermediate	Final
1	Increase employment	Reduce unemployment
2	Increase the number of start-ups	Increase stock of firms
3	Promote use of consultants	Foster growth in firms
4	Increase competition	Increase wealth
5	Promote 'efficient' markets	Increase wealth
6	Promote technological diffusion	Increase wealth
7	Increase wealth	Gain votes

Source: Storey (1995, p. 260).

twentieth century and release, or create, a spirit of enterprise. This led to unprecedented government intervention in education, creation of a supportive public, and partnership with the population leading to the establishment of an enterprise culture.

Thus, the objective of the resultant policies in the late 1980s and early 1990s was greater than simply to encourage more people to establish their own firms. A core theme was the promotion of a culture and environment whereby a wider section of the population would be stimulated into considering the 'entrepreneurial option'. Thus, they would become active partners with the Conservative Government in the process of cultural re-engineering.

In addition, the Conservative Government had identified the trend towards more flexible organizations and career redefinition. This trend gave further weight to the justification for the associated public policy, and put a higher premium on enterprise throughout the work force. Consequently, throughout the 1990s, policy had three main strands: influence on the general business and regulatory environment; promotion of an enterprise ideology; and direct specific assistance measures. The outcomes of these political intervention measures are discussed in detail later in this chapter.

The following illustration serves as an example of the current stage of political thought, relative to the stimulation of enterprise and entrepreneurship in Scotland. It demonstrates what is being done to create a stronger entrepreneurial culture and create a more favourable environment for enterprise. It can be observed that a number of elements are being combined to create an environment for enterprise. These include: the concept of personal enterprise is promoted to specific target audiences; development of effective formal and informal networks; and the provision of financial, managerial and technical assistance.

Illustration: Scottish Enterprise, political intervention

Scottish Enterprise's Business Birth Rate Strategy (1993) set out the main policy priorities:

- Unlocking the potential: persuading a larger number of people to set up a business.
- Improving the business environment: improving encouragement given to new starts by informal and formal business support networks.
- Improving access to finance: helping potential entrepreneurs gain access to appropriate funding to develop their business.
- Widening the entrepreneurial base: unlocking the untapped potential among women, the under-35s and non-home-workers.
- Developing start-ups in key sectors: obtaining more new starts in the important sectors of manufacturing, high-technology and business services.
- Supporting growing companies: increasing the number of starts which subsequently achieve substantial growth, across the spectrum of business activities.

These priorities have been addressed through the provision of appropriate formal institutions and programmes, accompanied by a more informal approach in acting as a catalyst to establish, for example:

- **The Business Forum**: modelled on the MIT Enterprise Forums in the USA, the forum provides a regular meeting-place for entrepreneurs. It provides support, practical case histories, promotes networking, and fosters links.
- **LINC Scotland**: LINC acts as the main body for promoting informal investment, and operates a database linking investors with investment opportunities.
- **National Seed Capital Fund**: the encouragement of new pre-start and start-up funds for growth-oriented businesses. Such funds make relatively small, early-stage investments in new and growing businesses, with conventional venture capital coming in at a later stage.

Source: Scottish Enterprise, 1993

These measures are an attempt to close the gap between Scotland and the rest of the UK in terms of the number of new businesses created. The objective is to at least equal the UK average of the number of new businesses created annually by head of population by the end of the 1990s. This currently implies that Scotland needs to achieve a 50 per cent growth in business start-ups per annum, which would involve the creation of an additional 25 000 businesses by the year 2000.

Industry sector focus

Over the two decades during which the Conservative Government concentrated on the environment for enterprise, a generally held consensus emerged. It is that political intervention should be less global and more industry-sector-focused in nature. In this way it has the potential to be tailored to special requirements, and the quality of the outcomes enhanced. Lead bodies within the hospitality, tourism and leisure industry strongly support such an approach. Thus, the special requirements of a sector can be identified and appropriate policy interventions made. This is viewed specifically in terms of developing co-ordinated and consistent policy relative to issues such as: taxation; licensing; de/regulation; and training and marketing incentives.

Thus, the industry supports the concept of political intervention, on the proviso that it is directed at addressing key issues of import. The following are two illustrations of industry responses which raise key issues for Government attention. The first was commissioned by the Joint Hospitality Industry Congress, and the second by the British Hospitality Association.

Illustration: Joint Hospitality Industry Congress, industry-sector policy focus

- Greater recognition of the importance of the hospitality industry given its significant role in employment and wealth creation.
- The desire for a unified approach to ensure co-ordination and consistent policy making including a review of government structures relevant to the hospitality industry.
- A review of transport policy, encompassing the requirements of domestic drivers and the impact of tourists.
- Further deregulation and revisions to Licensing Law.
- The development of fair and equitable taxation policies.

Source: Henley Centre, 1996

Deep!

Illustration: British Hospitality Association, industry-sector policy focus

- A thorough revamp of the Licensing Act 1964 and the Licensing (Scotland) Act 1976, bringing the law into line with social changes and consumers' needs.
- Deregulation to cut out red tape.
- A reduction in VAT on hotel accommodation from 17.5 per cent to 8 per cent, to bring the UK into line with the rest of the European Union.
- Appropriate incentives to train staff through S/NVQs and Modern Apprenticeships.
- Retaining the opt-out from the Maastricht Social Chapter.
- More backing for the British Tourist Authority for overseas marketing.
- A harmonized classification scheme based on stars, not crowns, to alleviate the confusion that these two separate schemes have caused.
- Improved access to the public-sector market for the contract catering industry by encouraging partnership and the use of audit procedures to encourage fair play.
- Clear and unambiguous policies for operators of motorway service areas, including planning criteria for future sites on motorways and intentions for motorway toll charges.

Source: Webster, 1996

At the time of writing it is too soon to ascertain the detailed impact of the new Labour Government's policy commitment to the industry. In one way it is encouraging that publication of *Breaking New Ground* (Department of Trade and Industry, 1996) has put tourism (including hospitality and leisure) firmly on the political agenda. It seems to indicate that the Government is committed to working with the industry to ensure the creation and maintenance of positive conditions in which both independent and corporate entrepreneurs can thrive. It has already been announced that a far reaching review of licensing legislation will take place. On the other hand, some argue that the very title of the Government's new Department of Culture, Media and Sport is a 'slap in the face' for the industry. Given that tourism accounts for 80 per cent of the Department's economic activity, it seems strange indeed that it does not figure in the Department's title!

Contribution of political intervention

The contribution of political intervention to the process of entrepreneurship in the UK is a complex and often controversial issue. It is recognized that the outcomes of political intervention, directed at the stimulation of an enterprise culture, were significant over the period in which the Conservative Party was in Government. Specific tangible outcomes are discussed later in this chapter.

However, Heelas and Morris (1992) identify a paradox in that the UK Conservative Government saw a need to enhance their power through political intervention in order to create an enterprise culture, against a need to diminish the role of the state in order to ensure that the enterprise culture really is enterprising. Thus, is enterprise seen as being a spontaneous human act, or an act contrived by the state? If it is spontaneous, then what was the need for public policy support? In order to justify intervention in a market economy, Storey (1995) asserts that it is necessary to identify precisely where the market failure exists and whether it is possible to rectify that market failure through intervention. The costs of intervention have to be carefully assessed and the benefits estimated. To date, there has been no such cost–benefit analysis in the UK. Thus, the rationality supporting political intervention can be regarded as somewhat dubious. It remains a question of belief, rather than a proven strategy.

Consequently, two related questions need to be posed relative to the past Conservative and current Labour Government's contributions to the process of entrepreneurship:

- Can they take sole credit for shaping an environment conducive to the process of entrepreneurship?
- Has Government policy been an independent force invoking change?

Burrows (1991) thinks not on both counts. Rather it is a result of the convergence of a set of contributory factors, including political and ideological practices. These have both mediated, and given expression to, socio-economic restructuring, which in all probability would have occurred without political intervention. Thus, the additional contributory factors in the transformation in the UK from a managerial to an entrepreneurial society are now identified and discussed. These are summarized in Table 4.2.

Table 4.2 Factors contributing to entrepreneurship

Contributory factors	Components
Political intervention	• macro policies, e.g. interest rates, taxation • deregulation and simplification, e.g. cutting 'red tape', legislative exemptions • sectoral and problem-specific, e.g. licensing law, VAT • financial assistance, e.g. Loan Guarantee Scheme, Employment Allowance Scheme • indirect assistance, e.g. information, advice, training
Entrepreneur's social development	• ideological practices • cultural attitudes, values and beliefs • personal motivations and characteristics • inter-generational role models • regional history and characteristics
Promoters/inhibitors of entrepreneurship in social structure	• employment patterns • industry-sector structure • corporate structure • economic structure • organization, production and distribution
Entrepreneurial behaviour mobilization	• political intervention outcomes • consumerism • financial resources

Discussion of these contributory factors is approached through a three-phase model presented in Figure 4.1. Incorporating the approaches adopted in Chapters 1 and 2 it combines: entrepreneur formation; entrepreneurship promotion/inhibition; and entrepreneurial behaviour mobilization of the entrepreneurship resource and behaviour within society. In this model, the social structure is recognized as being both an influencing medium and an outcome of an individual's social development. It both promotes and inhibits social action in the form of entrepreneurial behaviour. Furthermore, negative or positive outcomes, resulting from entrepreneurial behaviour, will feed back into the formation and promotion phases impacting on the degree to which future entrepreneurship mobilization is supported and encouraged within a society. Each of the phases are discussed in turn.

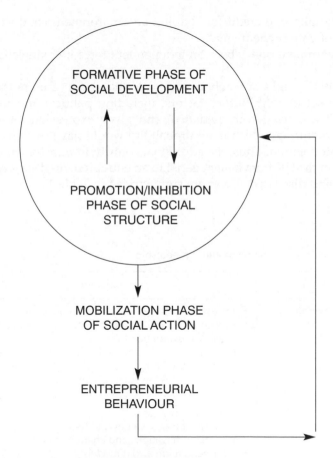

Figure 4.1 Social process of entrepreneurship

Formative phase of social development

It was proposed in Chapter 2 that entrepreneurial behaviour is a combination of born **and** made; thus, it is seen as both natural and cultural. Although people may be born with the innate spirit of enterprise, at some indeterminate point in time it may become promoted or inhibited through the social development process. Key social development influences were identified in Chapter 2, Table 2.3. Thus, the attitudes, beliefs, motivations, family background, and general socialization process of individuals within the population are significant to the understanding of entrepreneurial behaviour. In other words, the cultural context in which people are located plays an important influencing role. However, it is important to recognize that culture is not a static, but a dynamic variable. It can also be modified to the benefit of future generations, as advocated by McClelland (1961, p. 388):

> If man wants to control his destiny, he must learn to deal less in terms of the supposed reasonable consequences of historical events and more in terms of their often unintended or indirect effects on the motives and values of the next generation.

This was the perspective adopted by the Conservative Government from 1979, leading to the popularization of the term 'enterprise culture' in the UK. It can be defined as a culture in which a favourable social attitude towards enterprise is prevalent, enabling and supporting enterprise activity. It is an attempt to establish a regime whereby the individual, rather than the state apparatus can flourish, valuing the qualities and contributions of entrepreneurs and intrapreneurs alike (Heelas and Morris, 1992).

This was a response to the post-war years until 1979 which, according to Burrows (1991), were characterized in terms of the creation of an anti-enterprise, or dependency culture. This perspective was fostered by the Conservative Government, in the view that social democratic collectivism had lead to indulgence, degeneration and national demise. As such, the Thatcherite policies were presented as a painful but unavoidable 'cure' leading to the quasi-spiritual re-birth of enterprise. The aim was to effect a widespread industriousness, leading to regeneration and hence national recovery. Certainly there is a much more positive view of enterprise and entrepreneurship today.

Consequently, as discussed in Chapters 1 and 2, the prevalent culture of the 1990s in the UK is one which generally supports entrepreneurship, generating positive associated connotations. Attitudes, beliefs and motivations have changed to accept it as the norm, and not treat it as a marginal activity. This is promoted further by an inter-generational effect which provides young people with family entrepreneur role models to emulate. Unquestionably, these factors impact on the individual's social development process within the UK.

However, at a regional level attitudes towards entrepreneurship within communities vary significantly. For example, research shows that the Scots are noticeably more sceptical about, and less admiring of, the entrepreneur in their midst than people in England. Consequently, Scots have a stronger tendency to accord the entrepreneur a lower social standing. Furthermore, Scotland created 125 000 jobs from new ventures between 1978 and 1990. However, if that performance had matched Southeast England, the top UK region, an additional 195 000 jobs would have been created. Obviously, factors such as low population growth, and the lack of home ownership as a means of providing collateral and equity, skew these figures. Nevertheless, it is a fact that since the war, the Scottish economy has habitually under-performed, largely because of the failure of Scots themselves to renew their own business base. However, according to Anderson (1995, p. 8) this situation is slowly changing:

> The story of Scotland today is one which is changing its mind. For years, Scotland has lived with an extraordinary contradiction about itself – an unwritten understanding that personal enterprise and business acumen are better exercised outside Scotland than in it. At last, that culture is dying. In its place a native entrepreneurial dynamism is growing.

Thus, it can be proposed that entrepreneurial behaviour is linked to specific social structures of geographic regions, and the historical background of populations. Indeed the work of Hofstede (1980) supports such cultural specificity. He deepens our understanding of cultural issues in the provision of a framework for analysis which includes four cultural dimensions, as follows:

- **Power distance**: the degree of inequality among the people which the population of a country consider normal.
- **Individualism**: the degree to which people in a country prefer to act as individuals rather than as members of groups.
- **Masculinity**: the degree to which such 'masculine' values as assertiveness, competition, and success are emphasized, as opposed to such 'feminine' values as quality of life, warm personal relationships, service, etc. Hofstede indicates that in 'masculine' societies the differences between the men's and women's roles are larger than in 'feminine' ones.
- **Uncertainty avoidance**: the degree to which people in a country prefer structured over unstructured situations.

Clearly, each country has unique characteristics for which no one single model of entrepreneurship can account. Thus, it is apparent that the specific environment in which individuals are located is a powerful factor in the formation phase of the social development of the entrepreneur. Furthermore, it can be generalized that in the UK of the 1990s there exists a society which is going through a transition from a managerial to an entrepreneurial society. For example, this is evidenced in the 254 per cent rise in numbers of persons self-employed during the period 1980–1991, from 1.3 to 3.3 million (DfEE, 1996).

Consequently, within today's society new generations are being cut loose from the confines of traditional, expected roles. Societal norms are changing. Individuals are free to establish new social roles. Furthermore, the economic appeal of entrepreneurship is now culturally salient. This may lead to the emergence of a fresh resource of persons possessing a driving desire to achieve. Some of these young people will become entrepreneurs, directly active in the economic development process. The success of their activities will be dependent upon the factors at work within the social structure. These are now addressed.

Promotion/inhibition phase of social structure

Kirzner (1980) proposes that an economically successful society is one whose members pursue the 'right' set of co-ordinated actions. Thus, it follows that the ideal economic organization for a society consists of the pattern of institutions and incentives which will promote the pursuit of the 'right' set of actions by its members. This relates to structural considerations of: employment patterns; industry sectors; corporate organization; the economy; and organization, production, and distribution. These combine to form a pattern of institutions, conditions and incentives which may, or may not, promote a 'right' set of co-ordinated actions from members of the UK population. This pattern is now investigated. The degree to which entrepreneurship is promoted or inhibited within the UK today is summarized in Table 4.3.

Table 4.3 Structural promoters/inhibitors of entrepreneurship

Structural element	Entrepreneurship effect
Employment patterns	Current employment patterns promote entrepreneurship. This is due to the push/pull effect of self-employment as an alternative to unemployment, or insecurity within employment, accompanied by career redefinition to incorporate the concept of entrepreneurship.
Industry sector	The service sector in general promotes small-scale firms and entrepreneurship. It tends to have lower barriers to entry than those of the manufacturing sector, as such the potential volume of opportunities for new venture creation are numerous. However, competition is a fierce, challenging force.
Corporate	Restructuring is promoting entrepreneurship. As large corporations slim their operations to focus on core activities, there is the generation of a range of opportunities which can be addressed. These include creation of new firms, management buy-outs, and niche-market developments. Second, resultant flattened hierarchies recognize the value of the human capital of the employee, and the adoption of policies to encourage intrapreneurship.
Economy	A promoter owing to recognition of the distinct contribution made by individuals, and the multiplier effect experienced as a result of an increase in entrepreneurial activity. As a consequence of restructuring many firms faced financial failure. This may be seen as both a promoter and an inhibitor of future entrepreneurial behaviour.
Organization, production and distribution	Changes in organization, production and distribution within industry sectors both promote and inhibit entrepreneurship. These changes have been driven by technological developments but also by marketing through brand development. Changes can promote new business opportunities, they can also inhibit entrepreneurship in traditional enterprises, such as travel agents.

From Table 4.3, it can be observed that the forces at work in the social structure are strongly promoting entrepreneurship and intrapreneurship within the industry sector. Inhibitors are recognized as the failure factor, and a challenging competitive environment. Alternatively, given the entrepreneur's tolerance of uncertainty and ambiguity, it could be argued that these, in fact, are promoters. Each of the elements are now discussed in detail and related to the hospitality, tourism and leisure industries.

Employment patterns

The nature of work is changing. The proportion of the population who have full-time and permanent work is falling, though full-time employees still form a majority of the employment labour force (61 per cent). More people are now self-employed, or are moving to, and between, part-time and temporary jobs, or are in employment which is flexible in some other way (DfEE, 1996). This is evidenced in trends such as contracting out, management contracts, part-time arrangements, and job-sharing. As such, the concept of a job for life, with its planned career structure, no longer exists. This has led to a need to re-define what is meant by a 'career'. In particular as a consequence, self-employment is expected to grow substantially (13 per cent) during the period 1994–2001, about twice the overall employment rate. The following illustrates how changes in employment patterns and attitudes are encouraging more people, and specifically the young, into self-employment.

Illustration: Adventures in Golf, attitudes to self-employment

Adventures in Golf is a company owned by Jamie Gardner which organizes golf excursions and tournaments for individuals and groups. When it came to graduation he decided he did not want to do the traditional milkround: 'I just couldn't see any part of industry or line of work which was attractive to me'. From this it was a short step to self-employment. 'I had no ties and felt that this was the best time to start-up.' Initially, growth was slower than expected. He was under no illusions that it would be easy and as most of his marketing was by word of mouth, it took time to develop the leads. At the same time, it was hard to secure finance from banks as he had no track record. However, he overcame these problems through good financial management and tight controls on his expenditure.
Source: Scottish Enterprise Foundation, 1995

Industry-sector restructuring

During the 1980s, employment growth was totally dominated by the expansion of the service sector. Between 1981 and 1991 service industries increased their employment by almost 2.4 million. This outstripped the economy-wide increase in employment, which was only 1.5 million, because of the decline in primary and manufacturing employment. Over the period 1994–2001 it is predicted that manufacturing will lose 200 000 jobs from its total. By contrast the broad business and miscellaneous service sector is expected to gain over

1.1 million jobs (DfEE, 1996). Today, the vast majority (97 per cent) of British businesses have fewer than twenty employees.

This profile of services represents the typical pattern within the hospitality, tourism and leisure industries, with the majority of firms, such as bookmakers, leisure centres, travel agents, and bed and breakfasts, located at service points close to the customer. In ownership terms, firms range from international corporations to the self-employed independent operator. However, small and medium-sized enterprises continue to make up the majority of the operating units. For example, according to Keynote (1997) 68.7 per cent of hotels in the UK have a turnover of less than £250 000. Furthermore, the nature of the industry is such that there are few barriers to entry. Significant opportunities for entrepreneurs abound. Reasons for this are that services are generally geographically dispersed, service local market needs, and are often embedded in local culture. The vitality of many of these small business is recognized as a strength of the industry (Henley Centre, 1996).

However, as the industry matures there is creeping domination by large conglomerates, increasingly participating over more than one industry sector. For instance, Ladbroke (the betting company) owns Hilton International; Stakis Hotels also operate casinos; Bass (the brewer and pub operator) owns Holiday Inns; and the Rank organization operate Odeon cinemas, bingo, and multi-leisure centres. It is clear that there is a distinct blurring of spheres of activity. However, within the UK catering industry, for example, there are 300 000 outlets, and Granada as the largest single company owns only 750. Thus, there still remains room for the smaller operator to flourish. The following illustrates the typical role, characteristics, and contributions of firms within the industry structure.

Illustration: Bath, industry structure

Discovered by the Romans and transformed during the Georgian era into an elegant city, Bath has welcomed visitors for almost two millennia. In the 1990s, it is more popular than ever, with an estimated two million tourists flocking to soak up its history and culture every year. Not surprisingly, tourism provides a substantial boost for its economy, with some 79 per cent of the working population employed in the service industries. Approximately 3500 businesses are based within the city. A large proportion of local firms employ fewer than twenty-five people, reflecting the national trend. Job losses in manufacturing have been more than compensated by the boom in the service industries, hotel and catering in particular, and employment has increased significantly in recent years.
Source: Thompson, 1996

Corporate restructuring

Many corporations are either down-sizing, de-layering, out-sourcing, re-engineering, globalizing, collaborating, forming multi-disciplinary teams, and/or acquiring other companies. For instance, Granada acquired the Forte group for £3.9 billion in 1996, only to sell-off certain divisions, such as Heritage Hotels, as they did not add value to the company's portfolio. Successful businesses are recognizing the importance of the ability to focus on core activities, adapting quickly and innovating within specific niche markets. The entrepreneur is responding to opportunities which emerge from corporate restructuring in the form of new venture creation, management buy-outs, and niche market development. The illustration provides an example of corporate restructuring activity which has generated an entrepreneurial opportunity.

Illustration: BE Services, corporate restructuring

The Bank of England is preparing to shut down BE Services, its in-house catering subsidiary, which has fed the bank's 2500 City-based employees for the past two decades. The managing director and manager of catering services of BE Services are to carry out a management buy-out of the business, with financial backing coming from the bank. The bank's catering contract is believed to be worth around £1.5 million per year in turnover.

Source: Huddart, 1997

One of the consequences of corporate restructuring is that employees are working in flatter, more customer-focused structures, within which the value of human capital is being realized, both in terms of the entrepreneur and the intrapreneur. The intrapreneurs are directing policies at establishing cultures which support teams, autonomous work groups, reward systems and empowerment. Below is an illustration of employee empowerment, which we have earlier argued can be considered intrapreneurial.

Illustration: TGI Friday, employee empowerment

TGI Friday is one organization in the hospitality industry which aims to create the necessary sense of ownership and empowerment which will enable employees to act entrepreneurially. While service standards and production processes are highly standardized, elements of the service are customized to specific customer needs. Front-line staff are encouraged to develop a sense of ownership of the service encounter. Despite having a standard uniform they are able to customize their own appearance by personalizing their head gear and by adding badges to their braces. In addition, a system of individualized rewards gives employees a personal stake in meeting business objectives, and group dynamics are engaged through team briefing sessions. Strategies for the management of employees involve a package of recruitment and selection, induction, training, reward and appraisal processes, all designed to empower employees to act entrepreneurially.
Source: Lashley, 1996

Economic restructuring

Recognition of the distinctive contribution of the individual in the process of economic restructuring ensures that the process of entrepreneurship is supported by policy makers. According to research (Henley Centre, 1996) the hospitality industry has a significant multiplier effect on all aspects of the economy through the requirement for supporting products and services. The direct and indirect backward linkages include the food producers and manufacturers, transport companies, wholesalers, and related manufacturing industries. Thus, as an industry it is a major generator of both direct and indirect employment and contributes significantly to the flow of money in the regional and national economies.

The multiplier effect on employment alone is estimated to be around 1.3 additional jobs for every one directly employed in the hospitality industry. In financial terms the multiplier effect on the economy is estimated to be £1.75 for every £1 spent directly in a hospitality operation. The foreign earnings through the hospitality and tourism industry has risen and is calculated at £11.40 billion for 1995, a rise of 15 per cent over the previous year (Henley Centre, 1996). Consequently, as a result of globalization and competitive pressures, it is predicted that the hospitality, tourism and leisure industries will become increasingly important to the restructuring of the UK economy, both in terms of numbers of people employed and its contribution to the domestic product. Table 4.4 provides an example of regional income generation through tourism.

Table 4.4 Cumbrian tourism. Tourism volume and value, 1994

	Trips (million)	*Nights (million)*	*Spending (£million)*
UK residents	2.9	11.7	425
Overseas residents	0.30	1.3	53

Source: Caterer and Hotelkeeper (1996a).

The effect of the 1990s economic recession was compounded by less international travel because of the Gulf War in early 1991. As a result, the economic restructuring process claimed victims. Many businesses which had been bought at unrealistically high prices in the late 1980s based on inflated property values, and with large borrowings, failed. One illustration is that of Peter Tyrie. However, despite his negative experience, he clearly did not let it inhibit his entrepreneurial behaviour.

Illustration: Peter Tyrie, economic recession consequences

The 1990s 'have not been the happiest years of my life', admits Peter Tyrie. But after a period in which the former high-flyer's projects hit the rocks, he is back on the hotel scene with a vengeance. Tyrie is eager for the launch of the Regents Plaza in Maida Vale, which his Balmoral Hotels International will manage for developers Gainstride. It is a return to the form he enjoyed in the 1980s as managing director of Gleneagles Hotels PLC, which he launched with a buy-out from British Rail. Five years later the group included two hotels in Edinburgh and one each in London and Portugal. In 1986 he moved to Hong Kong as managing director of the Mandarin

Oriental group where he again enjoyed success and industry recognition for his achievements. Back in Scotland, he launched Balmoral International Hotels, developing the ex-Gleneagles North British Hotel as the luxury Balmoral. It was here, however, that things went wrong. He recalls: 'Gleneagles was a success at Mandarin, we tripled profits over three years. The Balmoral was a successful project which opened at a bad time, coinciding with the economic recession. We were badly let down through insufficient equity. That was a painful time. But life is about success and failure'.

Source: Legate, 1996

Currently, the economic downturn has reversed with fewer receivership appointments at hotel and catering companies in 1996 than for any other year in the 1990s. The total number in the hospitality sector was 89 in 1996, compared with 321 in 1992. This represents a fall of 72 per cent (Deloitte and Touche, 1997). Clearly economic changes and cycles, and the effect of government policies relative to the economy and exchange rate management, create both threats and opportunities for entrepreneurs. This has particular significance relative to the timing of the launch of entrepreneurial ventures, as was the unfortunate case for Peter Tyrie. However, we must not forget that the very same conditions worked to the advantage of Donald Macdonald in developing Macdonalds Hotels, referred to in Chapter 1.

Organization, production, and distribution

Changes in organization, production, and distribution within the industry sector has been intense. Changes have been rapid, their nature complex, and their implications for business success profound. They have been reflected in revolutionizing systems of production and distribution, organizational structures, and industrial relationships. Specific examples have been evidenced in a multitude of forms. These include privatization and outsourcing of services; technology-enabled food production and processing methods; radical changes in consumption patterns; electronic information distribution and transaction facilitation; forward and backward supply chain integration of catering manufacturing and provision; and joint ventures. Industry illustrations are now presented, exhibiting a meshing of these forms of change in the creation of timely, appropriate entrepreneurial strategies.

As a consequence of the introduction of Compulsory Competitive Tendering legislation in the early 1980s, there is a strong trend towards contractor-run outlets in the public sector. In the following illustration, the facilities management of a National Health Service hospital was put out to tender. This resulted in a joint-venture arrangement bringing together public- and private-sector organizations. (See page 87)

Developments in food production and processing systems, largely enabled by technological developments, have created substantial changes in the way in which the catering provision supply chain is organized. Specifically, the industry is seeing increasing forward integration of food

---

Illustration: Derbyshire Royal Infirmary, contracting-out of services

Derbyshire Royal Infirmary NHS Trust has withdrawn from direct operation of all non-clinical services by giving the responsibility to one contractor. In this instance, it is run by a partnership – Bateman Health Services and Tarmac Servicemaster, which have been handling the contract since April 1995. Bateman, the health service catering division of Compass Group UK, linked up with Tarmac Servicemaster, itself a joint-venture company looking after estate management, during the tender process. Each business was bidding separately and decided to improve its chances by forming a partnership. Together with the Derby-based trust, they created a Joint Partnership Body to administer the contract. Bateman is responsible for managing hotel services, while Tarmac concerns itself with estate management.
Source: Sutton, 1997

---

manufacturers, resulting in many kitchens now operating as assembly points at which to regenerate pre-prepared food items. Consequently, the emphasis is moving away from food production skills, to focus more on the logistics of operations. The following skychefs illustration is an indication of the changing nature of catering and consumption trends.

Illustration: SKY Chefs, organization, production, and distribution systems

LSG Lufthansa Services/SKY Chefs, the catering subsidiary of German national carrier Lufthansa, claims that its 33 per cent share of the airline catering market makes it the world's largest caterer. Fewer than 20 per cent of SKY Chefs' clients ask that their passengers be served meals which are in quantities too small for it to be efficient or practical to use either deep-frozen dishes or freshly prepared meals. LSG Lufthansa Services states: 'Today, since many products such as frozen meals can be purchased in large quantities, the caterer increasingly assumes responsibility for storage and transport. The consequence of this is that catering companies are tending to become logistics firms'. This trend toward logistics is seen as an evolving process that began when items arrived at the kitchens pre-peeled, then pre-cut and now they arrive packaged as a variety of ready-made, deep-frozen meals. For SKY Chefs, this is seen as the way forward, allowing it to concentrate on the logistics of receiving, storing and delivering the correct food to the right aircraft on time.
Source: Guild, 1997

Developments in communication technology have transformed the way in which firms distribute their products, by facilitating the flow of information and transactions on a global basis. As technology has continued to mature and advance, many travel agents may find themselves bypassed, as for instance, the Internet is accepted as a major business tool in the UK providing an international communications network. This has been supported by the hotel industry in the form of THISCO, a switch system, which has developed an industry site for the Internet called Travelweb. In 1996 Choice Hotels was receiving 55 000 enquiries a month on the Internet, and expects this to grow as a sales method eventually replacing the toll-free telephone system. The immensity of the Internet market and its potential are indicated in the following illustration.

Illustration: Internet, distribution systems

There seems to be a rush in the hospitality industry to get on the Internet. Everyone from fast-food outlets and bed and breakfast to tourist offices and hotel chains is doing it. With about 30 million people connected it is perhaps not that surprising. One of the advantages of the Internet is that small independents who do decide to go on-line have just as much chance of getting noticed as large chains.
Source: Drummond, 1996

These examples clearly illustrate the manner in which the organization, production and distribution of the industry has radically changed in recent years. For entrepreneurs, it presents a dynamic industry profile, fertile with new opportunities, and positively promoting entrepreneurial behaviour.

Mobilization phase of social action

Corresponding to the model presented in Figure 4.1 we have discussed how the entrepreneur has socially developed, and the pattern of structural promoters and inhibitors of entrepreneurial behaviour within the industry has been established. Attention now turns to the components which are required to mobilize the process of entrepreneurship. Conditions are influenced by the components of available resources and opportunities on the one hand, and by the patterns of consumer demand on the other. These are now investigated relative to support and opportunities arising. Specifically we will consider the public sector, consumerism, and financial resources.

Political intervention outcomes

As has been discussed in this chapter, Government policy has clearly been directed at supporting entrepreneurship. Outcomes resulting from policy intervention fall into four broad categories: financial assistance, education information, support and advice, and legislative changes. These are directed at mobilizing the entrepreneurship resource. Each category is now discussed.

Financial assistance

Three major programmes to help stimulate entrepreneurship currently exist. First, the Small Firms Loan Guarantee Scheme. By providing a Government guarantee against default by borrowers, the scheme enables high street banks and other financial bodies to lend between £500 and £250 000 to new and existing businesses. Repayment terms are two to seven years. Funds are lent at commercial rates, in addition, a premium of 1.5 per cent for variable interest rate loans. Unfortunately, changes effective from 1996 made some retailing and catering businesses ineligible. This is explored further in Chapter 5. Second, the Enterprise Investment Scheme (EIS) replaced the Business Expansion Scheme after the latter was withdrawn in 1993. The EIS is designed to encourage potential investors to invest small amounts of equity for small and growing firms. This is designed for 'business angels' who are prepared to invest in young firms with growth potential, and who may take a more active interest as a non-executive director. It is estimated that business angels invested £30 million in 1996 through individual investments ranging from £10 000 to £100 000. Finally, the Enterprise Allowance Scheme (EAS) was originally designed to encourage unemployed people to start up their own business. It amounts to approximately £2000, or £40 per week, in the first year of trading. In addition, there is a wide range of schemes initiated by local and central government and the European Union which may vary in nature regionally.

Owing to the lack of research regarding entrepreneurship in these industry sectors, it is not clear how influential these schemes have been in mobilizing entrepreneurial start ups. However, even if the direct impact turns out to be limited, the different schemes have certainly affected the entrepreneurial climate.

Education

The Government has implemented a number of policies to promote enterprise in schools (Young Enterprise), and to graduates (Graduate Enterprise Programmes). A product of a Graduate Enterprise Programme is Shahid Chowbury, who is discussed in the following illustration.

In addition, Education Business Links covers a wide range of initiatives aimed to strengthen links between education and the world of work. They are usually co-ordinated locally by Education Business Partnerships (EBPs), of which there are 128 nationally. Finally, the Enterprise in Higher Education initiative was the largest programme in the higher education sector. It aimed to enable higher education institutions to help students become life-long learners, develop enterprise skills, and be better prepared for working life.

Illustration: Shahid Chowbury, outcome of political intervention

For a number of years Shahid Chowbury was disappointed with the quality of Indian Restaurants in Scotland. He saw a gap in the market for an innovative concept of modern Indian cuisine served in a more appealing setting. Through the Graduate Enterprise Scheme he came up with the trading name and concept and was fortunate to find an excellent location. Funding was the biggest hurdle in getting off the ground, but he produced a winning business plan and secured finance from the first bank he approached. The concept has been successful financially. He is not content with this, however, and has now opened a Pakora Bar, which is another new concept he intends to franchise in the future.
Source: Scottish Enterprise Foundation, 1995

Information, support, and advice

The most far-reaching Government measure to involve and support entrepreneurs was the creation of Training and Enterprise Councils (TECs) in
England and Wales, and Local Enterprise Companies (LECs) in Scotland.
There are twenty-two LECs in Scotland. In England and Wales there are
eighty-one TECs, which in 1995 were responsible for £1.7 billion of public
funds invested in training, vocational education, and enterprise activities.
The mission of both the LECs and TECs is 'to provide the country with the
skilled and enterprising work force that it needs to sustain economic growth
and prosperity'(DfEE, 1996). At a local level the TECs and LECs are responsible for the implementation of government policy. An illustration of public-
sector provision of information, support, and advice measures is that of
Business Links.

Illustration: Business Links, public-sector support provision

Business Links were started in 1994 and there are now 240 centres nationally. They
offer a single point of access to the skills and resources needed to improve competitive performance. The services concentrate on functions which small firms cannot
hope to maintain effectively in-house. These range from financial advice to specialized training, marketing, and innovation. All have been available from a variety of
organizations in the past but finding, using, and paying for them often deterred
many firms.
Source: Crossley, 1996

Legislative changes

Specific policies have been directed at inflation control, taxation, and competitive practices relative to public-sector services and privatization of
former nationalized industries. It is clear that the Conservative Government
policies resulted in the generation of a range of opportunities for new
private-sector entrepreneurial activity. Illustrations of the ways in which
these have stimulated enterprise relative to public houses, contract catering,
motorway service areas, and transport catering are now presented.

Illustration: Beer Order, legislative changes

The major impact of the Beer Orders legislation and the Monopolies and Mergers
Commission report on the UK's pub market has been to create a new sector of independently owned pub chains. According to analysis by Marketpower, independent
pubs, including chains and single outlets, now number 27 350. This is up by
70.9 per cent on the situation which existed before the legislation which was
designed to loosen the big brewers' control of beer supply to pubs. It came into
effect in 1992.
Source: Caterer and Hotelkeeper, 1996b

Illustration: school meals, legislative changes

Scotland's private contractors involved in the school meals sector are faced with a frantic year as the government's moratorium on compulsory competitive tendering is lifted. Collectively the contracts due for retender, for which the private contractors can now bid, are worth £100m–£120m a year turnover. Although the rules for acceptance of tenders will change to reflect *Best Value* under the Labour Government, the competitive pressure and the climate of opportunity will remain.
Source: Shrimpton, 1996

Illustration: motorway service areas, legislative changes

The roadside catering market has become increasingly concentrated and competitive since 1993, according to the latest report on the sector by Minitel. While deregulation of Motorway Service Areas (MSAs) has allowed for their growth, the non-motorway-dedicated catering sector has contracted. Catering turnover at MSAs reached £203 million in 1996, revealing a 21 per cent growth since 1991.
Source: Jameson, 1996

Illustration: Snackline, legislative changes

In March 1995 Howard and Gail Roseman took a five-year lease from British Rail and purpose-built and opened a small café at Elstree and Borehamwood railway station in Hertfordshire. Until then there had been no catering facilities at the station, so the café, called Snackline, was welcomed by commuters. For the Rosemans it represented a venture into new territory. They had previously owned a mobile snack van, operating on registered sites. Business at the café has built up to 1000 customers a week.
Source: Sherratt, 1996

Thus, under the Conservative Government the outcomes of political intervention resulted in the merging of entrepreneurially positive elements, including financial resources, knowledge and training, information, and advice and support. There were also substantial legislative changes towards an environment conducive to stimulating and sustaining entrepreneurial behaviour. It is too early into the first term of the Labour Government to be in a position to postulate the effect of their future policies on the level of entrepreneurial behaviour in the UK hospitality, tourism and leisure industries.

Consumerism

Consumerism is a mobilizing factor for entrepreneurship as it lends itself to the flexibility, specialization, and innovatory capacity associated with current consumer demand. According to Henley Centre (1996), the hospitality consumer of the twenty-first century will be volatile, older, more discerning, and require a spectrum of convenient and entertaining services at almost any time and any place. Furthermore, the fragmentation in working structures, changing household composition, and increasing mobility are creating a society in which the traditional patterns of work and leisure are making way for an allocation of time and money at all hours and more varied locations.

With growing consumer confidence in purchasing, and widening choice in all markets, consumers will be demanding of value for time as well as value for money. Mere consistency, reliability, and efficiency are now no longer sufficient to maintain a competitive advantage. In such fast-changing markets, the entrepreneurial firm has the potential to create desirable new products/services which astonish customers and outstrip the competition. These changes are tied into what is termed 'post-modernism', where symbols have been elevated over substance. This will have implications for the consumption and marketing of goods and services, which are unlikely to revert to mass consumption patterns. Examples of such niche markets within the industry are presented in Table 4.5.

Table 4.5 Examples of niche market concept businesses

Sector	Business name	Description
Food, catering, and restaurant	Boy Stuart	• Biggest and freshest scallops, specially selected from the cleanest and richest waters in Europe
	Crepe a Croissant	• Over thirty different traditional French crepes to choose from, sweet and savoury
	Kompass Katering	• Anything afloat, anywhere … skippering, deckworking, cooking, cleaning, provisioning, budgeting, and menu planning
	Café Cyberia	• Internet cafés offer a stop-off for both seasoned Internet surfers and the uninitiated
Leisure	Backstreet	• Skateboard, snowboard, BMX, and hip-hop clothing and accessories
	Cape Sea Tours	• Cruise with MV *Kittiwake* for seabirds, seals, and scenery
	The Outdoor Survival Shop	• For all your essential outdoor clothing and equipment needs
Sport and fitness	Craig Robertson Coaching	• Badminton coaching – experience quality coaching, group or individual, from a top international
	Mirko Equestrian Services	• Classical art of riding. Enjoy training on performance horses
	Mogul Mouse	• Ski teaching and summer activity programme for kids aged 5–12 years
	BikeTreks	• World-wide road and mountain biking adventures, and women-only mountain bike clinics

In the 1990s a proliferation of cut-price airlines, are transforming holiday and business travel. The following illustration of EasyJet illustrates the shift in consumer values and attitudes towards travel and value for money.

Thus, it can be summarized that the features associated with current consumerism combine to present the entrepreneur with a mass of market opportunities at which to direct entrepreneurial energy and mobilize activities. These are further explored in Chapter 7.

Illustration: EasyJet, consumer values and attitudes

EasyJet's business concept is simple: a no-frills service between fixed destinations at the lowest possible price. By accepting minor concessions in luxury, passengers from Edinburgh and Glasgow can now fly south for as little as £29. Out went in-flight meals. Out went travel agents and their 15–20 per cent commissions. Out, too, went tickets and uniforms, together with any notion of a slick corporate image. Instead, they went to the local branch of Benetton and bought black jeans and orange polo shirts. So far it has worked.
Source: Nuki and Ellis, 1996

Financial resources

From the foregoing it can be surmised that the UK environment is generally supportive and the opportunities are prolific; however, in order to mobilize entrepreneurial behaviour capital needs to be raised. For many small firms, certain sources of finance are not available because of entry barriers. For example, some entrepreneurs are automatically excluded from financial sources such as the Stock Exchange. Others face difficulties raising certain types of finance such as long-term loans because of the automatically higher risk associated with firms who have little equity in the form of share capital. However, there are a variety of sources of finance available to the entrepreneur. These can be classified as internal and external (Deakins, 1996).

Internal sources of finance include the personal equity of the entrepreneur, usually in the form of savings, re-mortgages, or money raised from family and friends. After the initial start-up of the firm, retained profits and earnings provide internal capital. Principal sources of external finance are banks, equity from venture capitalists and informal investors, and short-term trade credit. Recently, the Alternative Investment Market (AIM) has been formed, designed for smaller firms as a means of raising equity through shareholders. In essence AIM introduces the entrepreneur to suppliers of capital. It seeks to promote trading in shares hitherto not associated with offers of investment, such as family-owned businesses, management buy-outs or buy-ins. This is the route which the Pierre Victoire restaurant group planned to take as a means of raising finance to fuel expansion plans.

Thus, while the new ventures may require to seek funds from less traditional sources than those associated with larger corporations, sources of finance do exist for those determined to mobilize the process of entrepreneurship. Furthermore, through the Pierre Victoire illustrations we are reminded that financial success and failure go hand in hand. Financial aspects associated with entrepreneurship are explained in more detail in Chapter 5.

Illustration: Pierre Victoire, alternative investment market

The founder of the Edinburgh-based Pierre Victoire restaurant group, Paul Levicky, announced in 1996 that his expansion plans were focused on the Continent and, in the longer-term, America, as he revealed that the company's flotation on the Alternative Investment Market was a step closer. It was planned that the company would come to the market in late October 1996 with a price of around 10 p per share. Before that, it was expected to announce a massive rise in pre-tax profits. The share issue looked set to be over-subscribed, valuing the company at around £15 million. The 36-year-old entrepreneur started his first restaurant in Edinburgh eight years ago with £70 capital and in 1996 controlled a business empire with a turnover of more than £40 million.
Source: Robertson, 1996

Note: Unfortunately this never happened and the company went into voluntary receivership in 1998. It was claimed that over expansion was to blame, but perhaps unsuccessful expansion is nearer the mark.

Summary

It can be concluded that the environment for enterprise in the UK is generally very supportive towards entrepreneurial behaviour within the hospitality, tourism and leisure industries. First, current ideologies and societal values promote the social development of potential entrepreneurs. Second, the nature of social structure combines employment patterns, industry-sector features, corporate restructuring, economic restructuring, and methods of organization, production and distribution in a way which, on balance, promotes entrepreneurial behaviour. Finally, entrepreneurs are mobilized into action through the availability of supportive political measures, market opportunities, and financial resources. Thus, it appears in the UK that there are few inhibitors to stifle entrepreneurship, and theoretically, limited barriers to those persons who wish to accept the entrepreneurial challenge. The possible effect, negatively and/or positively, of the newly appointed Labour Government may change this situation.

However, the danger is that this environment will result in many people being mobilized into entrepreneurship without the necessary management skills and financial resources to survive. As Deakins (1996) realistically points out, the associated suffering of families of failed businesspersons is frequently ignored. Families which may have enjoyed a good standard of living can, in some cases, be left destitute and with large personal debts. Second, the social costs of running a small business are often not appreciated, because of an emphasis on success and achievement. Costs include strains on married life and family relationships, long hours of work, and the lack of fringe benefits such as non-contributory pension schemes.

It is extremely easy to jump on the exciting roller coaster of entrepreneurship, with all the thrill, excitement, and energy and be totally sold on the adrenaline-pumping experience. The fervour and glamour of popular imagery which is currently associated with entrepreneurship is enticing.

However, it is important that the risks and consequences of failure should also be borne in mind.

Reflective questions

1 If entrepreneurial behaviour represents an essentially spontaneous human activity then why do governments feel the need to intervene in the process? Discuss.
2 Consider the degree to which the cultural context of an individual influences the degree of entrepreneurial behaviour exhibited.
3 Apply the structural elements which have been identified as promoting and/or inhibiting entrepreneurial behaviour to a specific business activity within the hospitality, tourism or leisure industries. Evaluate the balance between promoting and inhibiting influences.
4 Assess how effective UK government policy to date has been in creating an environment which stimulates entrepreneurial behaviour within the hospitality, tourism and leisure industries.
5 The 'dark side' of entrepreneurship is often overlooked. Discuss the features associated with negative entrepreneurship and its implications for society.

References

Anonymous (1996a) Cumbrian Tourism, Caterer and Hotelkeeper, p. 7.

Anonymous (1996b) Beer orders created independent chain, *Caterer and Hotelkeeper*, 8 August, p. 14.

Anderson, J. (1995) *Local Heroes*, Scottish Enterprise, Glasgow.

Beesley, M. and Wilson, P. (1984) Public policy and small firms in Britain, *Small Business Theory and Policy* (ed. C. Levicki), Croom Helm, London.

Burrows, R. (1991) *Deciphering the Enterprise Culture*, Routledge, London.

Crossley, G. (1996) Local boys make good, *Caterer and Hotelkeeper*, 11 July, p. 66.

Deakins, D. (1996) *Entrepreneurs and Small Firms*, McGraw-Hill, London.

Deloitte and Touche (1997) Industry suffers fewer failures, *Caterer and Hotelkeeper*, 23 January, p. 16.

DfEE (1996) *Labour Market and Skills Trends*, Department for Education and Employment, Nottingham.

Department of Trade and Industry (1996) *Breaking New Ground*.

Drummond, G. (1996) Untangling the net, *Caterer and Hotelkeeper*, 25 July, pp. 52–56.

Goss, D. (1991) *Small Business and Society*, Routledge, London.

Guild, S. (1997) Pie in the sky, *Caterer and Hotelkeeper*, 13 February, pp. 68–69.

Heelas, P. and Morris, P. (1992) *The Values of the Enterprise Culture*, Routledge, London.

Henley Centre (1996) *Hospitality into the 21st Century: A Vision for the Future*, Henley Centre, London.

Hofstede, G. (1980) *Culture's Consequences*, Sage, Newberry Park, CA.

Huddart, G. (1996) BE Services banks on MBO victory, *Caterer and Hotelkeeper*, 17 October, p. 9.

Jameson, A. (1996) MSAs take lead in UK roadside catering sector, *Caterer and Hotelkeeper*, 15 August, p. 14.

Keynote (1997) *UK Hotel Industry: Sector Analysis*, Keynote Publications, Hampton, Middlesex.

Kirzner, I. (1980) The primacy of entrepreneurial discovery. In *The Prime Mover of Progress: The Entrepreneur in Capitalism and Socialism*, Institute of Economic Affairs, London.

Lashley, C. (1996) Empowerment through involvement: a case study of TGI Friday restaurants, Nottingham Trent University, Nottingham, unpublished.

Legate, P. (1996) Return of the 80s men, *Hotel and Restaurant*, April, p. 9.

McClelland, D. (1961) *The Achieving Society*, Van Nostrand, New York.

Morris, P. (1991) Freeing the enterprise spirit. In *Enterprise Culture* (eds. R. Keat and N. Abercrombie), Routledge, London.

Nuki, P. and Ellis, W. (1996) War in the skies, *The Sunday Times*, 25 August, p. 3.

Robertson, R. (1996) Pierre Victoire set for logical step, *The Herald*, 29 August, p. 14.

Scase, R. and Goffee, R. (1989) *The Real World of the Small Business Owner*, Routledge, London.

Scottish Enterprise (1993) *Business Birth Rate Strategy*, Scottish Enterprise, Glasgow.

Scottish Enterprise Foundation (1995) *Graduate Entrepreneur*, University of Stirling, Stirling.

Sherratt, P. (1996) Expresso express, *Caterer and Hotelkeeper*, 21 March, p. 64.

Shrimpton, D. (1996) School meals contractors await tendering bonanza, *Caterer and Hotelkeeper*, 15 August, p. 80.

Storey, D. (1995) *Understanding the Small Business Sector*, Routledge, London.

Sutton, A. (1997) A question of trusts, *Caterer and Hotelkeeper*, 20 February, pp. 64–65.

Thompson, B. (1996) Team player. In *Signature Selects*, Diners Club, August, p. 7.

Timmons, J. (1994) *New Venture Creation*, Irwin, Boston.

Webster, J. (1996) New voice for hospitality, *Caterer and Hotelkeeper*, 15 August, pp. 60–61.

Part Two
Finance, Business Planning, Operations Management, Marketing and Strategy

5 Finance, business planning and entrepreneurship

The aim of this chapter is to develop an understanding of financial management and business planning issues which particularly affect entrepreneurship. Specifically, within the context of the hospitality, tourism and leisure industries, this chapter will develop understanding of:

* financial characteristics of entrepreneurial businesses;
* resource poverty, its implications and ways of avoiding it;
* sources of finance and their operational and ownership impact;
* business planning approaches;
* financial management in small entrepreneurial ventures.

Introduction

Lack of financial liquidity is the major cause of business failure in the hospitality, tourism and leisure industries. Of course, lack of funds can be a symptom of many different business problems; it may be that the financial planning and control function has been carried out adequately. However, if there is a problem with business marketing, quality control, or customer service, income generation will also fail to meet target. The business will suffer from a shortage of funds as soon as the start-up capital runs out. So, although it may be only the symptom of other deep-seated business problems, ultimately it is the lack of liquidity which forces businesses to admit failure and cease trading.

There are particular features of the hospitality, tourism and leisure business sectors which make them vulnerable to financial difficulties. Firstly, the fragmented nature of much of the industry means that it is a major entrepreneurial outlet for individual, as well as corporate, entrepreneurs. As we discussed in Chapter 3, established companies are often in a position where they have internally generated funds available to invest in potential new ventures. If these ventures are initially tested in a controlled manner, subsequent roll-out can be entered into with confidence, and the likelihood of financial difficulties being encountered is much reduced. In addition, the new venture will form an addition to an existing portfolio of business activity. If it goes wrong, the financial blow may be painful, but it is unlikely to be fatal.

With individual entrepreneurs the situation is quite different. Low financial barriers to entry mean that individuals with only a small amount of capital can start-up in a venture of their own. For example, the lease premium and ingoings for a fairly substantial pub business can be as little as £40 000. More modest pub businesses can be bought into for as little as £10 000. In the restaurant and take-away sector there are also a huge number of leasehold properties available on the market. To buy freehold may be beyond the means of the entrepreneur, but leasehold agreements make setting up the business possible. In the leisure sector, businesses such as fitness consultancies can be set up with minimal fixed-asset investment. Many small hospitality-, tourism-, or leisure-based businesses can theoretically be set up with mainly working, rather than permanent, capital since the fixed assets which the business needs to use are minimal.

There is therefore a situation where individuals with only modest amounts of their own capital will nevertheless be motivated to start-up a business. As a consequence, they will be in a situation where, in order to get started, they will need to maximize other sources of capital, relative to their own contribution. If this other capital is in the form of a relatively permanent injection of funds, such as additional share capital from a co-investor, or a low interest loan from a relative who is not particularly concerned when they are to be repaid, then the situation regarding repayment outgoings will be relatively relaxed. However, if the extra capital is provided in the form of a loan from a financial institution, the institution will want interest and capital, perhaps after an initial holiday period, to be repaid no matter what the business circumstances. In this situation the business has what is termed a high level of **financial gearing**. Its borrowed funds are at a high level relative to its permanent funds. This means that its interest and capital repayments are also high relative to the more lowly geared business. This situation increases the degree of risk of the new venture, since financial institutions are not renowned for their patience when it comes to recouping their money. Indeed, when a small business is forced into liquidation, it is often initiated by the financial institution lender who has lost confidence.

Non-financial barriers to entry are also fairly modest within the hospitality, tourism and leisure industries. For premises requiring a liquor licence, the requirement is that a licensee is a fit and proper person. Licensing magistrates are increasingly interpreting this condition to mean that the person should have some form of training, but it can be as little as a three-day British Institute of Innkeepers course. For businesses involving food, environmental health officers will require business operators to comply with food safety legislation, but this expertise can also be gained with short intensive training periods. For entrepreneurs setting up small leisure businesses or tour operations, it will be the insurance company and financing source which are the main controls over the extent of expertise which is brought to the venture. In the main, then, the controls over expertise tend to be focused on very narrow areas of technical knowledge. We seem to be a very long way from a situation where people require a proficiency-based **licence to operate**, such as exists in the Netherlands for example. Consequently, as well as low financial barriers to entry, there is the prospect of many entrepreneurs setting up in business with inadequate levels of business expertise.

Taken together, these two factors contribute to a scenario where many entrepreneurs have low levels of personal capital, and may enter into business with unproven levels of business expertise. This has been described by Welsh and White (1981) as **resource poverty**. Both financial funding and expertise are in short supply. Not a good prognosis for success, but a situation which offers unlimited entrepreneurial opportunity!

As well as capital requirements and barriers to entry often being modest, the cost structure of many businesses in the hospitality, tourism and leisure industries is often such that the level of fixed costs relative to variable costs is high. This has the effect of creating a high level of **operating gearing**. As Figure 5.1 illustrates, such a business needs to generate a relatively high level of sales income just to cover its fixed costs. Beyond this level of income it will quickly build up profits and cash flow. Below this level, it will lose money and its cash flow will be negative. There is therefore a particularly sensitive financial situation, linked to the level of trade. Not all hospitality tourism and leisure businesses will conform to this cost structure, but many do.

To an extent, **financial gearing** and **operating gearing** are linked, since a high level of borrowing compared to permanent capital will increase the ongoing interest payments of the business. Since interest is a fixed cost, higher operating gearing is a consequence of higher financial gearing.

A business with a high level of operating gearing has to operate at a high level of activity before moving into profitability. This is due to relatively high fixed costs impacting on the break even level.

The implications of this are that levels of initial start-up capital need to be adequate to cover the period where the trade is being built up and cash flow is negative. If this start-up capital can be permanent rather than through borrowings, then that eases the pressure of the situation. Financial planning also needs to take into account the sensitive nature of financial performance,

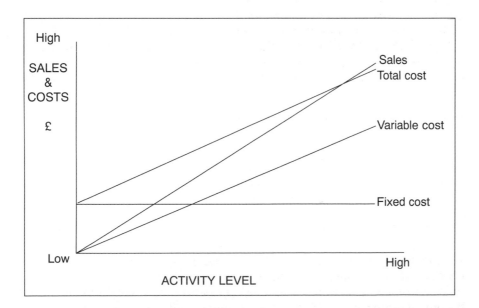

Figure 5.1 A high level of operating gearing

and ensure that estimates realistically reflect likely levels of income and expenditure. It is these aspects of financial management which will be considered further in this chapter.

Whilst it is the particular industry features emphasized in this introduction which can pose problems, the fact is that the sectors also have considerable attractions for lenders and external investors. It is the service sectors of the economy which are moving ahead most strongly. Therefore, counterbalancing any negative features is the over-riding positive influence of a strongly growing area of demand where there are many attractive investment opportunities, as identified in Chapter 4. Certainly in conducting the research which underpins the content of this chapter, we formed the opinion that the hospitality, tourism and leisure industries were favourably regarded by funding providers. Nevertheless, a cautious approach towards the provision of funds still prevails within most financial institutions.

Sources of start-up funding

An overview

Entrepreneurial firms typically operate in highly uncertain environments and with low levels of information. This has an impact on the type of finance used and the use to which it is put. Keasey and Watson (1993) attribute part of the problems in obtaining funding faced by small firms, in particular, to low information availability and the high fixed costs of obtaining such information. Furthermore, few entrepreneurs have the time available to search out information and process it. The government's Business Links mentioned in Chapter 4 were designed to act as **one-stop-shops** providing an information focal point for small businesses. However, as yet, it is believed that many entrepreneurs have not yet heard of Business Links!

During the 1980s and 1990s there have been major changes impacting upon the financial sector. Murphy (1996) identified the primary changes which are summarized in Table 5.1.

Table 5.1 Major changes impacting upon the financial sector

- Increased competition
- Greater technological applications
- Increased operational expenses
- Redesign of products and services
- Increase in bad debts

Source: Murphy (1996)

As identified by Murphy, the last recession accelerated some of these changes. It culminated in banks and other lending institutions being less willing to encourage small companies to extend their financial facilities and becoming more conservative in their general lending policies. This was particularly with regard to their exposure to lending to finance acquisition of fixed assets. This situation may now be easing slightly. However, even as late as 1995, banks were so wary of bad debts and businesses failures in the licensed-trade sector that it was very difficult for potential publicans to secure funding.

Most new businesses will require some injection of finance to facilitate the start-up and to begin trading. Even when selling **personal skills**, as in the case of a leisure or travel consultant, money may be needed to help set up the equipment base, recruitment of additional staff, and advertising. What the money is going to be used for determines the types of funding available. Typically, a hospitality, tourism or leisure business will require setting-up expenses, such as equipment purchases, premises purchase or lease, refurbishment of premises, legal and other professional costs, in addition to the multitude of other smaller expenses including purchasing stock, paying wages, etc., until the business begins to generate enough cash itself.

As identified in Chapter 4, sources of finance are internal and external in nature. Most businesses utilize a combination of both. Whilst many entrepreneurs would prefer not to have to rely on raising external finance it is unrealistic for most to expect to have sufficient internal funds available to invest. Deakins (1996) cited research from the Cambridge Small Business Research Centre identifying from where small firms receive external finance (Table 5.2).

Table 5.2 External finance and small firms

Source	Percentage respondents
Banks	83.7
Venture capital	6.5
Hire purchase/leasing	44.6
Factoring	6.0
Trade credit	8.5
Partners/working shareholders	19.5
Other private individuals	5.6
Other sources	9.7

Source: Deakins (1996)

As can be seen, bank lending and hire purchase/leasing are by far the most important sources of external finance. However, one of the messages of this chapter is that venture capital should be used to a greater extent, providing the business is truly entrepreneurial rather than a life-style type project. Whatever the source, funding certainly needs to be adequate to prevent the destructive effects of resource poverty.

One business-entry strategy is that of franchising which will be discussed in more detail in Chapter 8. The illustration of capital requirements for a Domino's Pizza franchise can be seen on the following page.

Potentially, therefore, there are a number of different sources of start-up funding available, depending on the specific nature of the new business opportunity. Though there is no data available regarding funding patterns for new venture start-ups across the hospitality, tourism and leisure sectors, from industry experience it is asserted that the majority of businesses are set

---

Illustration: Domino's Pizza, typical capital requirements (£, 1996)

	£
Building (approx. 700 sq. ft. store)	25 000
Equipment	42 000
Planning	2 000
Legal costs	4 000
Architect	1 000
Franchise fees	18 000
Training	3 000
	95 000

Domino's look for an internal investment from a potential franchisee of £40 000 unborrowed money. The remaining funds may be obtained through banks or building societies. They have already liased with lenders such as the NatWest Franchise Section – Small Business Services with regards to financial requirements and the particular details of the franchise arrangement. Domino's will also assist in preparing a comprehensive business plan for prospective franchisees to help secure external funding.

Source: Anonymous, 1996; Domino's Pizza Franchise Pack

---

up by means of direct personal funding, supplemented by borrowings from financial institutions (primarily clearing banks), leasing, and personal private contacts. An exception to the lack of data is provided by the public-house sector, where *The Publican* has investigated the extent and source of loans held by licensees of freehold, leasehold, and tenanted properties, as presented in Figures 5.2 and 5.3.

Size of Loans

Percentage of pubs

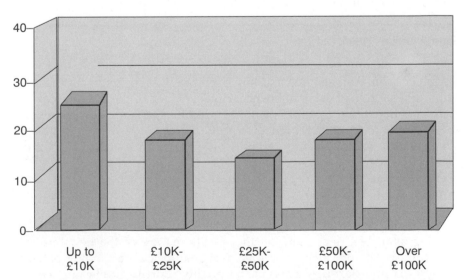

Figure 5.2 1996 Loan take-up by pub licensees. **Source**: *The Publican* (August 26th, 1996)

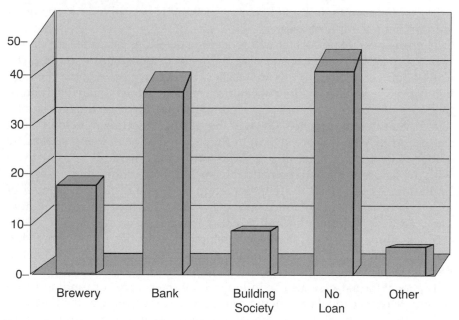

Types of Loan

Percentage of pubs

Figure 5.3 Loan sources used by pub licensees. **Source**: *The Publican* (August 26th, 1996)

The business plan

Before considering sources of funding in more detail, it is important to recognize the crucial importance of the proposed new venture's **business plan**. Without a credible business plan it is usually impossible to persuade any of the external sources to commit funding to a new venture, even in situations where considerable financial security is available. In any event, the production of a business plan is considered to be essential even if no external funding is required. Unless a plan clearly demonstrates that a business concept appears viable, offering potential returns significantly greater than low-risk investment alternatives, there seems little purpose in pursuing a venture unless it is for compelling life-style reasons.

The business plan may have been arrived at after initial work on a **feasibility study**. Such a study can consider different operating format and market response alternatives, working through their financial and other implications. Utilized in this way, the feasibility study can be used as a stage in the development of the final concept, testing out alternative ways forward, and considering their pros and cons within the context of different scenarios.

Detailed consideration of the business plan is beyond the scope of this text. There are high-quality publications produced by all of the clearing banks (see, for example, National Westminster's *Business Start-up Guide*, Anonymous, 1992). Additionally there are also many specialist books which deal with the writing of business plans. However, it is worthwhile considering the main features and content of the business plan in terms of its entrepreneurial implications.

The business' legal format will reflect the decisions taken regarding the ownership of the business and also the team responsible for putting the concept into operation. In this and earlier chapters we have noted the high level of risk associated with new venture creation. Whilst it may be thought that a limited company could provide some protection from the impact of a failed venture, in practice (as will be further discussed below) such protection may be illusory, owing to financial guarantees being sought by lenders. The decision regarding business format may therefore be more to do with the nature of the entrepreneurial team and their contributions than risk limitation. As identified in Chapters 3 and 6, it requires a wide spread of expertise to successfully launch and grow a new business. A team is more likely to have this than an individual. Participation in the capital of the business through actual share ownership, or potential share ownership through options, can both lock in and motivate key members of the entrepreneurial team.

The legal format may also be influenced by the sources of funding being sought. Venture capital providers will certainly want a share in the business. This is more practical with a company form of organization. Other sources of funding will prefer a more arms-length relationship. If future plans include high growth and take-off, then a limited company will provide greater flexibility in terms of future financing alternatives. A sole trader or partnership format is normally only suitable where future growth is not being sought and the entrepreneurial motivation is to create a life-style business.

Key people are probably the most important section of the business plan. The statement that the three most important factors (attributed to Conrad Hilton) for the success of a hotel are location, location and location is well known. In an amusing parody of this, a venture capitalist told us that the three most important factors that he considered when assessing the likelihood of a new venture being successful were – people, people and people!

In Chapter 2 we have noted that entrepreneurs come in many different forms and that it is difficult to generalize as to the personal traits and other characteristics which will lead to entrepreneurial success. To an extent, providers of funding may be flexible regarding the type of entrepreneur they deal with. However, they are essentially looking for strong indicators that they can be confident in the people to whom they are entrusting their money. Confidence will be generated if the members of the team have directly relevant and successful experience in similar ventures. Such key experience at least provides some indication that the people have the necessary technical skills. If they have progressed, or had a position of responsibility, in a related organization then the indication is also that others have already found them credible; others have been prepared to entrust them with responsibility for successful operation of an aspect of another organization.

This does not mean that the only people who can obtain business funding are those who have many years business experience. Those working in hospitality, tourism and leisure industries often acquire responsibility at an early age. The structure of the industries and the often high labour turnover, means that substantial experience can be acquired very quickly. Young people can either advance rapidly within the same organization, or by moving from one corporation to another. Furthermore, credibility is not just a question of people looking good on paper. At some stage the potential entrepreneur will need to sit across the table from those who may be providing funds. Here, the persuasiveness of the entrepreneur will be vital. If there are signs of nervousness, uncertainty, or a lack of commitment, then the weakness will soon be identified and the decision will be made not to risk the funds.

People are important both in their own right and also indirectly owing to their impact on the business concept development. Those who have good business experience will also tend to have sound business ideas that are based on their operational and market knowledge. They have learned about business operation using others' business vehicles as incubator organizations and are now motivated to take the risk of trying to create their own. The funding provider gains confidence from this practical exposure to business and gains reassurance that the new venture is likely to be in tune with what the market wants.

The business plan will need to set out the main features of the **concept** and its macro- and micro-**market.** As discussed in Chapter 7, the concept will require to offer attributes which are considered important by customers, which differentiate the venture from its competitors, and which are deliverable consistently. Increasingly, such attribute differentiation will be based upon intangible as well as tangible benefits. It is essential that the plan clearly identifies the main direct and indirect competitors to the new venture, and compares important features.

Communicating the key concept ideas through a business plan can be challenging. Photographs of other existing organizations with similar features can help. So can artist impressions of what is proposed. At the stage of direct negotiation with funding providers, it may also help if the funding provider is taken out into the business environment in which the venture will be located to help develop market knowledge and gain understanding of the concept in relation to its competitive context. A clear understanding of why the concept will enjoy competitive advantage over other existing business providers will need to be communicated. In the case of **imitative entrepreneurship**, which is discussed in Chapter 7, the task will be made easier. The success of an existing organization on which the new venture is being based can be demonstrated. The emphasis then switches to developing a case to show that the benefits delivered are not currently being made sufficiently available to meet demand in the proposed micro-market area.

As well as covering the main concept features from a marketing perspective the business plan will also need to demonstrate the **operational capability** to deliver them. Issues associated with this area are addressed in

Chapter 6. Operational systems require to be fully specified and key suppliers identified. Labour requirements should be detailed and schedules prepared which take account of the business fluctuations evident in many sector businesses. Key elements of the operation, such as peak capacity and service times, will have substantial impact upon the ultimate sales level. The previous key people section of the plan should have clearly demonstrated that the expertise will exist within the business to deliver the operational features fully and consistently. This helps avoid the quality problems that are an important cause of small business failure.

Equipment, fixtures and fittings, and property requirements should be specified in a section detailing the **capital expenditure** needed to realize the venture. These need to clearly relate to the delivery of the concept features. It is better to overstate rather than understate requirements, and to include a contingency for unexpected extra expenditure. The principal to be followed is that of avoiding under-estimation of the capital required at all costs. Such under-estimation is self deluding. If capital is fully estimated then it will show whether the return on investment really is commensurate with the risk. It will also go some way towards ensuring that the funding raised is sufficiently adequate to avoid the resource poverty identified earlier in the chapter as being the major problem which new ventures face.

If the intention is to move the venture into **take-off mode** and grow a substantial business concern, then the business plan should set out the **strategy** for achieving this. It requires to clearly identify the people, operational, capital, and funding issues associated with moving the business through different stages of business growth. For funding providers this may involve specifying **exit strategies** as well as details of future funding rounds. The tension of looking after the **mainstream** as well as any **new stream** needs to be addressed. It is likely that plans will require the taking on of additional expertise to anticipate the changing management requirements which will ensue.

The important **financial section** of the business plan will show the financial impact of the concept. This will include budget profit and loss, cash flow and balance sheets, usually for three years ahead, perhaps for five if a major growth scenario is anticipated. It is preferable if such projections depict **optimistic**, **pessimistic**, and **best guess** scenarios. If the project is viable even with a pessimistic scenario, then both funding providers and the venture initiators will be able to take up the business opportunity with confidence. It is important that such scenarios are developed from specific estimates. Sales scenarios should be based upon anticipated actual sales volumes and product/service item prices. Typical trading weeks can be used to illustrate sales income and mix under different trading conditions. These can then be consolidated into annual optimistic, pessimistic, and best guess estimates. In the same way, cost estimates should also be developed from a zero base which reflects anticipated activity levels and the **fixed, variable**, and **semi-variable** costs which it is estimated will be incurred. In particular, labour costs are normally very financially significant. Labour cost estimates should be based upon actual anticipated staffing schedules, labour hours actually required, and the rates to be paid.

The business plan should begin with a two- or three-page **business summary.** Unless this is particularly well written, the summary may be the only section of the business plan which is actually read! It requires to present a concept overview detailing its main features and the essence of why it will achieve competitive advantage. It should also give key financial ratios and details. It is important that the summary gives initial indications of the credibility of the key people involved. The emphasis of the summary may be changed somewhat depending upon the sources of funding which are being sought. For some providers of funds, growth potential will be the primary consideration. For others it will be the security of their investment.

The business plan is often produced in conjunction with accountants who will advise and support the new venture. If the right accountancy company is selected it will have extensive contacts amongst a network of potential sources of funding. Having the venture introduced by a well-regarded accountancy company can help substantially in access to funding. Its association with the venture will provide additional grounds for having confidence in it. Since the venture has passed through an initial screening by the accountancy company, its credibility will already be that much higher. However, it is important that in essence the business plan is produced by the individuals who are proposing the venture, rather than by its accountants. If ownership of the plan rests clearly with the venture initiators, it is much more likely that their passion for the opportunity will shine through. At the end of the day, funding decisions are about feelings and people as well as figures!

Sources of finance

Having established that a sound business plan is a necessity for obtaining any form of external finance, we are now able to consider in more depth the main sources of finance available and the implications of using them.

Banks

Most banks will lend money on both a short- and long-term basis. Short-term borrowing often follows the form of an overdraft which can cover a limited period or a temporary shortfall in funding, often necessary to cover working capital requirements. The benefits of overdraft borrowing are that it is quick and easy to set up. However, the upper limits can be quite low and restrictive. The interest rate for such unsecured borrowing may also be fairly steep, so it is not ideal for long periods.

Longer-term loans can be flexible but vary considerably between banks and depend heavily on your assets, track record, and business plan. The interest rate is usually negotiable and again depends on your particular situation and bargaining power. The rate may be fixed for the term of the loan, variable according to the current bank base rate, or stepped so that it starts off low but increases at set intervals to allow time for the business to establish. A capital repayment holiday may be negotiated allowing the business a certain period – usually three months – before it is necessary to start repaying the capital. In the meantime, only interest is paid

---

Illustration: The George Hotel, bank loan

Michael Slagle was general manager of the George Hotel in Colchester for a period back in 1979. Now he owns it. He bought the property from Queens Moat Houses in October 1994. For Slagle, buying the hotel was like taking a step back in time. The George did not seem to have changed in the fifteen years since he left and was in desperate need of modernization. So not only did he need to raise money for the purchase of the hotel, but also for extensive refurbishment. The refurbishment took place in 1995 and cost £1 million. Slagle financed it through a bank loan of £505 000 and the rest came from cash flow.
Source: Fox, 1997

In order to offer a loan, a bank would usually want to see a full business plan including projected trading figures and cash forecasts to ensure that the business is a viable venture and that they will be able to recoup their lending. The role of security is important in obtaining a loan as the bank typically wants to ensure that the entrepreneur has enough collateral to secure the loan. However, many entrepreneurs do not have sufficient assets to secure funding and thus have difficulties in raising enough money. Unsecured loans represent a high risk to the lender and lenders are reluctant to offer them. A small unsecured amount (approximately £5000–£10 000) may be arranged depending on the relationship between entrepreneur and bank and the reason for the loan. Owing to the high risk nature, the banks are likely to charge a high rate of interest in exchange for an unsecured loan.

The Small Firms Loan Guarantee Scheme and the finance gap

A gap can arise when the demand for finance from small companies is greater than the willingness of financial lenders to supply funding. For bank loan finance this gap can be termed **credit-rationing** (Deakins, 1996). The Government's Loan Guarantee Scheme is one initiative designed to close the gap, as is the development of the venture capital market.

The Loan Guarantee Scheme involves the Government providing a guarantee to cover a proportion of the loan – usually 70 per cent of the total loan. It is a joint venture between the Department of Trade and Industry (DTI) and the lenders. The scheme is designed for companies with viable business plans who are unable to secure sufficient funding through conventional loans owing to lack of security or business track record, or both. This enables banks and other lenders to lend up to £100 000 to new businesses with the government assuming the majority of the risk. If an established business is being bought, then the amount which can be guaranteed increases to £250 000 and 80 per cent of the total loan can be covered. The maximum loan period which can be guaranteed is ten years and the minimum two years. A capital repayment holiday of up to two years is permissible. Even though the loan is being guaranteed, arrangements concerning loan terms and capital repayment holidays all have to be agreed with the banks. A handling fee of up to 1.0 per cent of the loan is *able* to be charged by the banks. They can also choose not to charge it, so again, negotiation is necessary.

For variable interest loans a premium of 1.5 per cent on the cost of borrowing is payable to the DTI by the borrower in exchange for Government support. For fixed interest loans the premium is 0.5 per cent. This increase to the normal interest rate may make it quite costly in terms of repayments. However, the added expense needs to be balanced against the increased likelihood of getting the project up and running.

There are restrictions on the types of businesses eligible for support by the Loan Guarantee Scheme. Table 5.3 highlights some of the businesses **not** eligible for support.

Table 5.3 Businesses ineligible for Loan Guarantee support

Betting shops	Professional sports players	Sports promotions
Casinos	and sporting	Night clubs
Amusement halls	organizations	Taxi and cab-hire
Lotteries	Off licenses	Private members clubs
Public houses	Retail outlets such as	Ticket agents
Bars/clubs	clothes shops, sports	Travel agents
Restaurants and cafés[1]	shops, etc.	

[1] As of March 1996, catering activities such as restaurants and cafés were excluded from support under the Loan Guarantee Scheme, having previously being included.

As can be seen from Table 5.3, many new ventures in the hospitality, tourism and leisure industries are now excluded from the Loan Guarantee scheme. The rationale for the exclusion of restaurants and cafés in 1996 was that new concerns were simply displacing existing businesses. This is a view with which we have some sympathy and which reflects the particularly low barriers to entry identified in Chapter 7. Activity in this area is viewed as being sufficiently buoyant and so requires no encouragement!

However, there remains opportunity for many new ventures within the industry sector to qualify under the scheme. Table 5.4 identifies some of the kinds of venture within the industry sector which are supported. The DTI will provide guidance if an entrepreneur is uncertain as to whether a venture will qualify.

Entrepreneurs wishing to use the Loan Guarantee Scheme make all necessary arrangements through the clearing banks, who are authorized to

Table 5.4 Businesses eligible for Loan Guarantee support

Bed and breakfasts	Tour companies
Hotels	Leisure companies, e.g. golf courses, golf
Public houses with accommodation	driving ranges
Leisure and fitness centres	Fitness instruction
Equipment hire	Manufacture pre-prepared food
	Wholesaling pre-prepared food

administer it. Anecdotal evidence suggests that knowledge of the scheme amongst individual branches of banks varies considerably and that those seeking to use it should be prepared to educate the banks in some circumstances! Nevertheless the scheme can be extremely useful for entrepreneurs with limited capital and may certainly make the difference between a bank being willing or not willing to advance funding. Clearly the scheme will not be the answer in all cases and the entrepreneur will then need to look elsewhere for the missing funding.

Venture capital and business angels

Venture capital is funding which participates directly in the permanent capital funding of the business. This is as opposed to loan capital, which tends to be for a fixed duration. In fact, venture capital providers will want to plan at the outset of the arrangement for their exit from the venture. However, for the period they are involved, they are investing in the business directly, rather than entering into an arms-length financial contract. They are therefore fully exposed to the venture's risk. Venture capital companies are often only interested in more substantial propositions which require injections of capital over £100 000.

Business angels are wealthy private individuals who are available for smaller-scale venture capital investments. The distinction is becoming less clear-cut as some of the venture capital companies are also now willing to consider smaller-scale ventures and some private individuals have substantial funding available.

According to the British Venture Capital Association's (BVCA) informative web site (1996c), the UK venture capital industry is second only in importance to that of the USA and actually invests more in proportion to GDP. A record £2.5 billion was invested in over 1000 UK companies during 1995. Slightly more than half of the sum invested was for expansion of existing businesses, rather than start-ups. This partially explains why, despite its attractiveness, venture capital did not feature more prominently in Deakins' (1996) Cambridge research into sources of start up funding. However, it also seems that venture capital is not considered to the extent it should be by many entrepreneurs.

'Leisure and hotels' is the generic term used by the BVCA (1996a) in its report summarizing its investments in hospitality, tourism and leisure sectors. During 1995, these industries accounted for only 4 per cent of total venture capital company investment. This was a reduction from 11 per cent in 1994. The situation regarding the scale of investment by individual business angels is less well-documented, since not all investments are reported to the BVCA.

An entrepreneur considering venture capital has a major decision to make. Venture capital finance normally requires the entrepreneur to relinquish ownership over a share of the business. The venture will be set up in the form of a limited company and the venture capital provider (company or business angel) will take a proportion of the shares in exchange for the injection of funds. Psychologically, this can be very difficult. The entrepreneur has conceived the new venture and worked it up into a full business plan. There is naturally much enthusiasm and optimism about its prospects. It can be very difficult to hand over a share in a venture which is envisaged to create substantial wealth, simply in exchange for a share of the capital to get the show on the road. Yet, more often than not, this is exactly the right thing to do.

Whilst the new venture may have potential, at this stage it is nothing more than potential. The challenge is to convert the potential into reality. Venture capital can have a very positive impact on the chances of this happening. Whilst the venture capital company or business angel demands a share of the business, in exchange they are participating fully in the business risk. Unlike the clearing banks, they do not reduce their risk exposure by seeking personal guarantees and taking charges over the entrepreneur's personal assets. The venture capital provider's funds are at risk alongside those of the entrepreneur. In this situation it is surely equitable that there should also be proportionate sharing of the possible rewards.

It must also be considered that the inclusion of venture capital in the business can significantly reduce the overall risk as well as distributing that risk over a greater number of capital providers. Earlier in this chapter, we discussed how resource poverty contributed to the operating difficulties and ultimate demise of many small businesses. Venture capital can help ensure that the funding for a new venture is sufficiently adequate to see the company through the period where it is consuming, rather than generating, funds. It can provide valuable breathing space to get the venture operating effectively.

As well as providing funding resource, venture capital can also provide an invaluable injection of know how into the new venture. Business angels are often people who have become wealthy through their own business success. They can therefore make a real difference to the prospects for the new venture by passing on the benefit of their experience and expertise. Often a business angel will wish to formalize the advisory relationship through a non-executive directorship. Venture capital companies may also wish to

---

Illustration: Mercantile 100, venture capital

Mercantile 100 are venture capital specialists operating out of Glasgow. The organization was set up by Kidsons Impey, Chartered Accountants. The managers have a favourable view of the growth prospects for the hospitality, tourism and leisure industries and are reasonably encouraged by the sectors.

Recent venture capital projects include arranging the finance for the £3.5 million purchase of a pub estate. As is typical with this size of project, a portfolio of capital sources were used. Bank loans amounted to £2.75 million, the Brewery Supplier contributed £350 000 in the form of loan and advanced purchase discount, the Vendor helped bridge the funding gap with a £50 000 loan and a business angel invested £350 000.

A small Troon hotel wanting to expand by building ten new bedrooms found that it had a 20 per cent funding gap when it raised a commercial mortgage. The gap was covered by a business angel who invested the shortfall in return for a share of the business.
Source: Mercantile 100, Glasgow

appoint a non-executive director, particularly in situations where they think that there is an imbalance of expertise. Again the prospect of a different perspective and strengthening of the entrepreneurial team should be welcomed, rather than resisted. The entrepreneur has to be sufficiently open-minded to accept this and have personal confidence in the non-executive director.

In return for assuming this degree of risk, venture providers are naturally looking for good returns on their investments. The BVCA's *A Guide to Venture Capital* (British Venture Capital Association, 1996b) quotes a minimum Internal Rate of Return (IRR) of 20 per cent as being sought by venture capital companies. This does not mean that they will demand dividends on their shares, but that the total return, including exit arrangements, should equate to this. Some of the return can be via a formula to buy back the venture capital company's shares at a premium price, compared with their initial value. As such, venture capital is only suitable for truly entrepreneurial businesses which are intending to grow substantially.

The BVCA specifically differentiates between life-style businesses, where the business initiators are looking towards a particular way of life rather than to grow, and entrepreneurial businesses where the intention is to create serious wealth. This links to Chapter 2 where we discussed the difference between an entrepreneur and small business proprietor. It is not just a question of semantics. When it comes to funding, the difference is extremely important to the potential venture capital provider.

Going public

For truly entrepreneurial ventures, one way of providing an exit for venture capitalists, rewards for the entrepreneur, and funding for a further round of expansion, possibly all at the same time, is by going public.

The Alternative Investment Market (AIM) was designed to provide access to such funding, enabling small growing businesses to raise funds without the onerous requirements associated with a full stock exchange listing. The AIM has been used successfully by a number of hospitality, tourism and leisure companies seeking to expand. Obtaining capital through this route does have implications for ownership, but as the following illustration shows, this need not involve substantial dilution.

Illustration : Alternative Investment Market, Dragons Health Clubs

Health and fitness operator, Dragon Health Clubs floated on the AIM during 1997. It raised just over £1 million from the issue of shares, representing 17 per cent of its enlarged share capital. This added to the £2.3 million which had earlier been injected by a consortium of venture capital trusts.

The extra funding was used to acquire additional leisure clubs from another operator, giving it a strong London presence. The funding also enabled the company to spend money on the clubs' further development.

Opportunities, 2 May 1997

Illustration: Surrey Free Inns, full stock exchange listing

Surrey Free Inns (SFI) moved to a full stock exchange listing after a successful period of only twelve months on the AIM. The company has used its additional capital to further expand its branded operations, the Litten Tree pub brand and Bar Med café bar. The move to a full listing has been extremely positive and the shares are now up at a level 80 per cent higher than when the listing was obtained.
Opportunities, 8 August 1997

The idea of the AIM is that companies are able to experience a period of time when their shares are traded. They can then build upon this by progressing to a full stock exchange listing, expanding their capital base still further.

These examples illustrate that, for the truly entrepreneurial ventures, capital is available to develop businesses remarkably quickly. The above examples illustrate a classic development route, from venture capital to AIM to full listing. However, not all businesses are set up in such a way as to enable such dramatic development and for many businesses less high-profile sources of funding are more appropriate.

Hire purchase and leasing

These are financial facilities which enable an entrepreneur to use an asset over a fixed period in exchange for regular payments. With hire purchase the customer becomes the owner of the asset after all the payments have been made. This may be automatic, or after payment of an option-to-purchase fee. The primary difference with leasing is that the customer never actually owns the asset. With hire purchase the entrepreneur is treated as the owner of the equipment and so can claim capital allowances but with leasing, the leasing company claims the capital allowances and the entrepreneur can deduct the cost of lease rentals from taxable income as a trading expense.

Hire purchase and leasing can be used for most types of equipment such as cars, office equipment, kitchen equipment, and computers. It is only normally available for new equipment. The principal advantages and disadvantages of hire purchase and leasing, as identified by the Department of Trade and Industry (1995), are as follows:

- **Certainty**: these arrangements are a medium-term facility which cannot be withdrawn provided all payments are made as specified. Thus, uncertainty which exists with overdrafts, credit, etc., which are repayable on demand is not present.
- **Budgeting**: the payments are usually of a fixed sum and of a regular nature which helps a new business forecast cash flow.
- **Fixed rate finance**: in the majority of cases the payments are fixed so the business knows what the payments will be despite changes in interest rates. Some companies offer the option of variable interest rates but this makes it harder for the firm to estimate the level of payments required.

- **Effect on security**: the finance company retains legal ownership of the equipment until all payments are made which acts as security for the financing. This makes the company more willing to advance funds. However, the decision to provide finance to a business also still depends on the business' credit standing and potential. In the case of a new business, the credit standing of the entrepreneur is investigated which can pose a problem if the entrepreneur has had bad debts, county court judgements, or a bankruptcy in the past. The entrepreneur may additionally be asked to sign personal guarantees, even if of good credit standing.
- **Maximum finance**: by hire purchase or leasing, the entire cost of the equipment can be raised; however, most companies prefer to minimize risk and to see commitment demonstrated by requesting a lump-sum deposit from the entrepreneur.
- **Use of resources**: hire purchase and leasing can be a means for entrepreneurs to mix forms of financing, such as bank funding with medium-term financing. The primary benefit is that these methods remove the need to tie up resources in capital equipment initially and enable the firm to generate the revenue needed to repay the finance.
- **Tax benefits**: the entrepreneur has the choice of how to take advantage of capital allowances. If the firm is profitable then it can claim its own capital allowances through hire purchase or through outright purchase. If the firm is not yet profitable and thus not in a tax-paying position then a lease may be more beneficial to the business. The leasing company will claim the capital allowance and pass the benefit to the entrepreneur though reduced rental payments.

Supplier finance and trade credit

In some cases, suppliers may be a potential source of start-up finance or even expansion finance. The brewing and licensed trade industry is a prime case of supplier finance being a particularly important source for new business. The brewery, in many cases one of the major national brewing and pub retailing companies such as Scottish and Newcastle, may offer a loan at very favourable rates in return for a guaranteed outlet for its products. This type of loan agreement will usually have conditions attached to it. In this way the borrower will effectively be 'tied' into selling the brewer's products. The repayments are most likely to be connected to purchasing volumes of products, with each barrel sold representing a negotiated sum repaid off the loan. Thus, the loan is also likely to be connected to the borrower buying a stipulated amount of barrels over a fixed term. If the target figure is not reached then a higher rate of interest is charged to the loan. Usually, the higher the volume sold, the quicker the loan is paid off, providing a good incentive for both borrower and lender. Whilst some consider the 'tie' to be fairly onerous, in many cases the funding supplied by the brewer makes the difference between not being able to afford to set up the business and having sufficient finance. Also, the brewery loan will likely be at a lower rate of interest than most other sources of external finance. It is not uncommon for publicans to switch suppliers with the new brewery paying off the existing brewery loan in exchange for a re-negotiated deal.

Illustration: Stockport County Football Club, supplier and trade finance

In the early 1990s, Stockport County Football Club was a poorly performing club, both on and off the field. Commercial activities were minimal. The lounge area and bar in the club did not have a license and was run by the players who bought cans of beer and sold them for £1 each. All the profits went into the players' holiday fund. Whilst the club would have liked to develop the bar area, there was no capital available for capital expenditure – even paying the players' wages was difficult.

Greenall's, one of the smaller breweries, offered Stockport County a loan of £10 000 to refurbish the bar and purchase fixtures and fittings. This loan was to be paid back on barrellage at a very low rate of interest in exchange for selling the brewer's products. Following some mergers and take-overs between companies, Carlsberg–Tetley took over some of Greenall's interests and continued the loan. Recently, the club – now in Division One – has paid off the original loan and agreed an increased loan of £16 000 with Carlsberg–Tetley to assist the development of the new Earlam Suite; this is to be used as a catering and entertainment venue for the club.

In some instances, businesses can arrange contra-deals to help reduce expenditure. This is not often appropriate, but with a football club it is common. For example, Earlam Builders have agreed to carry out, free of charge, all the building work on the new Earlam Suite in exchange for having the suite named after them, season tickets, and advertisement hoardings around the pitch perimeter. Other such *ex gratia* deals include printers producing programmes, flyers etc. in exchange for advertisements in the programme and a weekly quota of 'free' tickets. Other businesses, such as McDonalds and Nynex are happy to be involved in sponsorship of schemes in order to generate publicity and positive PR.
Source: authors

Obtaining trade credit for supplies can potentially provide a useful form of working capital. However, as a result of the recession, supplying organizations are extremely careful as to how much trade credit they allow and to whom they advance it. Some companies will not give the usual thirty days credit unless six months audited accounts can be supplied, an obvious problem for a start-up venture. Others may be prepared to give credit subject to bank reference, or even personal guarantee. In this case, the length of time for which credit is allowed is very strictly controlled and supply will quickly be cut off if terms are not complied with. Even with such a short period, trade credit can be very useful. Certainly the hospitality, tourism and leisure industries convert physical stock into cash very quickly, normally in a few days. Even one month's credit can therefore have a very positive impact on cash flow.

Other loans

There are other types of loans available depending on the location and type of business. For example, The European Investment Bank – Capital Investment Loans are available to small and medium-sized firms in industry, services to industry, hotel and tourism, environmental energy, or infrastructure projects. These loans vary in terms of availability and timing.

Illustration: Premier Cuisine, grants

Premier Cuisine, a contract catering company, was started in 1996 by entrepreneurs Dennis Blades and Keith McDonald. Budgeted turnover for their first full year is £80 000. The partners initially invested a total of £10 000 and followed this by refinancing of the company with a £12 000 bank loan. In addition, they received a £1900 Tyneside Business Start-up Grant from the local enterprise company, Business Link Newcastle, and an equipment grant of £2500 from Newcastle City Council. **Source**: authors

---

Professional organizations and trade publications are the most likely source of up-to-date details.

Grants

A grant is **free money** in that the entrepreneur does not normally need to pay it back nor pay any interest (Caley, 1989). Any free money is clearly desirable! However, grant funding can be very difficult to obtain and the application process may be onerous. Industries such as technology and manufacturing tend to attract a large percentage of grant funds. The European Information Centre plus local Chamber of Commerce, Business Link etc. should be able to provide current details of any European Union-backed finance.

The Prince's Youth Business Trust offers small grants and start-up loans for people aged between 18 and 29, particularly those who have been unemployed for more than six weeks. Certain locations may attract grant funding to encourage the growth of new firms and jobs in inner city areas or poorer regions of the country. For example, the Regional Enterprise for Innovation covers up to 50 per cent of the total eligible cost up to £25 000 for small firms introducing new products or processes in a city challenge/task force area. Some entrepreneurs who run their businesses in historic, listed buildings may be eligible for a grant from Scottish or English Heritage who can provide funds towards the repair and preservation of historic buildings of grade I and II.

Family, friends, and contacts

Many entrepreneurs draw upon their personal network to supplement their funding for a new business. The advantages of utilizing informal methods such as family and friends are that they are more likely to **risk** their money without having security than are other sources. However, mixing family/friendship with business can be dangerous and heartbreaking. Many entrepreneurs lament the interference from family members who, having lent money to get the business started, were determined to be involved in the management and future of the business as they felt they held a stake in the company. Implications for family and friendship disharmony if the venture fails are also considerable. The primary recommendation when using family, friends, or contacts as a source of funding is that all loans should be made on a business-like basis, in writing, with legally binding contracts made for repayment, interest, and default.

Interestingly, ethnic minority entrepreneurs have a competitive advantage over many other entrepreneurs as they often have wide access to informal sources of finance in the extended network of family contacts that exist, particularly within the Asian community (Ward and Jenkins, 1984). It is common for members of the Asian communities to **club together** in order to set up a member in business. Partnerships between families and friends are also very common.

Bootstrapping

Despite the availability of the above sources of finance, the entrepreneur may nevertheless find that the dreaded funding gap still exists. Bootstrapping can be the last resort to get the show on the road, or what is turned to when funding is found to be inadequate in the early stages of operation.

Bootstrapping occurs when an entrepreneur supplements the working capital specifically provided to finance the new venture with funds from other sources. These sources unknowingly add to the funds flow into the entrepreneur's business. Such sources often involve utilizing the entrepreneur's private line of credit, intended for personal use, to support the business. Alternatively, credit arrangements entered into with suppliers may be exceeded without the explicit authorization of credit providers.

Clearly, this form of finance does generate some ethical debate, and in an ideal world such measures would not be necessary. Entrepreneurs would raise sufficient funds to cover both the initial capital expenditure connected with the new venture and its working capital requirements. In reality, resource poverty is the norm rather than the exception when a new business is started. It is more than likely that the entrepreneur does not have sufficient collateral to support the borrowings ideally required. Rather than forego the opportunity, the temptation is to try and make do with the funds that can be raised. Alternatively the entrepreneur's estimate of the length of time needed to reach a positive cash flow situation is over-optimistic and consequently credit arrangements subsequently prove inadequate.

The entrepreneur is left with a pretty desperate situation. Either the business is stillborn before it has a chance to become established, or corners have to be cut in order for it to survive. Having invested so much emotional energy in starting the business and risked so much, the decision is usually to cut corners and hold onto the dream. In reality the logic and ethics of this are not really that much different from those of a large organization trying to boost its cash flow by delaying payment to creditors. Both may act in ways that push back the boundary of behaviour that would normally be considered ethically acceptable.

A high profile entrepreneur provides an illustration of what can be done with bootstrap finance.

Illustration: Virgin Atlantic, bootstrapping

To launch Virgin Atlantic in 1984 Richard Branson needed £3 million. Despite the size of the Virgin Corporation, at that time it was short of cash. But Branson realized that while in most new businesses there are significant up-front costs that have to be paid before income begins to come in, that is not the case with an airline. Few of Virgin Atlantic's bills had to be paid far in advance. For the most part, the airline's inputs could be paid for either on delivery or afterwards. Its income from ticket sales, however, was a different matter: to make reservations, economy class customers had to pay when they booked – often weeks or even months in advance.

According to what Branson told the press a week from the inaugural flight, Virgin Atlantic had sold 25 000 tickets in advance. At a one-way fare of £219 that meant the company had already paid over £3 million into the bank. It had cost Richard Branson nothing to start up Virgin Atlantic! Its customers had loaned its working capital.

Source: Jackson, 1995

The main sources of bootstrapping capital are shown in Table 5.5. Essentially all of them involve the obtaining of capital to support the business from non-conventional sources that do not intend it to be used for that purpose.

Table 5.5 Bootstrapping: unofficial sources of capital for new ventures

---

- Personal credit cards
- Home equity loans
- Professional service providers at below competitive rates
- Working from home
- Personal savings
- Reduced, foregone, or delayed compensation

Source: Freer *et al*. (1995)

Personal credit cards can add up to quite an important source of extra capital. A typical person of good credit standing may have two or three cards with, say, a £1500 expenditure limit on each. Taken together these add up to quite a significant sum. This can be switched into the business either through financing living costs, rather than withdrawing a salary, or through using the cards to buy supplies for the business. Either use is a slippery slope to embark upon.

Extending the mortgage on the house through a re-mortgage is a strategy frequently used for raising initial capital. This can, to an extent, be self-defeating, since the equity in the house is no longer available to support other business loans. Either way, the house is at risk if the business fails!

Getting professionals to provide their services at nil or greatly reduced cost is another strategy for conserving precious cash flow in a start-up situation. One entrepreneur we worked with was particularly good at this. He was extremely persuasive and could get people to do almost anything.

The incentive was that there would be lots of subsequent business which would make the initial foregoing of fees worthwhile!

Whilst there is absolutely nothing wrong with trying to obtain the best deal possible and conserving precious cash, some of the bootstrapping methods are certainly a source of last resort. If the situation is such that the entrepreneur has to use them, as opposed to chooses to, it is a sure sign that the business is sailing very close to the wind and that the financial situation is very stretched.

Financial management

As we discussed in the introduction to this chapter, the nature of entre-preneurial enterprises in the hospitality, tourism and leisure sectors is that they are close to the customer and subject to all the operational and financial volatility which that implies. Financial problems and issues do not end with business start-up, it is simply the end of the beginning.

Dunn and Cheatham (1993) describe the particular financial challenges at different stages of a business' life. At the time of initiation of the business, there is the danger of under-capitalization. Inadequate estimation of initial capital and operating costs and revenue streams mean that there are cash flow problems right from the beginning. A second financial consideration often overlooked is the length of time taken to develop business and reach a stage where cash flow is positive. Some new businesses generate cash from day one, but others, which would develop to a successful level of trade, are not given the opportunity to prosper since inadequate provision for working capital has been made during the build-up period. Growth can bring its own problems. Many hospitality businesses can be cash generators in a growth situation, but a growing tourism or leisure business can involve heavy outlays before revenues start to fully flow. Finally, the small entrepreneurial business will experience the full impact of changes in the macro- and micro-environment, as discussed in Chapter 8. Such changes can cause wide fluc-tuations in levels of operation and subsequent cash flow.

Given this level of volatility, it is absolutely vital to have sound financial systems which will adequately control the business and enable difficulties to be anticipated and responded to early. The danger is that the demands on the entrepreneur in the hospitality, tourism and leisure sectors are so great that financial planning and control frequently takes second place to the operational activity. To an extent this is how it should be, since if the business is not operating well there is no cash flow to control! However, the demands of entrepreneurship in these sectors are such that a number of management functions need to carried out continuously, a feature that makes it so demanding. Demands on the entrepreneur's time can be compounded by resource poverty being such that the incentive is to do everything, rather than pay for it to be done by others.

The best advice is that financial management, above all others, is one area where it is imperative that false economies are not made. A good accountancy company, used to the demands placed upon entrepreneurial businesses, can provide invaluable advice. This will include specification of

---

Illustration: Fretwell Downing, financial management/operations management

Anthony Fretwell Downing was a director and manager in the family catering business. He recognized the operational importance of sound information and financial control and the potential impact of computer applications at a time when they were very new within the hospitality industry.

An opportunity to link up with a software writer provided a new business opportunity in software design and development and its installation in hospitality businesses.

Today, Fretwell Downing Computer Systems has grown to be a major MIS supplier to the catering and conference industries and to hospitals. It has far outstripped the original catering business.

Source: authors

---

the financial systems, knowledge of service providers for such activities as wages calculation, and frequent review meetings at which progress is assessed and the future is planned.

Summary

The nature of entrepreneurship within the hospitality, tourism and leisure industries is that financial management of new businesses in these sectors is always going to be exciting and extremely challenging. Businesses are rarely operating in some kind of steady state. The implication is that the entrepreneurial business will frequently swing from financial plenty, to famine, and hopefully back again! Raising money to start-up the business is frequently a major challenge. It is vital that the business is not under-capitalized. If this involves diluting ownership and equity in the business, then so be it. Providing the business moves into take-off there will be capital growth enough to satisfy all the investors. Effective continuing financial planning and control is essential, given the volatility which is likely to be experienced. Consequently, the ongoing support and expertise of a accountant specializing in entrepreneurial small businesses is invaluable.

Reflective questions

1 Consider the features specific to the hospitality, tourism and leisure industries which make entrepreneurial businesses particularly susceptible to financial difficulties.
2 Resource poverty has been recognized as a characteristic of entrepreneurial businesses. Given the nature of the entrepreneurial personality as discussed in Chapter 2, consider ways in which entrepreneurs generally address this characteristic.
3 Identify the different sources of finance potentially available to an entrepreneur to start a new venture, and evaluate the advantages and disadvantages associated with each.
4 Discuss the key functions of a business plan in the development and sustenance of businesses within the hospitality, tourism and leisure industries.
5 Identify the financial management challenges which may face the entrepreneurial business at different stages in its life-cycle.

References

Anonymous (1992) *The Business Start Up Guide*, National Westminster Bank.

Anonymous (1996b) *Guidelines for Prospective Franchisees*, Domino's Pizza Co.

British Venture Capital Association (1996a) *Report on Investment Activity 1995*, BVCA, London.

British Venture Capital Association (1996b) *A Guide to Venture Capital*, BVCA, London.

British Venture Capital Association (1996c) The UK Venture Capital Web Site: http://www.brainstorm.co.uk/BVCA/Welcome.html.

Caley, K. (1989) *Guide to The Structure and Financing of Your Small Business*, Lancashire Enterprises Ltd., Preston.

Deakins, D. (1996) *Entrepreneurship and Small Firms*, McGraw Hill, London.

Dunn, P. and Cheatham, L. (1993) Fundamentals of small business financial management for start up, survival, growth and changing economic circumstances, *Managerial Finance*, **19**, No. 8, 1–13.

Department of Trade and Industry (1995) *A Guide to Hire Purchase and Leasing*, March, DYI/Pub 1788/20K/2.96AR.

Fox, L. (1997) The secret's out, *Caterer and Hotelkeeper*, 12 June, pp. 64–65.

Freer, J., Sohl, J. and Wetzel, W. (1995) Who bankrolls software entrepreneurs? *Babson Frontiers of Entrepreneurship Research*, Babson 1995, pp. 394–406.

Jackson, T. (1995) *Virgin King*, Harper Collins, London.

Keasey, K. and Watson, R. (1993) *Small Firm Management*, Blackwell Business, Oxford.

Murphy , M. (1996) *Small Business Management*, Pitman. Publishing, London.

Ward, R. and Jenkins, R. (eds.) (1984) *Ethnic Communities in Business*, Cambridge, London.

Welsh, J. and White, J. (1981) A small business is not a little big business, *Harvard Business Review*, July/August.

6 Operation and management of entrepreneurial organizations

The objective of this chapter is to develop an understanding of the managerial and operational issues pertinent to an entrepreneurial venture within the hospitality, tourism and leisure industries. Specifically, this chapter aims to advance the understanding of:

- differences between the management and operations of small entrepreneurial ventures and larger, mature organizations;
- problems inherent with entrepreneurial management;
- organizational structure within entrepreneurial firms;
- entrepreneurial management and the organizational life-cycle;
- entrepreneurship and the issue of business failure.

Introduction

Many entrepreneurial firms die in their infancy. Dramatic, although dated, generic statistics indicate that only 50 per cent of new firms live as long as eighteen months and only one in five actually make it to ten years (Siropolis, 1986). The situation in the restaurant industry is even more daunting with 85 per cent of new restaurant establishments closing within five years and almost half not surviving the first year (Cullen and Dick, 1990). There are many reasons for this failure rate, however the overwhelming cause of failure has been identified as poor management. Many entrepreneurs are ill-prepared as managers. They may go into business with a good product idea but little or no business or managerial experience. One consequence of this, as discussed in Chapter 5, is that the capitalization of the business may be inadequate.

The very nature of the entrepreneur often plays an important part in the management of firms. Entrepreneurs, as identified in Chapter 2, typically exhibit characteristics such as initiative, independence, need for achievement, and optimism. Whilst these characteristics are important in the venture creation process they do not always fit into the management skills needed to take a business beyond infancy. An entrepreneur's job is traditionally seen as developing a new product or service, planning the business operations, and sorting out the money side of things. However, as Kao (1989) points out, entrepreneurs also need to define agendas, make compensation deals, establish standards, resolve conflicts, evaluate and develop key people, and so on. The issue of entrepreneurial management and operational control will be discussed throughout this chapter, commencing with the entrepreneurial skill requirements.

Entrepreneurial skill requirements

Given the high levels of competitiveness and environmental uncertainty that exist in the operation of a business today it is not surprising that many entrepreneurs lack the skills needed to operate their business successfully. Companies such as Whitbread and First Leisure employ many specialists in each functional area. Typically, a large organization would have a number of specialists in operations and other management functions, some of which are highlighted in Table 6.1.

Table 6.1 Specialist roles typically found within large organizations

Systems Analyst	Information Technology Specialist
Facilities Manager	Human Resource Manager
Financial Controller	Property and Estate Manager
Supply Chain Manager	Sales and Marketing Manager
Publicity and Public Relations Manager	Quality Controller
Purchasing Manager	Technical Engineer
Training Officer	Operations Planning and Forecasting Manager

Source: authors

Within the hospitality, tourism and leisure industries, whilst there are a large number of multi-national chains, the industries are still dominated by a substantial volume of small, entrepreneurial enterprises. Very few of these businesses actually grow significantly and thus the individual entrepreneur is required to possess multi-faceted skills in order to compete with the larger companies who employ specialist skills as shown above. In addition to employing specialists, the larger organizations clearly have the resources necessary to continually develop their staff through training and development programmes as highlighted in the following illustration.

> *Illustration: specialist training for management*
>
> The Carlton Inter-Continental Hotel in Cannes hosts a tailor-made management training centre for the company. Inter-Continental's middle managers go to Cannes to learn about issues such as the management of change, competitor profiling, staff attitudes, and business practice which are covered in a five-day integrated business management programme.
> **Source**: authors

Consequently, in order to compete with the big companies in the industry, the entrepreneur must be able to handle a wide variety of problems and situations. The entrepreneur has to be their own systems analyst, 'hirer and firer' of staff, quality controller, and in some cases even legal specialist. Running a small, entrepreneurial business requires different operational and managerial skills to running a large corporation with experts available to call upon. In order to survive and grow, the entrepreneur must identify the type of help needed at different stages. However, this is one of the primary failures of entrepreneurial management. The concept of **'know what you do not know'** is forgotten as in many cases the entrepreneur will think that they can manage and is typically very reluctant to 'admit defeat' by bringing in specialist help. This is termed **'entrepreneurial immaturity'** and is discussed in further detail later in the chapter.

Many entrepreneurs perceive that they are the only ones who can do a particular job well and that in the time taken in asking an employee to do a job, they could easily have done it themselves. Furthermore, they believe if they are not there supervising, the job does not get done to the right standard. In some cases their fears are well founded. Most people can relate occasions they have gone into a restaurant when the owner was there and had an excellent meal; going back another time they have had a poor meal, only to find out that it was the owner's night off.

Given the limited resources generally available to entrepreneurs, they have no choice but to define their operation in terms of skills needed, as opposed to the specialists available. It is safe to assume that the entrepreneur will rarely have the resources available to afford a full-time accountant or a full-time market research specialist. Table 6.2 presents a list of typical skills required in setting-up and running a hospitality, tourism or leisure operation. We have assumed that in each case, the entrepreneur will have some relevant skill but, as can be seen, a wide range of other specialists may also be needed.

Illustration: Rocky Mountain Diner, skill gap

A sad case of an entrepreneur not having the skills needed to succeed is that of the Rocky Mountain Diner. The Rocky Mountain Diner closed down in 1996 following a long, lean spell in which the owner put all his money (including his house as collateral) into the business. The restaurant was a diner themed around skiing, Colorado, the Rockies, etc. It was located in a good position on one of the main roads leading from Sheffield city centre. Whilst the product itself was perfectly acceptable, the diner suffered from not having a clearly focused customer group. Instead of attracting either shoppers, students, or business people the diner tried to appeal to all of them, unsuccessfully. The owner was so concerned with trying to generate extra money – for example offering a delivery service – and working himself to reduce staff costs, he could not see why his business was losing money. He did eventually seek specialist help from Sheffield Hallam University. Their advice was to remove the dated theme from the diner and re-focus towards targeting the student market. However, it was too late. The business had to close before the bank foreclosed. The irony in this case is that this area of Sheffield has just recently become one of the 'in' places for drinking and dining out. There are currently two major brewery-driven investment projects underway and a new Pierre Victoire restaurant just completed within walking distance.
Source: authors

Table 6.2 Identifying skill needs

Step number	Description of step	Skill need	People best suited to met need	
			Entrepreneur	Other
1	Decide to go into business	Raising finance	✔	Banker/ accountant
2	Analyse yourself	Knowledge of self	✔	
3	Pick product or service	Knowledge of industry sector	✔	Business advice agencies
4	Research the market	Knowledge of marketing research/hospitality, tourism or leisure industry	✔	Market researcher/ other operators
5	Forecast sales revenues	Knowledge of marketing research/finance	✔	Market researcher/ accountant
6	Select site	Knowledge of property markets	✔	Business sales/ estate agent
7	Develop operations plan	Knowledge of hospitality, tourism or leisure operations	✔	Technical experts/IT specialists/ equipment specialists/ consultants
8	Develop marketing plan	Knowledge of marketing	✔	Marketing consultants/ PR agencies/ business advice
9	Develop organizational plan	Knowledge of skill needs and human resources	✔	Human resource consultants
10	Develop legal plan	Knowledge of law	✔	Accountant/ Solicitor
11	Develop accounting and financial plan	Knowledge of accounting and finance	✔	Accountant
12	Hiring and training staff	Knowledge of human resources and relevant legal issues	✔	Solicitor/ training company

Source: adapted from Siropolis (1986)

Griffin (1987) believes that in order to identify the type of help required, the entrepreneur must plan the business as though specialist help can be afforded. Only by going through this process can the entrepreneur be sure that required skills are not overlooked. Specialist help can come from a variety of sources and need not cost much money, if any at all. For example, members of the Sheffield Chamber of Commerce (annual membership around £100 for small businesses) have access to a free legal helpline number with Hambro Legal Protection Limited providing legal advice twenty-four hours a day. The Chamber of Commerce offers many other free services to members, such as sourcing suppliers of any given product and having specialist advisors available for consultation. Sources of advice are mentioned in Chapter 3; these include Business Link, Training and Enterprise Council, the Small Business Bureau, banks, and industry professional organizations such as the British Institute of Innkeeping (BII) and the Hotel and Catering International Management Association (HCIMA).

The hospitality, tourism and leisure industries have low barriers to entry and many new businesses are created as a result of identifying an opportunity following experiences as a consumer. Furthermore, these low barriers to entry give rise to many new businesses built on the back of a hobby or interest. Barriers to entry are considerably lower than those in manufacturing or engineering businesses. For individuals with no business or industry background, many of the skills have to be learnt whilst 'on the job'. The popularity of franchises, as discussed in Chapter 8, illustrates that many entrepreneurs see the benefits of buying in specialist skills such as new product development, operational controls, marketing expertise, etc.

Illustration: management inexperience

Fifty-two-year-old Henry Tonga founded the all-suite town house hotel, 22 Jermyn Street, London, which opened in 1990. His background as a property investor gave him good business experience and he had worked in restaurants throughout his youth. However, as he stated, '*I was very experienced in property, interested in decor, experienced in staying in hotels – but very inexperienced in running one!*'.
Source: Tarpey, 1996

The above scenario is not uncommon in the hospitality, tourism and leisure industries. For many people, starting a business is the result of identifying an opportunity following experiences as a consumer, or through identifying a gap in the market. When individuals have no business or industry background, taking a franchise may be a suitable approach. As described in Chapter 8, there is a caveat – prospective franchisees do need to ensure that the market for the franchise is not overcrowded.

Management expertise – name of the game

Haswell and Holmes (1989) found that managerial inadequacy, incompetence, inefficiency, and inexperience to be a consistent theme in explaining the failure of entrepreneurial ventures. Peterson *et al.* (1983) identified that the primary causes of entrepreneurial business failure were the lack of management expertise and finance-related factors. Entrepreneurs in the hospitality, tourism and leisure industries are particularly vulnerable. As discussed previously, the barriers to entry in the industry are considerably low. Greene King, the brewing and pub retailing company, operate their Greene Start programme aimed at providing opportunities for potential licensees for as little as £5000 capital investment. Licensees are given a three-day training induction which covers finance, training, cellar management and food hygiene. Clearly this is not a substantial training experience for would-be entrepreneurs! Whilst the company does provide further support for its licensees, it does mean that many of the managerial skills will need to be acquired by the licensee during their tenancy, if not already possessed.

Table 6.3 identifies the many management skills and competencies required for effective management. In a large organization, where there are teams of individuals all offering different skills and competencies, the majority of these will be covered. In an entrepreneurial organization, where the entrepreneur is the only or primary decision-maker, the responsibility for these competencies and skills may fall to a single person. Some of these skills and competencies do not necessarily fit with the hallmarks of the typical entrepreneur, such as risk-taking, innovation, creativity, adaptability, and task orientation.

Table 6.3 Management competencies and skills

• Vision	• Motivation skills
• Innovative capability	• Positive attitude
• Lateral thinking	• Self-confidence
• Creative talents	• Intellectual ability
• Co-ordination skills	• Foresight
• Intelligence	• Intuition
• Leadership skills	• Analytical thinking
• Communication skills	• Judgement

Source: Carson *et al.* (1995, p. 102)

Bovee *et al.* (1993) identified the six most common characteristics of entrepreneurs which have an impact on their management of business:

1 **Energy level:** it is not uncommon for entrepreneurs to throw themselves into their business, spending in the region of seventy hours per week working. Many entrepreneurs find it difficult to recognize that employees may not share this same commitment and energy level. Even the entrepreneur may find it difficult to sustain. A further effect of this degree of commitment is that the entrepreneur's management style will almost certainly be very hands-on. As explored further in Chapter 8, finding space to think strategically about the business can also be a problem.

2 **Need for achievement:** as discussed in Chapter 2, typically entrepreneurs have a high drive to achieve. They set ambitious targets which challenge them and often they are not happy with a single unit and plan to grow the business. In some cases, entrepreneurs are so keen to succeed that they grow and expand before the operation is ready and the appropriate controls are in place.

> *Illustration: challenge of business*
>
> In an earlier illustration we noted that Holiday Inns were founded in the USA in 1952 by entrepreneur Kemmons Wilson. He retired in the early 1980s following a heart attack. Instead of being content with golf, tennis, and an easy life, he found himself missing the business challenge. He decided to set up a new chain of budget-priced hotels called Wilson Inns. When asked why he was doing this so late in life he stated '*I just love to build … I love to create*'.
> **Source**: authors

3 **Level of risk:** many entrepreneurs are so committed to their idea or business that they are prepared to put all their money and assets into the business to get it going. It can be difficult for first-time entrepreneurs to raise sufficient money to get their venture off the ground and, as identified in the previous chapter, it is common to find that many entrepreneurs put their house and life savings into the venture as collateral. This level of exposure will inevitably mean that the entrepreneur has to think very short term and put the immediate survival of the business at the very top of the management agenda. Such short-term thinking can mean that there is no time to experiment with changes to the business format. On the other hand it does focus the mind wonderfully!

4 **Self-confidence:** entrepreneurs are typically confident about their market, idea, or product. In some cases, this high level of self confidence is a detriment as they can be a 'know it all' and be so confident about the product that they refuse to listen to advice from others. Banks and other lending institutions recognize this level of self-confidence and belief in the business idea and try to view each business plan by considering the worst-case financial scenario as opposed to the often inflated financial projections supplied by the entrepreneur.

> *Illustration: self-confidence*
>
> The up-market fish and chip restaurant in London's St. Katherine's Dock, M Fish, has closed after seven months of trading. The primary reason cited by Managing Director Terence Bramble for the demise of M Fish was the 'seasonal trade at the dock'. The lunch-time trade was good and the restaurant had a good reputation but they were not busy enough, doing very little trade at all during the day (except for lunch) and evening. Despite evidence of there not being sufficient trade in the area at these times, the company are looking for new backers to try and get M Fish open and trading again.
> **Source**: authors

On the other hand, self-confidence is absolutely vital to the establishment of a new venture. It can also be self-fulfilling in that a confident entrepreneur is likely to attract a good team and give a good impression to customers.

5 **Locus of control:** many entrepreneurs believe that they have control of their life and are prepared to take the future into their own hands. They feel that they have to make things happen themselves. This can result in a very hands-on management style. Again, there are both advantages and disadvantages to this. Certainly a highly involved entrepreneur is likely to achieve tight control over operating standards. On the other hand, they may not necessarily get the best out of those who work for them, particularly as the business grows.

6 **Tolerance for ambiguity:** entrepreneurs are usually good at making decisions in an uncertain and ambiguous environment, with little information available. They often have no alternative! Setting up a new business is fraught with uncertainty. Welsh and White (1981) state that the owner-manager needs to have the broad thinking of a generalist and be able to tolerate ambiguity, put up with switching between roles, and stick to fundamental issues. They also postulate that owner-management of a small business is a distinct discipline characterized by severe constraints on financial resources, lack of suitably trained staff, and a short-term perspective imposed by operating in a dynamic and turbulent operating environment. Whilst this sounds interesting, it does not make for a consistent management approach!

The term **entrepreneurship** itself seems to imply an informal approach to management. It also appears to imply at an extreme, the total lack of management in a new business – which can sometimes be found! Many successful businesses start with few or no managerial skills. However, these skills are an essential component of a firm's growth and progression through the organizational life-cycle. Appropriate management, systems, and procedures are a prerequisite to a successful, growing, professionally managed business. However, many entrepreneurs often fail to recognize their importance.

Illustration: inadequate management

Bill Smith was a hotel school graduate who developed a successful fast food concept on the East Coast of the USA. He expanded the company quickly and soon had twenty-two units within a 100-mile radius. His master plan was to franchise the concept and open over 400 units within five years. Today Bill is bankrupt. In an analysis, the following points were identified. Bill could not understand why things were not going to plan as he started to experience declining sales in some of the twenty-two units. He was also finding it hard to get everything done within the day. He was involved with visiting all units, which did not leave time for formal planning, cash flow analysis, marketing plans, or any of the activities usually performed by chief executives. Bill was trying to duplicate his management efforts from his first unit into all his units – attempting to manage twenty-two units in exactly the same way as he managed one. The major problem identified was that he was unable to think conceptually in a way that would enable him to see that he had to adapt his management style, delegate some of the more minor jobs, and bring in specialist help in areas such as marketing and finance.
Source: Olsen and Schmelzer, 1988

Entrepreneurial immaturity

The illustration on the previous page clearly shows that the entrepreneur lacked the depth of managerial skills necessary for running a multi-unit business. The common view held by entrepreneurs is that they managed to get this far without specialists and are wary particularly of the **'money men'** – bankers and accountants. This can be called **'seat of the pants approach'** to management or **'entrepreneurial immaturity'** as termed by Olsen and Schmelzer (1988). Many entrepreneurs revel in the seat of the pants approach, which really comes to the fore during the opening of a new operation.

Illustration: 'seat of the pants approach' to management

'I found it compelling', stated Stephen Bull, when speaking of opening a new restaurant. When he first opened his restaurant in remote Wales in 1974, he confesses that he really did not know what he was doing and knew nothing about cooking (but he planned to do the cooking himself without the help of a chef!). *'The nuts and bolts of running a restaurant are a nightmare, frankly'*, says Bull. *'Opening them is a big buzz, but it is the six months afterwards that are horrendous.'*
Source: Stringer, 1996a

This need for the entrepreneur to keep up with the complexities in management, such as the company organizational structure, is described by Olsen and Schmelzer as the move towards entrepreneurial maturity. This takes place when the entrepreneur is ready to delegate responsibility to other managers and specialists in the organization and recognizes that specialist help is essential to the growth of the business. Greiner (1972) termed this as crises of leadership. This is a critical juncture in a new organization's life-cycle as it marks the point when the entrepreneurial drive needs to be balanced with day-to-day management and leadership. The successful companies are the ones who recognize the need for strong management executives to manage the company and bring in required expertise.

Illustration: employing specialist expertise

Max Griggs, president of Dr. Martens Footwear, is also the Chairman of Rushdens and Diamonds Football Club which is a semi-professional outfit in the GM Vauxhall Conference. When developing the football ground he recognized that he knew absolutely nothing about catering so he brought in Scott Benham, manufacturing kitchen designers to design, plan, and install the entire catering facilities at the ground. Max Griggs identified the need to bring in expertise in order to produce the most appropriate and efficient catering operation for the club.
Source: authors

Controlling the business

The need for strong operational control cannot be understated. Without control, all other management functions become ineffective. Entrepreneurs typically have a dislike of numbers – except the bottom-line profit figure! This is due, to some extent, to inexperience and the low educational attainment of many entrepreneurs. Entrepreneurs in hospitality, tourism and leisure are particularly susceptible to this owing to the 'craft' nature of many enterprises. It is possibly also due to the family business environment where staff are hired from within the family (nepotism) and may not be the most suitable or skilled for the job.

Hospitality tourism and leisure students provide a good case study. The weakest academic subject amongst hospitality students tends to be finance and accounting. Consequently, when these students graduate into the market place and open their own operations, the financial weakness is carried over.

Illustration: insufficient financial control

The ignorance and dislike of financial issues is highlighted by Angus Boyd who co-owns, with his wife, Mitchell's Restaurant and Bar in Glasgow. Boyd is a trained chef and a veteran restaurateur. He has many ideas for boosting the low sales and for turning the £200 weekly loss into a profit. His biggest self-confessed failing is his grasp of the statistical and financial side of the business. Boyd agrees that he is ignorant of crucial information, such as average spend or cover turn per session. It is clearly evident that all the good ideas in the world are not sufficient if the sums do not add up at the end of the day.
Source: Tarpey, 1995

There is the misconception by many entrepreneurs that financial control is a function carried out by large organizations. Many fail to see that control is the way that they can assure themselves that they, and their employees, conform to their plans and strategy. Other issues, such as the mis-management of working capital and failure to use efficient accounting practices, also lead to difficulties for entrepreneurs. Small companies often have difficulties in collecting debts and do not have the procedures in place to implement swift invoicing and money collection. The Bolton Report (H.M. Government, 1971) identified a number of areas in which small entrepreneurial companies could improve.

One key area was finance. The report acknowledged that many small companies lack knowledge of alternative sources of finance and different methods of raising capital. Secondly, the report identified that cost control and costing data are often so poor that the entrepreneur frequently learns of an impending crisis only when the bank bounces cheques. In less serious cases, the lack of costing data makes it very difficult for the entrepreneur to monitor factors such as the product mix, credit and stock control, and profit percentages. Compounding this is the group of 'old school' entrepreneurs who are reluctant to implement any form of computerized control system.

Welsh and White (1981) identified the major distinction between large organizations and small entrepreneurial operations as being that smaller companies are considerably more likely to experience 'resource poverty' than the more financially stable large organizations. This was discussed in Chapter 5. One reason is high levels of competition to which the small firm responds by cutting prices, thus reducing profits and cash flow. The effect of this is felt more by companies with small amounts of working capital. One of the primary outcomes of resource poverty, other than the demise of the firm, is the 'burn out' of the entrepreneur. The entrepreneur attempts to do more and more to overcome the resource poverty and eventually burns out.

Drucker (1985) highlights the case for managerial skills even within a new venture. It is not sufficient to have a superb business idea, the ability to generate the necessary resources and to play 'the boss'. Indeed, managing does not mean being the boss. Drucker identifies four requirements for entrepreneurial management:

- a market focus;
- financial foresight and planning;
- building a management team;
- decision on own role and responsibilities by the entrepreneur.

The new venture needs to focus on the market and anticipate responses from competitors. There is a need for environmental scanning, as discussed in Chapter 8. Many entrepreneurs have skills in recognizing market opportunities and capitalizing on them. However, many also possess tunnel vision when it comes to managing their business. As a company begins to grow, one of the most serious issues, as already identified, is the lack of financial foresight by entrepreneurs. As profits are often the focus of attention, areas such as cashflow, capital and controls are often forgotten. A growing venture needs financial feeding.

Building a management team is crucial as the company grows as, often, the company outgrows the entrepreneur. Drucker (1985) recommends that an entrepreneur starts building a top management team *before* the need is critical, as they take time to assemble. The management team can be established informally by ensuring that the right people are in the organization ready to be called upon as senior managers when the time is appropriate.

As the company grows, the time comes when entrepreneurs need to make a decision as to their role and responsibilities within the company. A decision must be made as to whether a professional management team and leader should run it. Understandably, many entrepreneurs are reluctant to let go and are often instrumental in destroying the business they set up. It is important for them to recognize their own skills and where they are best able to contribute, as the following illustration highlights.

> *Illustration: relinquishing control to professional management*
>
> Although Ray Kroc of McDonald's remained President of the company until he was over eighty years old, he put a top management team in charge of the company and made himself the company's 'marketing conscience'. He continued to visit outlets, check quality and standards, and talk to customers, leaving the top management to deal with the management issues. This contribution by Ray Kroc enabled McDonald's to retain an entrepreneurial approach and make any changes necessary to retain its dominance of the fast food industry.
> **Source**: authors

The entrepreneur and human resource management

The Bolton Report in 1971 stated that small entrepreneurial companies have advantageous characteristics, such as loyal employees, which lead to harmonious industrial relations. These advantages are reduced as the company grows. However, other researchers, such as Rainnie (1989), have found that small companies may exploit employees through the sweatshop environment and can include autocratic relationships between workers and employers.

Human resource management is clearly an important area for any business. However, in many cases, entrepreneurs are not particularly well-skilled in dealing with other personnel and employees. There are two stereotypes of employee relations for small businesses, as identified by Stanworth and Curran (1989), which represent the extreme situations.

Firstly there is the sweatshop image, where the entrepreneur exploits employees by offering low wages and long hours. This is typified by the 'villain' entrepreneur, as played by Mike Baldwin in *Coronation Street*. He is portrayed as a slave-driving boss running a clothing factory exploiting female semi-skilled workers. The sweatshop image is present in the hospitality and tourism industries possibly more than in the leisure sector. The use of young unskilled workers working long hours in exchange for a minimal wage is prevalent. Both large companies and the smaller entrepreneurial operations can be guilty of this.

> *Illustration: use of young workers for low wages*
>
> Anabel Carter decided to work as a tour rep for a year to gain experience and travel the world. She was employed by a small tour company and was sent to work in Turkey. She received a basic wage of £50 per week plus her accommodation. For this she had to work from 6.30 a.m. to 12.00 p.m. six days a week and be on call for the remaining time. Such problems as complaints from guests about taps dripping at 4.00 a.m., and people wanting to divorce their partners and be on the next flight home were not uncommon. Also, as a twenty-two-year-old she had to deal with guests being taken seriously ill and even death. A lot of responsibility and work for a very low wage.
> **Source**: authors

A second alternative stereotype is when the small entrepreneurial firm is perceived as 'small is beautiful' and the perfect environment with highly satisfying and conflict-free relationships (Stanworth and Curran, 1989). The problems of communication are nil as the employee is able to approach the entrepreneur in a friendly manner, and the low rates of pay are counteracted by a family and homely working environment.

Contributing to the image of poor human resource management by entrepreneurs is the theory of dual labour markets proposed by Kreckel (1988). This theory suggests that large firms have a preference for certain types of employees – well-qualified, experienced, members of professional organizations, and with a stable work history. Given that the smaller firm cannot offer the same remuneration and benefits offered by the large enterprise, they are inclined to recruit from the secondary labour market. This means that they typically look to younger, less-qualified and less-experienced employees, many of whom do not have a stable work history. Of course there are notable and successful exceptions to this.

In most small operations, the primary control of the operation is in the hands of the entrepreneur. Consequently, the personality and psychology of the entrepreneur has an impact on employee relations and operations in the entrepreneurial firm, as discussed in Chapter 2. Kets de Vries (1977), in a summary of literature, noted that in many entrepreneurial ventures the managerial style is autocratic, impulsive, egocentric, and unpredictable. He found that:

> What we frequently encounter in an entrepreneurial organization is an organizational structure and work environment completely dependent and totally dominated by the entrepreneur ... We are also faced with an individual who refuses to delegate, is impulsive, lacks any interest in conscious, analytical forms of planning, and engages regularly in bold, proactive moves ... [which] ... make for the initial successes and may contribute to the continued success of the enterprise, but due to the absence of a conscious planning effort also carry a high risk component ... Within the organization power depends on the proximity to the entrepreneur, is constantly changing and creates a highly uncertain organization environment. This state of affairs contributes to a highly politically charged atmosphere where changing coalitions and collusions are the order of the day (p. 160).

This is compounded by the frequent lack of any formalized job description and job definition in an entrepreneurial operation. The result is that employees have to be a 'jack of all trades' working with a high degree of role ambiguity. This can provide role conflict and a difficult working environment, but it can also prove to give excellent opportunities for career succession if the organization goes on to be highly successful.

Hodgetts and Kuratko (1992) suggested that there are three human relations skills particularly necessary for successful entrepreneurs – communication, motivation, and leadership. Communication involves the transmission of messages between two or more people. Many employers are not natural communicators as they often make decisions without much input from other employees. The informal structure of the entrepreneurial organization plays an important role, as there are typically no recognized lines of communication. Motivation of staff is necessary for a successful business. Growth firms will involve entrepreneurs who have the ability to motivate their staff to achieve high performance (Deakins, 1996). As the firm grows, the call for the entrepreneur to delegate authority increases, and the importance of motivated staff cannot be underestimated. Independence is a motivating factor for entrepreneurs but can actually act as a demotivating factor for employees, who generally dislike working on their own with little guidance. In any business, an entrepreneur with a good, positive leadership style is likely to have positive results. Entrepreneurial leadership often differs from leadership in larger organizations as entrepreneurs tend to be autocratic, commanding, and expect employees to work with only little feedback. One major reason for this is rooted back in the entrepreneurial personality and traits such as need for achievement, strong internal locus of control, and a driving ambition. They expect others to work at the same level and pace as themselves.

Illustration: delegation of authority

Saxon Inn's Managing Director, Ulsterman John Connell, worked for Scottish and Newcastle Brewery before opening his own chain of pubs. He places strong emphasis on staff relations. *'Most breweries are highly centralised … the guy running the retail outlet is the lowest form of life at the bottom of the heap.'* Connell cherishes his staff and has empowered unit managers to make more decisions.
Source: Stringer, 1996b

Other issues relating to human resource management within entrepreneurial organizations include staff turnover, absenteeism, and staff training. In entrepreneurial organizations staffing levels are usually very tight, with just the bare minimum of staff necessary to do the job and keep the costs down. Thus, when staff are absent the remaining staff are asked to work even harder or work extra shifts, which can affect overall product quality. A typical case is a bar and restaurant we know in Sheffield. One chef walked out on a pre-booked, full restaurant on Christmas Eve over an overtime pay dispute. The result was that the manager had to work in the already short-staffed kitchen leaving insufficient control in the bar and restaurant. The food and service was so poor that after waiting over two and a half hours for a meal, most of the customers left without paying! These customers are unlikely ever to return. Finally, training new staff in an entrepreneurial operation can be costly and time consuming. As many entrepreneurs do not possess good training skills, staff training is often ignored, placing undue strain on both new and existing employees.

Organization structure

Entrepreneurs tend to run informal and unstructured organizational structures. The entrepreneur is the primary decision maker and typically there is no recognized chain of command other than to approach the entrepreneur. In some cases, the entrepreneur is the *only* decision maker. Usually entrepreneurs prefer a large horizontal span of control and tend to have an in-built aversion to structured companies. Greiner (1972) identified a crisis of autonomy as the business grows. With the introduction of mainstream management, the organization needs to adopt a more formalized organization structure. The requirement for a more formalized structure is clear but a potential impact is that it can inhibit creativity and start to demoralize lower-level management and employees. This is especially true for those members who have been with the company from the beginning, and indeed may have been attracted to the informal and unstructured nature of the organization.

Structures can range from one which is unplanned and sporadic to a recognized line organization.

1 **Pioneer structure**: this is when the entrepreneur is the total centre of the operation and all decisions radiate from the core (Figure 6.1).

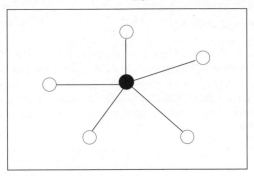

Figure 6.1 Source: Greiner (1972)

2 **Unplanned structure**: this occurs when the structure of the organization tends to evolve haphazardly with little conscious planning. As the company grows, people who initially started performing certain functions within the small company tend to retain these functions, often outside their skill levels. Within this type of structure, the entrepreneur may find positions for people as favours, or because they are the most available person at the time, rather than them being the right person for that job. This type of structure can work while the organization is still small, but once the firm grows beyond a certain size an organizational change is necessary for success (Figure 6.2).

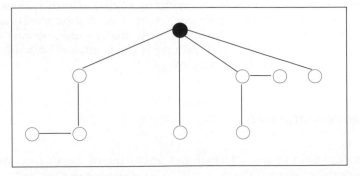

Figure 6.2 Source: Greiner (1972)

Illustration: unplanned structure

In 1990 Stockport County Football Club were in the fourth division of the Football League and had been for many years. With the club losing thousands of pounds per week, short of a miracle, it seemed that they were condemned to this situation for ever. The employees were mainly ex-footballers willing to accept low wages in exchange for remaining in a business that they loved. These employees were hired as favours to long-serving players past their prime. Whilst these employees, several of whom were in high positions in the club (Commercial Manager and Chief Executive), were well motivated, they had insufficient experience to enable them to perform their jobs effectively. When an ambitious new Chairman took over the club and injected a large amount of capital to improve the facilities, the team, and the prospects for the club, many of the existing employees were unable to handle the challenge. Whilst they were able to survive in a small, stable business environment, when faced with computerized accounting systems, weekly sales targets, and a more formalized organization structure, they were out of their depth. Rightly, the new Chairman recognized that the organization needed personnel with management training and expertise to manage what was becoming a complex and dynamic business.
Source: authors

3 **Formalized structure:** a more formalized structure is where a specific chain of command exists, typically in a small firm in a line management configuration (Figure 6.3).

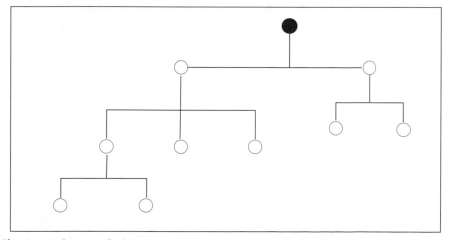

Figure 6.3 Source: Greiner (1972)

In small entrepreneurial companies there is the tendency to be informal and ignore organizational lines. Where an entrepreneur is actively involved in a hands-on manner problems can arise if employees are dealt with directly, without going through the appropriate line manager.

Delegation of authority

Typical of an entrepreneurial operation is the reluctance of the entrepreneur to relinquish authority to line managers. This represents a weak link in small businesses. For many entrepreneurs, the business is 'their baby' and they do not want to let go. This is evident when the entrepreneur has previously been responsible for the tasks him/herself and wants to retain control. The 'headless chicken scenario' develops where the entrepreneur tries to do everything him/herself, leading to a poorly organized operation and often physical and mental burnout. The background of the independent entrepreneur is a contributing variable to this. Frequently the entrepreneur is the one who created the business, made all the contacts, and knows more about it than any other person and, in order to protect the business, wants to hold onto the reins of leadership (Broom *et al.*, 1983). The upshot of this is that too much time is spent dealing with day-to-day matters which can lead, not only to breakdowns and burnouts, but to neglecting planning, financial, and personnel issues.

In his research, Deakins (1996) has identified that the problem of delegation and loss of control has actually served as a constraint for entrepreneurial companies with the potential for growth. This ability to delegate is critical and enhances the importance of forming a management team that can participate in decision making. Greiner (1972) termed this as a **crisis of control**, typified by entrepreneurs not wanting to relinquish the reins, and trying to re-centralize in order to try to restore a sense of control. This type of organization can be a difficult working environment for employees. The entrepreneur often hoards information in an attempt to retain control, and they can exhibit erratic behaviour, leaving employees not knowing where they stand. Furthermore, the entrepreneur may play 'favourites' with certain members of staff and create an 'inner circle' of employees, ignoring any organizational structure.

Entrepreneurial decision making

Illustration: delegation of authority

Many successful entrepreneurs have recognized that they cannot continue to do everything as the company grows. Adrian Barbieri is the Chairman and Managing Director of Figaro Trading. The company includes Fuego, a Spanish restaurant and tapas bar, Shangri-La a frozen Chinese food company and French Fauachon producing gourmet foods. Barbieri is a firm believer in devolving tasks to staff and rewarding them with profit-sharing incentives. He states that the choice is 'delegation not abdication' for the entrepreneur with a growing company.
Source: authors

Decision making generally is determined by the type of decision to be made, i.e. from simple to complex, and the time available, i.e. the degree of urgency of the decision.

The entrepreneurial approach to decision making is normally made against the background of limited margins for absorbing error but with equally limited time to seek quality information to help with those decisions. There are two broad bands of decision making for entrepreneurs. First, there are those decisions made on a continuum with highly structured planning at one side and informal unplanned decision making at the other. Second, there are those decisions where, at one extreme, the entrepreneurial character is reflected in a haphazard and uncoordinated approach which tends to be reactive and where the level of risk is low. The other extreme is where the opportunistic approach tends to be proactive and where the amount of risk is substantially higher (Carson *et al.*, 1995). This corresponds to the entrepreneur-trustee–entrepreneur-visionary continuum presented in Chapter 1.

Carson *et al.* (1995) developed a matrix identifying four categories of entrepreneurial decision making. This is presented in Figure 6.4.

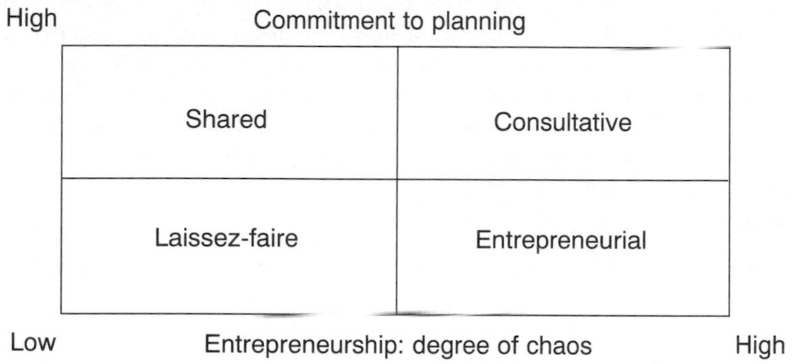

High   Commitment to planning

Shared	Consultative
Laissez-faire	Entrepreneurial

Low   Entrepreneurship: degree of chaos   High

Figure 6.4 Matrix of entrepreneurial management decision-making styles.
Source Carson *et al.* (1995)

Laissez-faire decisions

There are always some simple and easy jobs in any environment which need little skill and supervision. These jobs are highly routine and non-urgent, low-risk areas of decision making. An example of such a task would be to count the number of towels returned in a leisure centre at the end of the day. Any junior member of staff could perform this task without much concern from the entrepreneur.

Shared decisions

These are routine decisions with a strong operational focus. These decisions are of low urgency, complexity, and risk. Typically, such decisions may deal with improvements to routine tasks. For example, altering the fitness class timetable to accommodate an extra step class.

Consultative decisions

These are important decisions which have the potential to impact on the future prospects of a business. The level of risk of these non-routine decisions is high and, as they are of a strategic nature, they are more complex and the outcome is somewhat uncertain. The availability of up-to-date quality information is crucial and sufficient time is needed for the decision-maker to consult with colleagues before making the ultimate decision. A typical example is when an entrepreneur wishes to diversify the firm's product or service.

Illustration: consultative decision making

The Ball family who own and operate the pub/manor house hotel Calcot Manor in Gloucestershire decided that, following a decline in turnover, it was time for diversification. They raised over £1 million to build a wing onto the side of the hotel to house a pub called The Gumstool and a new conference facility. This new pub's restaurant does not cannibalize sales from the hotel restaurant but is popular with local trade. Economies of scale were created by doubling up the hotel and Gumstool kitchens. In addition, as children were not accepted into the hotel restaurant, the Gumstool helps broaden the hotel's appeal by also catering for the family market whilst retaining the hotel's current trade.
Source: authors

Entrepreneurial decisions

Entrepreneurial decision making is usually highly personalized. It can also be autocratic, when the individual entrepreneur makes critical decisions with little information and within a turbulent environment. These decisions tend to be *ad hoc* and made with gut feeling and intuition. Entrepreneurs, by their very nature, are often risk takers and thus thrive on the challenge presented when making such decisions.

Reactionary and gut feeling as operational advantages

Small firms are often the first to offer new products, innovative themes, and revolutionary concepts in the market place. One of the primary advantages entrepreneurial firms have operationally is that they can respond far more quickly than big companies and they can adapt their products and services at a lower cost than their larger counterparts. The entrepreneurs are close to the market, can 'feel' intuitively trends as they evolve, and are closer to true customer feedback. This enables them to redefine their product/service speedily whenever and however necessary.

Illustration: capitalizing on market trends

Some entrepreneurs are capitalizing on the popularity of ethnic dishes whilst taking advantage of the increasingly sophisticated market for international cuisine. Xantia and Stefanos Hamawi saw a gap in the market for good 'Hellenic' cuisine, utilizing food and recipes from their homeland, mainland Greece. The Hamawis wanted a more up-market and sophisticated operation than the typical Greek-Cypriot Taverna prevalent in the UK. They created the up-market Café O in the salubrious district of South Kensington, London. Café O fills a niche in the market by offering traditional, yet exciting Greek dishes in an elegant and cultured environment.
Source: Lyons, 1996

Recognizing this strength, even some of the standardized franchise operations allow the franchisee a certain level of flexibility. Interestingly, Subway is recruiting master franchisees in the UK to cover a particular geographical area. The master franchisee is then responsible for 'subfranchising' to other individuals within that area or developing units themselves. The responsibility extends to finding suitable sites. The requirement is that the master franchisee lives in the geographical area so therefore they are close to the market and understand the consumer. They are the best-placed person to identify the most suitable sites for development. Furthermore, each unit manager can include two menu items of his choice – specials which he feels would best suit the local custom.

Illustration: inability of large organizations to quickly respond to trends

McDonald's is the world's largest restaurant company with over 18 000 units worldwide. It has approximately 650 units in the UK, most of which are franchised. The company is now so large that any new product developments have to be researched and introduced with great care. The recent introduction of the Vegetable Deluxe veggie burger in the UK is the result of four years of research and trials. Their successful McSalads were some ten years in research and testing.
Source: authors

For the same reasons, entrepreneurs are the most effective in locating a niche in the market. Modern pub retailing is a very competitive environment and it is all about finding a place in the market and filling it. Sometimes the niche is not easy to spot – it is sometimes a question of market knowledge, confidence, and guts. For example, Billy Lowe and Kenny Waugh created their Thistle chain of pubs in Edinburgh by buying up business-failure pubs and turning them around by upgrading the pub and making it appealing to the local market.

Illustration: flexibility of entrepreneurial operations

The Flexible Food Company was set up by two female entrepreneurs, Liz Beauchamp and Ruth Nightingale, as a contract catering operation targeting business and industry contracts within Central London. Their strength is that they pay attention to detail and offer more flexibility in an industry dominated by large operators such as the Compass Group, Gardener Merchant, and The Sutcliffe Catering Group. *'Small contract caterers will fill the gap being created as the giant companies swallow up the middle ground'*, states Beauchamp.
Source: Huddart, 1996

Recent years have seen the expansion of multi-national companies, such as McDonald's, Marriott Corporation, and the Rank Organization, and much has been written on their new products/services. However, it is those companies, large or small, which remain entrepreneurial who are at the frontiers of innovation. Their closeness to the market and customer, plus their willingness and ability to experiment, results in innovative concepts and services.

Teamworking

Entrepreneurship is usually associated with one individual setting up a new business. However, as noted by Lyles *et al.* (1994), new ventures are just as apt to be started by a team of entrepreneurs. They identify that in the USA, three-fifths of new ventures are started by teams. Recent research indicates that approximately a quarter of new businesses in Britain start as a partnership. The primary belief is that, in joining forces with another person with different but complimentary skills, the sum of human capital will be greater than the parts (Kochan, 1996). Partnerships are often the only way entrepreneurs can raise sufficient capital to start their own business. Research by the University of Warwick shows that partnerships with three or more partners have a better chance of survival than the more typical two-person business. The primary reason being that there are more heads focused on each issue and less risk of confrontation than in partnerships between two people (Kochan, 1996).

As identified, the team approach may often be the most effective way of generating sufficient resources to get the new venture off the ground and to add a broader variety of skills to the new venture. One of the most critical issues for new firms is achieving management depth and finding talent. This can be resolved through teams of entrepreneurs as opposed to the individual (Kamm and Nurick, 1993). Furthermore, Deakins (1996) states that firms founded by teams of entrepreneurs are more likely to grow than those founded by an individual. Not only do team start-ups have a higher level of capitalization but when entrepreneurs bring in complimentary skills they are less likely to be overstretched by the opening and running of a business, as can be seen from the following example:

Illustration: teamworking

Vong is one of London's 'buzz' restaurants at present. It is located in the basement of the Berkley Hotel and the owners, the Savoy Group, pay Vong's creator and master chef, Jean-George Vongerichten, a percentage of turnover as a royalty for operating the business. Vong is one of London's most innovative restaurants combining French and Oriental (particularly Thai) cooking. The success of Vong is huge and they are serving over 300 covers each day.
Source: Anonymous, 1996

Cromie (1990) identified the major benefits of a partnership as being a mix of skills, motivational support from a partner in what can be a very lonely and stressful time, a continuing source of, and sounding board for, new ideas, plus double the amount of commitment, energy and drive. Cromie did identify the negative aspect of the approach as being the desire for autonomy many entrepreneurs possess which can lead to disharmony between partners. The entrepreneurial personality may be extremely self-confident and results-orientated, making it difficult to work as a team player. Ego and single-mindedness often separate two partners in an entrepreneurial venture, as one or both entrepreneurs decide to go it alone. For this reason, many people advise against taking a partner and many entrepreneurs remain adamant that they would be unable or unwilling to enter into a partnership even if it was a very good opportunity. The following illustration is of a successful partnership – so far!

Illustration: an effective partnership

Peter Dyer and Darko Emersic together were responsible for founding Crystal Holidays in the early 1980s. The company has grown and become one of Britain's top ski operators. Both entrepreneurs were disenchanted employees of a large tour operator and left together to create their own business. They have developed an excellent and effective partnership. The success of the partnership can be attributed to the fact that they liaise closely with each other but do not interfere with each other's areas of expertise.
Source: authors

Entrepreneurs and quality management

Quality management represents a large operational challenge for entrepreneurs. Whilst many entrepreneurial companies are able to achieve high levels of product quality, the difficulty lies within the area of achieving *consistently* high levels of quality. Within service businesses it is relatively difficult to consistently achieve quality, as highlighted by the following points:

- service workers are often viewed as short-term, disposable workers and as such are often undertrained and unmotivated;
- there is more chance of making errors in service operations owing to the complexities of production and delivery process and the involvement of the customer during the process;
- the customer consumes the service as it is produced which does not always allow time for the producer to correct mistakes.

Controlling quality is one of the most important management responsibilities, given the competitive nature of the industry and the increasingly sophisticated and discriminating consumer.

Illustration: quality management in practice

Stoll Moss Theatres have introduced a service quality management approach into their business. They manage eleven of London's West End theatres and realize the importance of the overall experience of theatre-going in creating repeat business. They have introduced a system of regular checks on the state of the theatres based on a fast food franchise audit. Standard setting and staff training are both designed to improve and maintain the quality of the service.
Source: Morgan, 1996

As highlighted in the above illustration, entrepreneurs can ensure a consistent level of quality. Murdick *et al.* (1990) make the following suggestions for assuring quality, shown in Table 6.4:

Table 6.4   Quality Assurance: scope and task

Task	Method
Identify customer expectations	Use focus groups, suggestion cards, discussions with customers, interviews
Design the service to meet customer expectations of quality	Involve the customer in the service process, e.g. Brewer's Fayre where the customer actually places the food order themselves at the bar. Inform the customer what is expected, e.g. through table tent cards
Design and implement a quality appraisal programme	Monitor guest comments, talk to guests, customer trails, mystery customer programme, visit competitors
Design and implement a quality training programme	Create a 'service culture', develop a customer care programme, reward staff upon achievement
Design and implement a quality control programme	Keep records and data, monitor any complaints, regular inspections, mystery customer programme

Source: Murdick *et al.* (1990)

There is nothing intrinsic in these tasks and methods which make them more difficult to implement in new entrepreneurial ventures rather than in established organizations. Yet we have already noted that many entrepreneurs prefer a 'seat of the pants' approach rather than the more systematic approach described here. The entrepreneur's closeness to the market, owing to the hands-on involvement with the business, may however keep them in tune with customers and compensate for the lack of a strategic approach to quality systems.

The entrepreneur and management of the life-cycle

The entrepreneurial characteristics needed to create and get a new operation off the ground, as identified in the early chapters of this book, are often not the same characteristics required to manage a growing organization. In many cases the entrepreneur is not able to make the transition from a small organization to one that is growing in size and complexity. As identified in Chapter 2, the management style of the entrepreneur needs to change as the organization progresses through its life-cycle and the entrepreneur needs to plan its further development systematically and apply management controls effectively (Burns, 1989).

Dynamics of the life-cycle

Introduction/creation stage

This is the birth of the organization. The founder – the entrepreneur – recognizes a market opportunity and offers a service, usually at a single location. Sales are low and profits are either low or non-existent. Most companies are struggling just to stay alive. Typically this is the period when eighteen-hour working days are common to get the business up and running. The entrepreneur will be personally responsible for all major decision making and will be in full control. The organizational structure tends to be highly centralized. The entrepreneur will determine the culture and team spirit within the organization. Employees will be hired who best fit with the entrepreneur's personality and philosophy. Most employment of staff will be done on an informal basis with few entrepreneurial organizations having contracts of employment, job descriptions etc. At this stage in the life-cycle, there is little complexity in the organization, with the management functions performed by a small core of personnel, closely supervised by the entrepreneur. Generally there will be low formalization within the organization with a few systems and procedures.

Illustration: entrepreneurial enthusiasm and drive

When he was first creating and developing the successful Domino's Pizza business Thomas Monaghan worked seven days a week for seven years. Even now he gets up at 5.45 a.m., runs three miles on three mornings a week and still gets to the office by 8.00 a.m.
Source: authors

Growth stage

This is the stage when the product or service starts to become popular and sales start to grow rapidly. In food service and hotels the growth stage of a business is when a single operation grows to two or more units, often by replicating the original unit in a different location. Franchising or licensing arrangements may be a very successful way of expanding a business quickly without requiring a vast capital investment. This is increasingly popular within the hospitality, tourism and leisure industries and is discussed further in Chapter 8.

Illustration: growth through franchising

In exchange for about £7500–£8000 an investor can purchase a franchise to run a five-a-side football league. The Elms are selling a proven format developed over three years and are seeking to expand their five-a-side football league through franchisees. In exchange for the franchise fee, they provide support such as PR and advertising, computerized back-up, an equipment pack, fixture and results service, liaison with the Football Association and a training programme. The Elms charge 15 per cent of total annual income as a management service fee and a further 2 per cent of total annual income as a marketing levy.
Source: authors

At this stage, most entrepreneurs must start to delegate some responsibility and qualified managers need to be recruited. The new, growing firm operates in an uncertain, unpredictable, and often ambiguous environment. The entrepreneur needs to remain the risk-taker searching for new market opportunities but also develop the team and delegate responsibilities (Burns, 1989). Emphasis shifts from the entrepreneur to the management team as specialist skills are brought in to support finance, marketing, and human resource activities. Communication channels require to be formally defined and structured training introduced. Strategic planning, not something generally considered to be a particular skill of entrepreneurs, is necessary to manage the company's growth. This stage of the life-cycle often attracts new 'me too' entrants to the industry, therefore monitoring of the competition is essential. The operations of the business become more complex as the entrepreneur has to maintain the smooth running of the business whilst continuing to find new sites. Operations may still be fairly informal but some thought needs to go into standardizing operating procedures. Operations usually becomes the first managerial function to be fully delegated and signals the transition of the organization from a simple structure to a more complex form.

It is at the growth stage where many entrepreneurial operations become over-ambitious and grow too quickly. Many over-extend themselves financially and do not develop the management structures necessary to run a more demanding and complex business. Furthermore, when companies grow quickly they frequently lack the formal control systems necessary and the entrepreneur is more concerned with day-to-day issues as opposed to strategic and operational planning. As the organization moves towards greater complexity and decentralization, different challenges are presented for the entrepreneur. The entrepreneur must strive to achieve higher level thinking, that is, rise above the operational thinking which may be based largely on common sense and intuition, towards more complex issues such as financial accounting, marketing planning, and strategic planning. It is at the growth stage that many entrepreneurs are either pushed out of the company or feel that they are better suited elsewhere. The formalized and bureaucratic structure of a large organization typically stifles entrepreneurship and creates an environment which is the opposite of what the entrepreneur set out to create in the first place.

Maturity stage

As the market becomes saturated, sales and growth tend to level off. This period may last for many years or can be relatively short. It is at this stage when marketing comes into its own as advertising and promotional efforts are devoted to boosting revenues. Financial control is crucial as the organization tries to manage variable costs and, in many cases, a need to consolidate. Some streamlining of staff may be required and few new people will be hired. Issues such as quality control and productivity now play a more important role than location analysis, etc. It is at this stage that the company often strives to rekindle the entrepreneurial spirit which may have been lost as the company increased in formality and complexity during the growth stage.

Decline and failure

A report by Stoy Hayward (1996) researched the reasons for business failure and found that the hotel and catering sector had a different profile of causes of business failure than other industries. Generally, the most frequent cause

---

Illustration: importance of operations management

The trendy Forum café bar in Sheffield is popular with students and young drinkers. Sales of 'soul food' are booming. However, in 1995 the owners could not work out why they were not making any money from food sales despite rave reports from satisfied customers. Not having much catering experience they decided to employ two local chef/entrepreneurs to act as consultants. Immediately, the consultants identified the major problems as no portion control (some days customers would get massive sandwiches), too much food wastage through inadequate control, and poor purchasing. Without the alcohol and beverage sales, the Forum would never have survived with the existing food operation. Fortunately, the owners recognized a problem early enough to change it. The difficulty was reducing and then controlling the portion sizes without upsetting the customers who were more than happy with the existing value for money!
Source: authors

Table 6.5 Reasons for business failure in the catering, hotel and leisure industry

Reason for failure	Primary factor %	Contributory factor %	Sector ranking	Global ranking
Undercapitalization	64	74	1	1
Poor operations management	46	62	2	2
Poor state of local economy	30	46	3	7
High gearing	30	50	4	6
Poor chief executive officer	28	38	5	5
Poor management accounting	24	38	6	3
Short-term liquidity	24	38	7	4
Poor marketing/sales management	14	38	8	8
Misguided diversification	12	14	10	12
Other personnel reasons	12	14	10	12
Increased competition	10	26	11	11
Poor facilities and machinery	6	20	12	17
Poor quality product	6	12	13	16
Theft and dishonesty	6	10	14	9
Poor labour relations	4	4	15	19
Problems with suppliers	4	20	16	21
Bad debts	4	4	17	10

Source: Stoy Hayward (1996, p. 20)

of failure is undercapitalization, particularly significant in industries such as construction and manufacturing. In the hotel and catering sector, however, operations and management problems were also a primary cause of failure in over half of businesses studied (Table 6.5). This reflects the fact that these businesses are difficult to control. Since the entrepreneur is often physically involved in the entrepreneurial venture, problems can all too easily result in fatigue and the neglect of management issues.

The entrepreneur and business failure

Long ago, Larson and Clute (1979) researched the role of the entrepreneur in firm failure. The researchers found that many firm characteristics – particularly decision-based ones – were directly related to entrepreneurial characteristics. These included lack of insight, inflexibility, and emphasis on technical skills. Additionally managerial deficiencies and the financial shortcomings of the entrepreneur also contributed to failure. Little seems to have changed. Other researchers (Peterson *et al.*, 1983; Wichmann, 1983) have found support for the case that lack of management expertise along with financial matters were the most common causes of business failure. Haswell and Holmes (1989) and Weitzel and Jonsson (1989) were among those who found that poor management skills were most frequently identified as a common theme in small business failure.

Birley and Niktari (1995) identified seven potential reasons for failure connected with the characteristics of the owners, and four reasons connected with the management team (Table 6.6).

Table 6.6 Importance of owner and management team factors to failure (1 = to no extent; 5 = to a very great extent)

Factor	Score					
	1	*2*	*3*	*4*	*5*	*No.*
The owner factor						
Owner inflexible to change	24.6	28.6	25.5	13.7	7.6	475
Resisted advice from qualified sources	25.4	24.1	23.5	15.6	11.4	473
Problem of an autocratic dominating principal owner-managed	43.2	18.9	17.9	10.2	9.8	470
Owner did not seek outside help and advice	19.4	22.4	31.4	16.7	10.2	474
Owner did not innovate	30.4	28.5	21.7	13.1	6.3	474
Decision-making based upon intuition/emotion	14.5	20.1	24.3	22.9	18.2	477
Excessive remuneration paid to owner-manager	50.2	13.3	14.2	8.9	13.3	472
The management team factor						
Poor operations management	13.6	18.6	27.0	25.5	15.3	478
Owner had insufficient management experience	8.6	14.3	27.0	28.9	21.2	477
Management teams were not balanced	16.6	13.2	26.2	30.3	13.6	469
Inability to delegate managerial responsibility	34.1	26.4	22.0	11.1	6.4	469

Source: Birley and Niktari (1995, p. 23)

The dominant issue that emerged from this research was that the attitudes and actions of the entrepreneur rather than their technical managerial skills were to blame for the decline. The most serious problems were reliance on intuition and emotion in decision making and the inflexibility of the entrepreneur. (However, reported research considered in Chapter 7 considers intuitive decision making to be potentially rewarding, at least in terms of concept development.)

Table 6.7 illustrates the primary causes of small business failures as divulged in research by Griffin (1987).The findings are quite damning!

Larson and Clute (1979) identify the personal and managerial characteristics leading to failure as:

- exhibits exaggerated opinion of business competency based on knowledge of some skill;
- limited formal education;
- inflexible to change and not innovative;
- uses own personal taste and opinion as standard to follow;

Table 6.7 Causes of small business failure

Percentage	Causes of failure	Explanation
44 per cent	Incompetence	Lack of fitness to run the business – physical, moral, or intellectual
17 per cent	Lack of managerial experience	Little, if any, experience managing employees and other resources before going into business
16 per cent	Unbalanced experience	Not well-rounded in marketing, finance, purchasing, and production
15 per cent	Inexperience in line	Little, if any, experience in the product or service before going into business
1 per cent	Neglect	Too little attention to the business, resulting from bad habits, poor health, or marital difficulties
1 per cent	Fraud or disaster	Fraud; misleading name, false financial statements, premeditated overbuy, or irregular disposal of assets
6 per cent	Unknown	Disaster; fire, flood, burglary, employees' fraud, or strike (some disasters could have been insured against)

Source: Griffin (1987, p. 689)

- decision making based on intuition, emotion, and non-objective factors;
- oriented to past, ignores future;
- does little reading in literature associated with business;
- resists advice from qualified sources but will accept it from the least qualified.

Overall, there seems to be little consistency in research findings regarding business failure. The research area is, in any case, fraught with difficulty since people are naturally reluctant to talk about the traumas of failure.

A further management trap for entrepreneurs is when a hobby is converted to a business. This is especially so in the hotel, tourism and leisure industries. There are many cases where new businesses are started on the back of a hobby, e.g. sports gyms and restaurants. The entrepreneur may have little or no business acumen, just a love for the activity. There are numerous cases where a person loves cooking or has a deep interest in wines and decides to 'do it for real' by setting up a business. Where there is such deep feeling, judgement may become very cloudy.

The entrepreneur and business growth

Churchill and Lewis (1983), in their analysis of small business growth, identified five stages of development – existence, survival, success, take-off, and

---

Illustration: running a business as a hobby with little experience

One interesting case is that of *Coronation Street* actor Phil Middlemass and *Minder* actor Gary Webster who, together with a third partner, bought the Grant Arms in the quiet town of Ramsbottom, Lancs. They spent over £400 000 refurbishing the history-rich fourteen-room inn and the actors themselves worked shifts behind the bar to attract publicity and business. Unfortunately the trade just was not there in such a sleepy town and no matter what they did, the pub could not attract enough trade to sustain the investment. The pub went into voluntary liquidation two years after opening.
Source: authors

---

resource maturity. The authors proposed that small business owners who can assess the stage at which their companies are operating can use the framework to enable them to better understand any existing problems and help anticipate future challenges. Churchill and Lewis' framework is illustrated in Figure 6.5.

Each of the five stages of growth is characterized by an index of size, diversity and complexity and described by five management factors – managerial style, organizational structure, extent of formal systems, major strategic goals, and the owner's involvement in the business. An alternative life-cycle is presented by Burns (1989) as illustrated in Figure 6.6. This model identifies the primary management style and organization required at each stage of introduction and growth in addition to the marketing and financial problems likely.

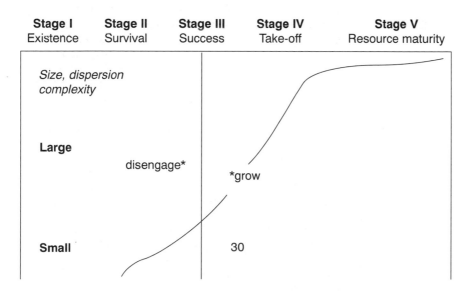

Figure 6.5 Churchill and Lewis' framework of business growth. **Source**: Churchill and Lewis (1983)

As already highlighted, many businesses in the hospitality, tourism and leisure industries may never progress beyond the initial existence stage, where the entrepreneur performs all important tasks individually. Many such organizations do not have sufficient customer acceptance and/or product capability to become viable.

If the organization makes it to the survival stage, the key problems centre around revenues and expenses. Many small businesses sit well into this category, earning marginal returns on time and capital. The third stage – success – requires the decision to be made whether to exploit the company's success and expand, or keep the business as a stable base for alternative

	Introduction	Take-off	
OBJECTIVE	**Phase 1** *Survival*	**Phase 2** *Consolidation and control*	**Phase 3** *Control and planning*
MANAGEMENT STYLE AND ORGANIZATION	• Owner *is* business • Owner does everything • Direct supervision of staff • Simple organization • Informal systems • Opportunity driven	• Owner *is* still the business • Simple organization • Informal system • Some supervision and control • Cash-flow planning	• Recruit staff • Delegate to staff • Encourage staff to develop and grow into new jobs • Tighten controls on staff • Strategic planning
MARKETING PROBLEMS	• Getting customers • Developing unique selling propositions	• Generating repeat sales • Proving unique sales proposition	• Proving ability to combat competition • Further, steady market penetration
ACCOUNTING AND FINANCE PROBLEMS	• Cash flow • Testing projected margins and break-even	• Cash flow • Proving margins and break-even • Greater financial control	• Tighten financial control • Improve margins • Control costs
	• Owner's funds • Borrowed resources – leasing – subcontract • Bank borrowing	• Owner's funds • Borrowed resources – leasing – subcontract – suppliers • Greater bank borrowing	• As before but search for expansion capital • Possible first phase venture capital

Figure 6.6 New business life-cycle: introduction and take-off. **Source**: Burns (1989, p. 43)

Illustration: insufficient customer acceptance

Sustenance is a small sandwich take-away shop set up towards the end of 1996 by a single entrepreneur – John Stephenson. The outlet is conveniently located in a very small unit on a pedestrian thoroughfare in Sheffield City Centre. John had experience with other small businesses, mainly in the motoring industry, but had never before worked in a catering outlet. He approached the new venture with confidence 'How hard can it be to make a sandwich', was his comment. He felt that the area needed a more 'trendy' alternative to the nearby bakery-style sandwich outlets, offering a better variety of speciality products. John converted the unit himself over a two-week period spending as little money as he possibly could. The menu was developed mainly around the existing equipment left behind by the previous occu- · piers. No formal approach to pricing or research was adopted, basing prices on 'feel'. The main difficulty currently being experienced by Sustenance is that very specific times of the day (1.00–2.00 p.m.) are busy, but if people see a queue of more than a handful of people they will pop into the nearby Marks and Spencers instead. Furthermore, the market is much more price sensitive than John initially perceived and he is finding that he either must drop prices or reduce the portions to make a profit. He is disappointed that the customers are so fickle and that they do not appear to appreciate a good product. He is considering closing the outlet as it is not generating enough money to be worth his effort.
Source: authors

---

owner activities. This is a critical time as the management challenges are very difficult, often requiring a change of ownership or management, delegation, and substantial cashflow. The final stage, resource maturity, is mainly concerned with consolidating the previous rapid growth stage and ensuring sufficient human and financial resources. Formal planning and systems are key issues.

Eggers *et al.* (1994) sought to update Churchill and Lewis' (1983) typology of business growth. They found that there was still support for the original typology but that there was considerable variability and individuality in the way some firms develop. The authors suggest that companies may not follow the same life-cycle sequence and that the most common conditions originally referred to as 'Stages of Growth' should be referred to as 'Phases of Management' instead. Figure 6.7 and Table 6.8, from Eggers *et al.* (1994), provide further detail.

As can be seen, the situation regarding business growth in today's trading conditions is far from stable. Organizations are quite likely to prosper and fall away in dynamic ways over short time-frames. The complexity and challenge of managing entrepreneurial firms during such intense changes is very considerable.

Summary

The hospitality, tourism and leisure industries, like many others, have their share of successful and unsuccessful new ventures. Entrepreneurial firms are

Table 6.8 Top ten management/leadership skills per phase

Conception	Survival	Stabilization	Growth organization	Rapid growth	Resource maturity
Communication	Financial management	Financial management	Communication	Communication	Communication
Administration	Communication	Vision	Motivating others	Vision	Motivating others
Vision	Marketing	Planning and goal setting	Financial management	Motivating others	Vision
Time management	Vision	Communication	Vision	Planning and goal setting	Financial management
Planning/ goal setting	Motivating others	Motivating others	Planning and goal setting	Financial management	Planning and goal setting
Human resources	Planning and goal setting	Relationship building	Relationship building	Problem solving and decision making	Problem solving and decision making
Business and technical knowledge	Customer and vendor relations	Problem solving and decision making	Business and technical knowledge	Relationship building	Customer and vendor relations
Financial management	Employee development	Employee development	Problem solving and decision making	Motivating self	Ethics and organizational culture
Problem solving and decision making	Problem solving and decision making	Marketing	Leadership and management skills	Leadership and management skills	Motivating self
Leadership and management skills	Business and technical knowledge	Business and technical knowledge	Human resources	Human resources	Leadership and management skills

Source: Eggers, Leahy and Churchill (1994) p.137

different from their larger, established counterparts in many ways, not least in their management and operation. Not only are appropriate management skills needed to successfully get a new business up and running; but also to enable the company to move beyond the initial stages of the life-cycle towards growth and investment realization.

Many entrepreneurs are simply unaware of the managerial and operational skill requirements of a business. They try to muddle through without ever acquiring the necessary skills. Others find that the management and operation of a business require skills which are opposite from those which assisted and motivated them to set up a new organization in the first place.

A large proportion of problems experienced by entrepreneurial ventures centre around management-related issues, such as inappropriate organizational structure, reluctance to delegate, absence of operational controls, and

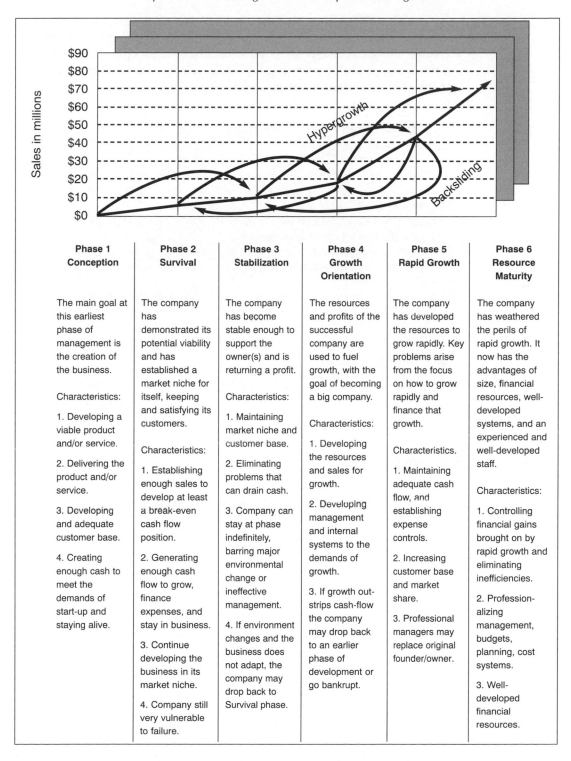

Phase 1 Conception	Phase 2 Survival	Phase 3 Stabilization	Phase 4 Growth Orientation	Phase 5 Rapid Growth	Phase 6 Resource Maturity
The main goal at this earliest phase of management is the creation of the business. Characteristics: 1. Developing a viable product and/or service. 2. Delivering the product and/or service. 3. Developing and adequate customer base. 4. Creating enough cash to meet the demands of start-up and staying alive.	The company has demonstrated its potential viability and has established a market niche for itself, keeping and satisfying its customers. Characteristics: 1. Establishing enough sales to develop at least a break-even cash flow position. 2. Generating enough cash flow to grow, finance expenses, and stay in business. 3. Continue developing the business in its market niche. 4. Company still very vulnerable to failure.	The company has become stable enough to support the owner(s) and is returning a profit. Characteristics: 1. Maintaining market niche and customer base. 2. Eliminating problems that can drain cash. 3. Company can stay at phase indefinitely, barring major environmental change or ineffective management. 4. If environment changes and the business does not adapt, the company may drop back to Survival phase.	The resources and profits of the successful company are used to fuel growth, with the goal of becoming a big company. Characteristics: 1. Developing the resources and sales for growth. 2. Developing management and internal systems to the demands of growth. 3. If growth outstrips cash-flow the company may drop back to an earlier phase of development or go bankrupt.	The company has developed the resources to grow rapidly. Key problems arise from the focus on how to grow rapidly and finance that growth. Characteristics. 1. Maintaining adequate cash flow, and establishing expense controls. 2. Increasing customer base and market share. 3. Professional managers may replace original founder/owner.	The company has weathered the perils of rapid growth. It now has the advantages of size, financial resources, well-developed systems, and an experienced and well-developed staff. Characteristics: 1. Controlling financial gains brought on by rapid growth and eliminating inefficiencies. 2. Professionalizing management, budgets, planning, cost systems. 3. Well-developed financial resources.

Figure 6.7 Phases of management. **Source**: Eggers, Leahy and Churchill (1994) p. 136

predominance of informal decision making. For organizations to progress beyond survival requires not only possession of management skills but also a change in management skills and leadership to include more defined human resource skills, planning and goal setting, financial management, and the ability to 'manage' people effectively.

Reflective questions

1 To what extent would the expertise required to manage a hospitality, tourism or leisure business differ depending upon whether it was independently owned or part of a chain?
2 Discuss the extent to which the entrepreneur is the best source of expertise relevant to the starting up of a new venture.
3 Identify an independently operated entrepreneurial business. To what extent is the entrepreneur engaged in the day-to-day operation of the business? What is the effect of this?
4 Review the rates of pay and working conditions in an independent entrepreneurial business with which you are familiar. How does this compare with chain operations? What effect does any difference have?
5 Review common causes of business failure and review their implications for the planning of a new venture.
6 With reference to an entrepreneurial venture with which you are familiar, discuss the applicability and implications of Eggers *et al.*'s 'Phases of Management'.

References

Anonymous (1996) *Caterer and Hotel Keeper*, 1 February, p. 96.
Birley, S. and Niktari, N. (1995) *The Failure of Owner-Managed Businesses: The Diagnosis of Accountants and Bankers*, The Institute of Chartered Accountants, London.
Bovee, C.L., Thill, J.V., Burk Wood, M. and Dovel, G.P. (1993) *Management*, McGraw-Hill, New York.
Broom, H.H., Longeneckers, J.G. and Moore, C.W. (1983) *Small-Business Management*, South-Western Publishing, Cincinnati, OH.
Burns, P. (1989) Strategies for success and routes to failure. In *Small Business and Entrepreneurship* (eds. P. Burns and J. Dewhirst), Macmillan, Basingstoke, pp. 32–67.
Carson, D., Cromie, S., McGowan, P. and Hill, J. (1995) *Marketing and Entrepreneurship in SMEs: An Innovative Approach*, Prentice Hall, Hemel Hempstead.
Churchill, N.C. and Lewis, V.L. (1983) The five stages of small business growth, *Harvard Business Review*, **61**, No. 3, 30–50.
Cromie, S. (1990) The problems experienced by young firms, *International Small Business Journal*, **9**, No. 3, 23–61.
Cullen, T.P. and Dick, T.J. (1990) Tomorrow's entrepreneur and today's hospitality curriculum, *The Cornell HRA Quarterly*, August, pp. 54–57.

Deakins, D. (1996) *Entrepreneurship and Small Firms*, McGraw-Hill, London.

Drucker, P.F. (1985) *Innovation and Entrepreneurship*, Harper and Row, New York.

Eggers, J.H., Leahy, K.T. and Churchill, N.C. (1994), Stages of small business growth revisited: insights into growth path and leadership/management skills in low- and high-growth companies. In *Frontiers of Entrepreneurship Research*, Proceedings of the 1994 Babson Entrepreneurship Research Conference, Wellesley, MA, pp. 131–144.

Greiner, L.E. (1972) Evolution and revolution as organizations grow, *Harvard Business Review*, **49**, 37–46.

Griffin, R. (1987) *Management*, Houghton Miffin, Boston.

Haswell, S. and Holmes, S. (1989) Estimating the small business failure rate: a reappraisal, *Journal of Small Business Management*, **27**, 68–74.

H.M. Government (1971) *The Committee of Enquiry on Small Firms (The Bolton Report)*, HMSO, London.

Hodgetts, R.M. and Kuratko, D.F. (1992) *Effective Small Business Management*, Harcourt Brace, Orlando, FL.

Huddart, M. (1996) *Flexible Food Service Management*, February, p. 4.

Kamm, J.B. and Nurick, A.J. (1993) The stages of team venture formation: a decision making model, *Entrepreneurship Theory and Practice*, **17**, No. 2, 17–27.

Kao, J. (1989) *Entrepreneurship, Creativity, and Organization*, Prentice-Hall, Englewood Cliffs, NJ.

Kets de Vries, M.F.R. (1977) The entrepreneurial personality: a person at the crossroads, *Journal of Management Studies*, **14**, No. 1, 34–57.

Kochan, N. (1996) Teamworking and partnerships, *Director*, August, pp. 44–47.

Kreckel, R. (1988) Unequal opportunity and labour market segmentation, *Sociology*, **14**, No. 4, 525–550.

Larson, C.M. and Clute, R.C. (1979) The failure syndrome, *American Journal of Small Business*, **iv**, No. 2, 35–43.

Lyles, M.A., Carter, N.M. and Baird, I.S. (1994) Partnering in establishing new ventures: the experience of Hungary. In *Frontiers of Entrepreneurship Research*, Proceedings of the 1994 Babson Entrepreneurship Research Conference, Wellesley, MA, pp. 430–444.

Lyons, (1996) *Caterer and Hotel Keeper*, 11 January, p. 54.

Morgan, M. (1996) *Marketing For Leisure and Tourism*, Prentice Hall, Hemel Hempstead.

Murdick, R.G., Render, B. and Russell, R.S. (1990) *Service Operations Management*, Allyn & Bacon, New York.

Olsen, M.D. and Schmelzer, C.D. (1988) Entrepreneurship and the organization life cycle. In *Proceedings of the International Conference on Entrepreneurship in the Hospitality Industry*, June 8th–10th, Queen Margaret College, Edinburgh.

Peterson, R.A., Kozmetsky, G. and Ridgway, N.M. (1983) Perceived causes of small business failures: a research note, *American Journal of Small Business*, **8** (Summer), 15–19.

Rainnie, A. (1989) *Industrial Relations in Small Firms*, Routledge, London.

Siropolis, N.C. (1986) *A Guide to Entrepreneurship*, Houghton Miffin, Boston.

Stanworth, J. and Curran, J. (1989) Employee relations in the small firm. In *Small Business and Entrepreneurship*, (eds P. Burns and J. Dewhirst), Macmillan, Basingstoke, pp. 158–177.

Stoy Hayward (1996) *A Study to Determine the Reasons For Failure of Small Businesses in the UK*, Stoy Hayward, London.

Stringer, J. (1996a) Bullish outlook, *Caterer and Hotel Keeper*, 21 March, p. 68.

Stringer, J. (1996b) *Caterer and Hotel Keeper*, 11 January, p. 63.

Tarpey, A. (1995) Survival strategy, *Caterer and Hotel Keeper*, 27 July, pp. 46–47.

Tarpey, A. (1996) *Caterer and Hotel Keeper*, 4 January, p. 63.

Weitzel, W. and Jonsson, E. (1989) Decline in organizations: a literature integration and extension, *Administrative Science Quarterly*, **34** (March), 91–109.

Welsh, J. and White, J. (1981) A small business is not a little big business, *Harvard Business Review*, July/August, pp. 18–34.

Wichmann, H. (1983) Accounting and marketing – key small business problems, *American Journal of Small Business*, **7** (Spring), 19–26.

7 Marketing and entrepreneurship

The objective of this chapter is to develop a critical awareness of the relevance of specifically selected marketing concepts and techniques to the entrepreneurial process. The chapter will develop understanding of:

- competition in relation to hospitality, tourism and leisure markets;
- market orientation, positioning, and segmentation;
- concept development and differentiation;
- contemporary developments in marketing theory;
- implications for entrepreneurial activity in the tourism, hospitality and leisure industries.

Introduction

Considering entrepreneurship in the hospitality, tourism and leisure industries, what can be learned from a study of contemporary thinking in marketing? An entrepreneurial approach implies taking advantage of market opportunities in a dynamic, proactive way. This can sit uneasily alongside the analytical corporate approach evidenced amongst much marketing literature. However, the discipline of marketing has itself been undergoing a metamorphosis as it takes on the challenge of the ever-increasing pace of change. To prosper in this dynamic environment requires a reappraisal of marketing concepts and techniques. As the literature has begun to catch up with modern-day business conditions, it has become more relevant to those wishing to operate proactively.

Marketing is absolutely central to the entrepreneurial process. Knowingly or intuitively, successful entrepreneurs and intrapreneurs are people who follow marketing principles. For a new venture to be viable, customers have to desire what it is being offered, in sufficient numbers, and be prepared to pay an economical price. This is at the heart of the marketing concept. However, there is increasing evidence that traditional marketing techniques may not be the ideal way of anticipating consumer preferences in present-day society. Such evidence may actually be good news for entrepreneurs. There undoubtedly still exists much scope for individual flair in developing propositions that have market appeal.

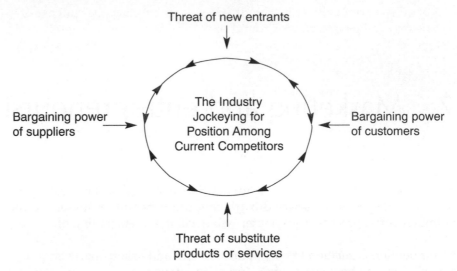

Figure 7.1 Forces governing competition in an industry. **Source**: Porter (1985, p.5)

Marketing and competition

Entrepreneurs in the hospitality, tourism and leisure industries are operating within sectors where competition is extremely fierce. Porter (1985) identified the forces governing competition in an industry. These are shown in Figure 7.1.

All of the forces which Porter identified impinge upon the hospitality, tourism and leisure industries in a powerful way. In combination, they provide a business operating environment where competition is extremely intense and sustained. A brief examination of each of the competitive forces serves to illustrate this.

The **industry** itself comprises thousands of organizations in both public and private ownership. As Porter identifies, these are all jockeying for position in order to attract customers and achieve success. Whilst endeavouring to do this, they are constantly exposed to the threat of new competitors entering the market.

Illustration: Center Parc, industry competition

Scottish and Newcastle's Center Parc operation has enjoyed great success by providing a pleasurable oasis from the stresses and strains of modern life for its 'middle class' customers, who often visit in family groups. Resort occupancy and profitability have been extremely high, even throughout the recession. Indeed, Scottish and Newcastle sold its highly successful Thistle Hotel chain in order to concentrate on its development. Such success inevitably attracts envious eyes and in autumn 1995 Rank announced that they had obtained planning permission to build a new all-year-round resort on the lines of Center Parc south of Penrith, close to the Lake District. More Rank resorts are likely to follow. Competition in the all-year-round, all-weather resorts will inevitably become fiercer.
Source: authors

Not all new ventures in these industry sectors are so capital intensive as setting up a large-scale all-year-round resort. Capital barriers to entry are, in many instances, relatively low. A modest legacy, or even a redundancy payment, can be sufficient to launch a new restaurant or small hotel. As we discussed in Chapter 5, ventures such as a fitness class, may actually require no investment in fixed assets and very little working capital. For more ambitious and capital-intensive projects, sources of venture capital funding are available. As a consequence, there are always new entrants arriving to add to an already competitive situation. Some newcomers will be more effective and professional than others, but even a poorly run operation will be a threat in the short-term.

As well as new entrants providing similar products and services, there is also the **threat of substitute products or services.** This can be simply a question of geography. A hotel offering a weekend break in the Yorkshire Dales can be in competition with others offering weekend breaks in the Cotswolds. Holidays in Greece compete with substitute holidays in Spain. Alternatively, the substitution could be a completely different service. Rather than go away for a weekend break, potential customers can just as easily undertake a range of recreational and cultural pursuits whilst remaining within their own residential area. The opportunity for such switching within these different industry sectors is limited only by the imagination.

Suppliers to the industry are also operating in a generally very competitive situation. **Supplier bargaining power** is often low owing to the existence of a wide range of alternative suppliers to which the operator is able to turn if dissatisfied. Since the suppliers are in such a competitive situation they will strive to keep costs, and hence prices, down. Suppliers are hungry for new business and are eager to open new accounts, even though they know that new ventures can be risky. They are also constantly innovating as they seek to be competitive. As a result, new products and services are always being made available to the retail end of the industry, reinforcing the competitive situation.

The **bargaining power of customers** within this competitive situation is very high. Even one individual customer is effectively in a strong position since operators are aware of the power of word of mouth in creating, sustaining, or destroying reputations. In the packaged holiday and hotel sectors, customer bargaining power is reflected in extensive price discounting. In the restaurant sector, bargaining power is reflected in meal **deals** and a consumer willingness to complain if quality falls below that expected.

Generally, all this adds up to a situation where **the customer** is in an extremely powerful position. If what is on offer is not acceptable, then there are a myriad of other attractive propositions vying for customers' business. Satisfying the customer is therefore of prime importance to successful entrepreneurship. Marketing theory and techniques have a useful role to play in achieving this. Though, as we will consider, meeting market needs can be a question of flair and intuition, as much as of analysis.

Marketing and markets

Given this constant striving to deliver what customers want, it is only to be expected that, when aggregations of activity are produced, some markets are found to be declining whilst others are expanding. The rate of expansion or decline can also vary considerably from market to market. Such trends and developments in markets have significant implications for entrepreneurs.

Illustration: Fast Food Market, market trends

In 1994, the Fast Food Market increased total sales by 6 per cent to £5.1 billion after holding sales in real terms during the preceding recession (MSI, 1995). However, within this total market increase, some sectors of the Fast Food Market were increasing at a much faster rate than others. For example, sandwich sales were estimated to have risen by 48 per cent between 1991 and 1995 as a result of the consumer trend towards healthy eating and the demise of the working lunch.
Source: Anonymous, 1995

This example powerfully illustrates how market developments can be extremely dynamic and have considerable impact. Here there was an opportunity for new product/service providers and a challenge for those sectors heavily dependent on the traditional, more substantial, meal-based, working lunch market.

Table 7.1 Forecast Fast Food Market, £million

Sector	1996	1997	1998	1999	2000
Sandwiches	2003	2085	2157	2207	2255
Hamburgers	1122	1169	1204	1237	1268
Pizza and pasta	834	882	920	957	996
Fish and chips	663	671	669	661	640
Chicken	355	366	378	384	389
Chinese	381	390	395	394	388
Indian	204	209	212	214	212
Total	**5562**	**5770**	**5935**	**6054**	**6148**

Source: MSI, quoted in Anonymous (1995, p. 16)

Table 7.1 shows how MSI forecasts that the Fast Food Market will change in the years up to 2000. All sectors of fast food are expected to grow, except for the fish and chips sector where competition from other fast food sectors, and where large chains will increase activity, is expected to have an adverse effect.

Of course, the demand within a sector is only one side of the equation. As we have already identified, barriers to entry in the hospitality, tourism and leisure industries are generally low and supply can come on stream at speed.

During 1994, MSI estimated that the total catering market grew 3 per cent to £34.2 billion, however the total number of catering businesses, as opposed to outlets, increased by 4 per cent to 115 000. Put another way, increased supply as measured by the number of businesses grew at a rate 33 per cent higher than the increase in the size of the market! Since some new businesses will have multiple outlets, total supply will actually have grown by more than this.

Given this situation, either everyone does 1 per cent less business, or something has to give! In the fast food sector of endless shake out, it is the latter. Porter's **jockeying** results in winners and losers. However, even within a market in decline it is perfectly feasible for a particular operation to strike a chord with customers and for an organization to grow whilst others fall away. Within the fish and chip sector, Harry Ramsden's expansion is a clear example of this happening. Conversely, within a growth sector, not every operation will succeed. Much of the growth in the sandwiches sector has been within multiples such as Marks and Spencers and the supermarket chains. Unfortunately, a number of independent operators have failed.

Market conditions, both demand and supply, are important for entrepreneurs to consider. The hospitality, tourism and leisure industries are ones where there is constant change. Customers change their habits and preferences. Supply of new concepts and business formats can be brought on stream very rapidly. All this results in constant change. Entrepreneurship within these industries is not for those who want to contrive to do things the same way. Those who choose to be small business proprietors, operating in a fixed rather than entrepreneurial way, run the risk of the market turning against them. However, it does seem to be the case that successful operations can make headway even in seemingly adverse circumstances. These operations must, in some way, be meeting market needs in a superior or different way, as is illustrated by the budget hotel accommodation sector.

Illustration: budget hotel accommodation, market conditions

The British hotel market is widely considered to be in its mature phase. Yet some areas of the market are experiencing very strong growth. Deloitte Touche (1997) predict that the supply of available budget hotel rooms will double by the millennium. Since overall demand for hotel rooms will certainly not increase by 100 per cent during this period, there will inevitably be losers as well as winners. One sector widely predicted to lose out is the traditional town or city centre two- or three-star hotel.
Source: Deloitte Touche, 1997

Market orientation

At the core of the marketing concept is the idea of satisfying customers' needs in a new or better way. This implies having a sense of what the market wants. In the situation where a completely new product or service is being considered, it is having a sense of what the market **will** want, once it sees what is on offer. Sometimes this successful orientation to the market is a happy accident – the entrepreneur happens to want to provide what the market happens to want! In this situation, there is no attempt to gauge market needs and preferences beforehand. Such entrepreneurs simply have an intrinsic belief in what they are providing, are dedicated to developing it, and trust that others will have the good sense to appreciate and buy it! This is the case with the New Indian Garden Restaurant in the following illustration.

Illustration: New Indian Garden Restaurant, a market 'happening'

The Bangladeshi owner of the New Indian Garden Restaurant certainly did not approach the development of his business with any formalized knowledge of marketing. However, his dedication to providing wonderful food and well-kept drinks ensures quality core products. At the same time, a keen personal sense of the importance of value ensures that the restaurant is competitive price-wise. The non-tangible aspects of the service delivery are rather idiosyncratic!

Certainly some aspects of the operation would be disapproved of by the marketing professional. Service staff's shirts are usually slightly crumpled and their image is one of untidiness, rather than casualness. Often the order-taking process is pressurized for the customers, through the staff wanting to rush. Surroundings are far from immaculate and the menus handed to customers are somewhat dog-eared! Yet the overall experience is appealing. People keep on going there. The idiosyncrasies are cause for amusement rather than complaint. As a consequence, the restaurant works well and is successful. This is not the result of a carefully worked out marketing strategy, but is due to a combination of dedication, intuition, and good fortune in giving the market what it wants in a way that sets it apart from many competitors. Given this approach, success is in some ways a happy accident. However, as we will see from consideration of contemporary marketing theory, it may be a question of synergy between the entrepreneur and the market rather than pure luck.

Source: authors

In other circumstances, success comes about through consciously applying marketing principles to the development of a new venture or innovatory endeavour. In this case, the market has been monitored and the conclusion drawn that some needs remain to be satisfied. It may even be that where the new development is particularly innovatory, consumers do not realize that they do need it until it is there, as was the case with the budget accommodation concept.

As Lambin (1993) has identified, a marketing strategy which is guided by market wishes tends to favour minor or evolutionary innovation. A strategy based on technological or creative advance is more likely to lead to a breakthrough innovation which is more difficult for other entrepreneurs to emulate at speed. We therefore need to be aware that too much focus on specific existing customer needs may lead to incrementalism, rather than more fundamental innovation. Such fundamental innovations can extend to leaps forward in competitiveness and productivity, as well as to new products or service features. For example, our illustration of the development of budget hotel accommodation, with the innovation of prefabricated hotel building combined with carefully thought-out cost-effective designs, resulted in a revolutionary new concept. Owing to the associated low-cost operating procedures and overheads, budget hotels achieved a market breakthrough based on new building technology. No fresh needs were being addressed, but consumers suddenly found they were able to have their accommodation requirements satisfied to an acceptable extent, but at a much lower price than had previously been on offer in the market place.

In contrast, the impetus for a new concept may come purely from the provider's creative urge, as with the New India Garden illustration. Fundamental breakthroughs are not confined to the harnessing of technology. They can extend to design of product/service concepts which are different in some radical way, but because of the creative application of the ideas incorporated in them, rather than the use of technology. Creativity is by no means limited to the technology dimension. As Searles (1980) identifies, it is clear that artists are not concerned about the marketing problem, they create without worrying whether their work will please or not and this is their social function. However, in the case of business creativity, we would argue that to be successful the creator must consciously or intuitively have had a **sense of the market** and what is required. If the market is ignored a major risk is being run in that customer response may not be sufficiently positive to bring about success.

Hence, the challenge for the entrepreneur is to maintain creativity and innovation alongside a market orientation, rather than trust to the happy accident. We hypothesize that it is when these conditions are present simultaneously that success is most likely to ensue. The creative process is being triggered by an awareness of the market, new ways of satisfying it, and an openness to change. In this circumstance, creativity can stem from intuition or **gut feel**, but nevertheless remain in tune with actual or potential market needs. This can particularly apply when it is a new concept which is being created. The flair of an individual in harmony with societal trends can move things on in a quantum leap, whereas traditional marketing theory would simply lead to incremental development. The prime illustration of Sir Terence Conran is considered later in this chapter.

Entrepreneurship writers as far back as Schumpeter in the 1930s were highlighting the importance of intuition in entrepreneurial activity. Despite this, there has been a general tendency to underplay the intuitive, non-cognitive skills and behaviours very necessary for entrepreneurial success. Recently Horner (1997) showed via a survey of tour operators that their new product development was based upon intuitive feel, rather than on formal market research. It may be that new concepts generally are developed much more on the basis of 'feel' than text books would have us believe.

Market positioning and segmentation

What does marketing positioning and segmentation theory contribute to an understanding of the entrepreneurial process?

Lewis (1985) has demonstrated that consumers respond to products and services offered in terms of attributes or benefits which are perceived as being delivered. For example, pizza home-delivery customers may be seeking attributes which include convenience, speed, nutrition, lifestyle association, tastiness, and value for money. In seeking to develop or modify a concept, marketing theory tells us that certain attributes can be more important to specific groups of customers than to others. It therefore makes sound business sense to develop concepts which are perceived to deliver those attributes of significant importance to the customer groups which a business is setting out to attract. That is to say, the concept is positioned in the market place aligned to the attributes and benefits sought by the target market. The difficulty for the entrepreneur lies in gaining accurate knowledge of these features.

Almanza *et al.* (1994) demonstrated that this approach can be shown diagramatically. They carried out research amongst customers of a University food service operation and used semantic differentials to discover those features of food service which were perceived as most important. They also combined these with the customers' perception of the extent to which the food service operation delivered against the desired features. Figure 7.2 shows features mapped in terms of both importance and deliverability.

This approach is all very good in theory. However, in the case of this research, there was an easily identifiable customer group, probably exhibiting reasonably homogenous characteristics. In commercial locations open to a wider customer base, customer groups may be more heterogeneous than homogenous. In such situations it may be relatively straightforward to identify attributes which are significant to the overall customer base. However, linking attribute preferences to more focused and meaningful market segments and customer groups can be more problematic.

This moves the focus of marketing theory to address customer groups, or segments, in a quest to gain the valuable knowledge the entrepreneur needs to achieve product/market alignment. Traditionally, customer groups have

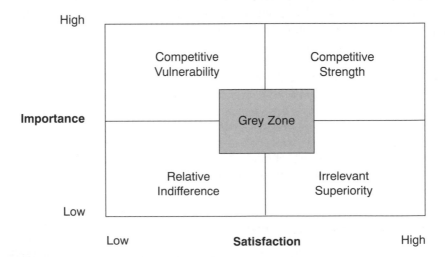

Figure 7.2 Service attribute matrix for ranking satisfaction and importance
Source: Alamanza et al (1994)

Table 7.2 Traditional customer groups: socio-economic grouping and occupation

Grouping	Occupations
A Quite rare	Barrister, Bishop, Pilot, Principal-Grade Civil Servant, Lt. Colonel in Army, MP, Consultant Physician, Wing Commander RAF
B Most professionals and business people – usually with degree or professional qualification	Solicitor, Accountant, Bank Manager, Lecturer, Clergy, Stockbroker, Marketing Manager, Company Director, GP, Pharmacist
C1 White collar/office	Secretarial, Clerical, Administrative, Teacher, Engineer, Nurse, Social Worker, Police, Fire Service, Ambulance Service, Estate Agent, Computer Programmer, Sales People, Travel Agent, Student
C2 Factory/manual – skilled trades people	Painter and Decorator, Electrician, Plumber, Carpenter, Builder, Welder, Joiner, Fitter, Plasterer, HGV Driver, Tailor, Foreman, Printer, Sheet Metal Worker, Telecom Engineer, Service Engineer, Nanny, Market Research Interviewer, Retail Assistant, Chef, Baker
D Unskilled	Driver, Window Cleaner, Post People, Milk Delivery, Waiting and Bar Staff, Caretaker, Porter, Childminder, Housekeeper, Warehouse Operative, Store Staff, Cleaner, Farm Hand, Messenger, Packer, Labeller
E Non-salaried	House wife, unemployed, on benefit, retired (though social class normally taken from previous occupation)

been classified according to their socio-economic status as either A, B, C1, C2, D or E, as presented in Table 7.2.

Clearly, it might be useful to know that you are aiming a product or service at a particular socio-economic group, if only because the grouping will, to an extent, equate with spending power. However, this will apply only at very broad aggregate level for the overall group of occupations which together form a particular socio-economic group. Hence, alternative forms of segmentation have been used to try and identify markets more precisely.

For example, the ACORN market classification system is extensively used by UK chain restaurant, pub and leisure operators. The classification breaks down customer groupings into segments according to a neighbourhood classification system. Neighbourhoods are groups of around twenty-five households, the smallest unit for which census data is analysed. By carrying out extensive market research against this classification system, CACI are able to associate neighbourhood groupings with quite specific consumer behaviour. For example, the extent of their expenditure on eating out, number of holidays taken and price paid, and leisure participation and frequency patterns. Analysis of neighbourhoods at different radii around specific locations can therefore predict total buying power available for particular kinds of expenditure. This can be particularly useful to those entrepreneurs planning new ventures or repositioning existing ones. It helps both to define and quantify the nature of the market available.

However, it again needs to be stressed that demand is only half of the equation. A golden opportunity exists where there is **high aggregate demand** combined with **low supply**. If there is high supply in the form of many competing businesses, then prospects for individual businesses may be poor even though a strong overall demand situation exists. Conversely, opportunities exist for entrepreneurs to spot situations where demand has not already been met. This does not necessarily mean creating something completely new. **Imitative entrepreneurship** is quite legitimate. Legal passing off restrictions mean that a new concept cannot make out that it is really an expansion of an existing business. However this does not mean that the ideas of existing successful businesses cannot be taken on board. Imitative entrepreneurship can therefore involve identifying that a particular area has unmet demand for a business format which is already established and successful elsewhere.

Illustration: 'Quaglinos', imitative entrepreneurship

Howard and Paul Bossick are to open a 110-seat restaurant in Croydon, intending it to be a pilot for a chain of restaurants on the south side of the Thames. They are particularly interested in sites in the south London 'village' areas. The concept is 'Quaglinos' for South London. *'I think we have found a niche in Croydon for good food and good service'*, said Howard.
Source: *Caterer and Hotelkeeper*, 17 April 1997

Useful though the ACORN system is, in terms of marketing utility, other segmentation models can sometimes provide additional or different insights. These may be based upon alternative socio-economic classifications.

Illustration: female hotel guests, segmentation by sex

Callan reported on research carried out amongst hotel guests showing that female guests desire similar attributes in hotel service to those desired by males. However, compared with men, females put a heightened emphasis on security and privacy. They also place more importance on their first impression of the hotel and its service providers. Characteristics such as cleanliness, friendliness, politeness, and communicative ability are particularly important.
Source: Callan, 1995

Callan's research provided a great deal of other specific information useful to those hoteliers seeking to provide an improved level of service to female guests. It clearly illustrated the power of research in enabling concepts to be designed and engineered in such a way that consumers needs and aspirations are met. Such research is expensive to carry out and may be beyond the scope of an individual entrepreneur seeking to put together a new venture. However, much useful information can be gained from secondary sources, as discussed in Chapter 8.

In addition, segmentation which provides greater insight into psychological beliefs, motivations, and behaviour (psychographic segmentation) can, potentially, be useful to those designing or modifying concepts. In contemporary tourism literature, researchers have investigated whether a relationship exists between individual psychological characteristics, consumer behaviour, demographic characteristics, and the types of tourism experiences desired. For example, Weaver *et al.* (1994) attempted to identify four market segments in relation to seven attributes considered important in selecting a family vacation destination. The segments were investigated using psychological, behavioural, and demographic variables. Cluster analysis was used in an attempt to produce different profiles in terms of the destination attributes sought. However, only three variables, two behavioural and one demographic, were found to be statistically significant. No significant psychological variables were discovered, illustrating that a qualitative basis for meaningful segmentation can prove elusive.

Thus, it can be observed that marketing segmentation practice is made more problematic if this view of an increasingly complex, sophisticated and heterogeneous consumer clientele is accepted. It can be much more difficult to identify and target the specific customer groups who are likely to be attracted, particularly when potentially more relevant psychographic or lifestyle segments may well cut across traditional segmentation boundaries such as age and socio-economic groupings. Nevertheless, segmentations based on broad aggregations can be useful. Certainly, many of the retail

---

Illustration: Tom Cobleigh, positioning and mixed segmentations

A good illustration of how a concept can be designed to appeal to different target customer groups for different occasions is provided by a new Tom Cobleigh pub/restaurant development.

The pub/restaurant is located close to both a University campus and a large city Hospital. It is also adjacent to student and middle-class residential areas. Its concept offering is positioned to appeal to different groups at different stages in the mid-week trading day. At lunch time and early evening the emphasis is on food. The extensive use of value promotions attracts retired 'greys' at lunch time and early evenings. Family groups also take advantage of the early evening high-value children's menu, combined with adult meal deals. Mid-evening diners are presumed to have less price sensitivity and to be dining for social or special occasion reasons. Large tables, friendly service and ambience enhanced by atmospheric music are the concept features which are given prominence. Late evening, the concept switches to more of a drinks-led social occasion. The music is turned up louder and special drinks promotions are often used to attract high student numbers and ensure a lively atmosphere.
Source: authors

chains in our business sector use ACORN analysis on the assumption that a given population, in a particular mix of housing within a given radius, will contain sufficient potential customers to support the development of a particular new concept. However, concepts may need to be sufficiently flexible to attract different customer segments at different times.

The post-modernist consumer challenge

Planning and implementation of the marketing activities of the entrepreneur is further complicated by what is termed the **post-modernist consumer challenge**. The essence of this challenge is that today's consumers have become far from straightforward to define and categorize, extremely heterogeneous, open to new experiences, and volatile in their consumer behaviour. Of course, this is necessarily a generalization, but few experienced entrepreneurs would disagree that today's customers are far more idiosyncratic, sophisticated and discerning in their approach to purchasing goods and services than in the past.

Although subject to widespread debate within the literature as to its specific nature, indeed some writers even refute its existence, Brown (1993) has attempted to define the nature of post-modernism, as shown in Table 7.3.

Table 7.3 Nature of post-modernism

Modern/modernity	Post-modern/post-modernity
Order/Control	Disorder/Chaos
Certainty/Determinacy	Ambiguity/Indeterminacy
Fordism/Factory	Post-Fordism/Office
Content/Depth	Style/Surface
Progress/Tomorrow	Stasis/Today
Homogeneity/Consensus	Heterogeneity/Plurality
Hierarchy/Adulthood	Equality/Youth
Existence/Reality	Performance/Imitation
Deliberate/Outer-directed	Playful/Self-centred
Contemplation/Metaphysics	Participation/Parody
Congruity/Design	Incongruity/Chance

Source: Brown (1993, p. 22)

Brown (1993, p. 99) summarizes the implications of this transition as being:

> post-modernists prefer disorder to order; ambiguity to certainty; form to content; surface to depth; present to past and present to future; heterogeneity to homogeneity; conflict to consensus; differences to similarities; complexity to simplification; rhetoric to logic; individuality to universality; customization to commodification; and, not least, consumption to production.

Quite straightforward really isn't it? Indeed, in a later publication, Brown (1995) comments that the inherent eclecticism of the post-modern moment might lead many to conclude that it is not worth the trouble! We believe this would be a mistake. The emergence of the post-modernist consumer represents a sea change in the way that consumers respond. It has considerable implications for those developing concepts or bringing new ones to the market.

The thrust of this change can be generalized as being towards a situation where the post-modern consumer is more individualistic, and is increasingly being stimulated by perceived aesthetics rather than by functionality. Functionality of products and services is more or less taken for granted. It is the intangibles, and their association with style, that enables consumers to act out their desired socio-cultural roles. It has long been a truism that you **sell the sizzle**, not the steak. However, this perhaps misses the post-modernist point. The sizzle, although in itself an intangible, must also be considered within its aesthetic context. A sizzle in one setting may evoke a very different response from that in another!

Romm (1989) has argued that aesthetics are partly brought about by the physical environment, such as design and decor, but also by the quality of the social interaction between staff and customers. He maintains that, in the restaurant sector, this is often given insufficient management attention. Romm proposes that managers should view restaurant service as a theatrical performance and help service staff play their part in ensuring a good customer experience. Our view is that restaurants are increasingly recognizing the multi-faceted contributions towards the overall guest experience, and that his criticisms regarding lack of attention to the aesthetics are no longer so valid. **Soft system** elements of service delivery seem to be increasingly recognized as important in achieving customer satisfaction. The following illustration provides a reflection of one response to the post-modernist challenge.

Illustration: Yo! Sushi, aesthetics

Customers dining at Yo! Sushi could soon find themselves being verbally abused by talking robots. Three automatic guided vehicle robots are programmed to carry drinks along a pre-set route through the 100-seat restaurant. The original concept was that staff would help customers get drinks from the robotic trolleys, but customers want to serve themselves. Robots are part of the hi-tech experience at Yo! Sushi. Other state-of-the-art equipment includes a 60 m conveyor belt which travels the length of the restaurant carrying colour-coded plates of sushi, priced from £1 to £2.50. In the middle of the restaurant, chefs work in an open-planned sushi-making area. A bold move is the restaurant's lack of decoration. *'It's a food factory. There is no decoration, the technology becomes the decor'*, says Simon Woodroff, Yo! Sushi's owner and designer.
Source: Fox, 1997a

Cova and Svanfeldt (1993) have claimed that the aestheticization of everyday life and consumption are possibly the strongest characteristics of post-modern European societies. The post-modern human being is free to pursue choices which can turn each day into a work of art, resulting in

general stylistic promiscuity and playful mixing of codes. Faced with this rich canvas, a post-modernist consumer could adopt seemingly aberrant consumer behaviour, out of type from what would be expected. Nevertheless, such behaviour may well have a hidden consistency within the context of a lifestyle in which different roles, occasions, and motivations interweave in a complex and fast-moving way.

Firat *et al.* (1995) associate post-modernism with a fragmentation of experience, together with the growth and efflorescence of multiple, highly incompatible lifestyles, ideologies, and myth systems. Within this context, consumption is the means by which individuals define their self-images for others and for themselves. Self is in fact a marketable entity to be customized, positioned, and promoted in the same way as any other product. Such active acting out of complex images inevitably brings with it juxtapositions of opposites in statements of style. Post-modernist consumers will often have multiple, even contradictory, projects to which they are marginally and momentarily committed.

According to Foxall (1993), like any other biological species, consumers also react and adapt to their environment – even the fickle post-modernist. The Behavioural Perspective Model of Purchase and Consumption (Figure 7.3) relates patterns of consumer choice to their different environmental consequences.

The **current behaviour setting** consists of the physical, social, and temporal influences which signal the likely consequences of behaving in a particular way. In other words, all the various influences which affect the way that we see the world. The **consumer learning history** is the cumulative effect of rewarding and punishing outcomes to past behaviour. What worked for us? When did we feel good? When did we suffer disasters? These influences will impinge on the consumer's own behavioural predispositions, for example the predisposition to adapt or to innovate. If our experiences of change have been favourable, we are likely to continue experimenting, if that is in our nature. If we are naturally conservative, then we are likely to

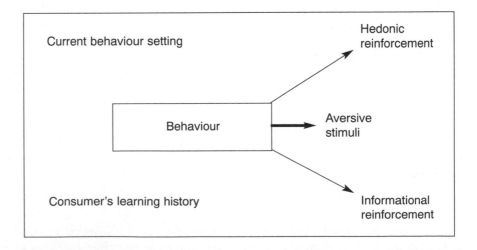

Figure 7.3 Summary of the behavioural perspective model.
Source: Foxall (1993, p. 10)

stay with the tried and tested. Just because one thing brings a good outcome does not mean that another will! Accordingly, individual consumers will process the same information, but in different ways, leading to different conclusions and behaviour. Such behaviour will, in itself, adapt over time. It will be directly influenced by the **hedonic reinforcement** deriving from the extent of satisfaction and utility within the service. **Informational reinforcement** feedback on such issues as social status and style will also positively affect future consumer behaviour.

Whether what we choose to do meets with the approval of significant others and receives positive reinforcement from the media images to which we are exposed, is also important. Counter balancing these will be **aversive stimuli**. These will include the necessary foregoing of alternative products and services and other costs of consuming. These can be very important in the hospitality, tourism and leisure industries. For example, a holiday can actually be competing with alternative leisure pursuits as well as with other holidays.

The following illustration presents one businesses approach to assessing customer behaviour.

Illustration: People's Palace, customer behaviour

Restaurateurs face some obstacles to obtaining customer information, but EPOS (Electronic Points of Sale) systems like the Sulcus Squirrel system installed in the People's Palace restaurant on the South Bank of the Thames can help. The People's Palace is operated by the Capital Group, founded by a leading hospitality industry entrepreneur, David Levin.

Manager, Joseph Levin, is building sales tactics around his ability to analyse customers' eating and drinking habits. '*It won't tell us their names and addresses but it tells us what they eat and drink, when they eat and drink it and how they settle their bills,*' he says. With that he tracks the different tastes of business and weekend lunch and dinner clients, and pre-concert evening diners, as they spend up to £5.5 million per year in the 200-cover restaurant.

Source: Kimber, 1997

As industries inextricably linked with lifestyle and aesthetic associations, the hospitality, tourism and leisure sectors can expect to feature ever more significantly in the post-modernist consumer's consumption behaviour. Health, style, taste, excitement, and adventure are all likely to have a place in the post-modernist portfolio of self-image components and our industry is well placed to supply them. Furthermore, the fragmented, disparate ownership structure of these industry sectors is an extremely fortunate feature in terms of meeting post-modernist consumer aspirations.

Consequently, the dynamism and diversity inherent in post-modernism create a wealth of fertile opportunities for individual entrepreneurs to develop concepts which have customer appeal. These enable customer interaction with the industry sectors in a way that provides a powerful statement of individual taste, attitudes, and beliefs. The recreational pursuits we enjoy, the kind of holidays we go on, and the restaurants, cafés, and bars we frequent are important and evocative images and statements of how we see ourselves in the world.

In a situation where customer tastes are so heterogeneous, the entrepreneur's individual intuitively based flair and creativity may match evolving customer preferences just as well as a carefully researched chain concept based on well-established market desires. In the previous New India Garden illustration we saw how a restaurant had wide appeal despite being idiosyncratic in some areas of its operation. There is virtually unlimited scope for those who have flair and imagination to meet customers' needs in innovative ways that capture customers' imagination and ultimately lead to success.

All in all it is obvious that there is a complex and dynamic web of factors influencing consumer behaviour in the post-modernist society. Entrepreneurs need to be aware of this. One implication is that public relations and other promotional activity which influences consumer perception is vitally important for business success. It is no longer sufficient to simply get the concept delivery right. It also requires the active influencing of customer perception. The concept needs to be presented and reinforced as being congruent with the lifestyle, social, and cultural aspirations of targeted customers. Furthermore, Foxall's behavioural perspective model is important as it reminds us that meeting the needs of customers is not a question of addressing a static portfolio of wants and desires. The goal posts move continuously! As they move, they create new opportunities and challenges for the entrepreneur.

In meeting these challenges, it may be that much marketing theory has lost some of its utility. Elliot (1993) maintains that many of the traditional marketing concepts regarding consumer behaviour, consumption activities, and marketing research are now in need of fundamental reassessment. In a post-modern world characterized by the consumption of symbolic meaning and construction of multiple realities, meaning is negotiated by consumers rather than determined by marketers. An entrepreneur with affinity to the market place and technical expertise, may intuitively create attractive concepts with broad appeal. In the illustration opposite did Sir Terence Conran use affinity to the market place, technical expertise, or intuition, or a combination, to develop the Quaglinos concept?

In seeking to understand consumers it is perhaps all too easy to get carried away with behavioural and cultural theories and to lose sight of the fact that, for most people, expenditure in the hospitality, tourism and leisure industries is discretionary expenditure. Consequently, whilst these motivational influences have potentially wide-ranging impact, such effect presupposes the economic means to act out the desired consumption scenario. The recent recession showed that post-modern consumers are willing to substantially cut back on discretionary expenditure in these industries when faced with uncertainty and economic loss.

Nevertheless, given the economic means, it does seem that today's consumers are able and willing to play their part fully in an incredibly rich performance based on improvisation rather than a fixed script. This post-modernist poetry, quoted in Brown (1993, p. 22), perhaps encapsulates the essence of the situation and its implications for marketing:

> God is dead
> History is dead
> Theory is dead
> And, I'm not feeling too good myself!

Illustration: Quaglinos, post-modern consumer behaviour

Sir Terence Conran has a remarkable track record in opening new ventures which break the mould of existing provision. When Quaglinos opened in 1993, it was the first of London's mega-restaurants. Seating around 420 people, it was a brave development in the midst of the recession. With Sir Terence's background in design it was inevitable that the general aesthetics and style of the venture would command attention as much as the food.

Whilst the food never attracted rave revues, it was sufficiently competent for people to feel that the overall offering was desirable. The sunken restaurant is overlooked by a large bar and performance area. Pre- and post-dinner drinkers can gaze down the white staircase to see who is present. The staff are mainly young and all incredibly good looking, as well as being extremely competent. Presumably the 15 per cent service charge on the £40-plus average spend for dinner makes it a good place to work as well as a good place to frequent.

Whatever the key components, the fact is that, overall, Quaglinos has worked. It rapidly became one of London's most important and busiest eating-out venues. Customers (sometimes described as the gold bracelet brigade) learned it was a place to see and be seen in. They enjoyed the occasion and felt that being associated with taste and success reflected their taste and success. 'It made eating out more of an event than it has been for years' (*Time Out* – 13 September 1995).

Three years on Sir Terence opened the 700-seat Mezzos in Soho, aiming for 2000 customers a day! As reflected in its name, Mezzos is designed to be a lot of interrelated activities in one big air-conditioned envelope (the essence of post-modernism!?). These include a restaurant, café, bread shop, patisserie, and bakery. Though design is of course important, Sir Terence has claimed that *'Food is the most important thing; everything else, even service and look comes second'*. Undoubtedly food is important and for a time it was uncertain whether this functional core to the concept would support or undermine the venture.

Critic's verdicts were mixed. Caroline Stacey in *Time Out* (18 October 1995) described it in glowing terms. *'The place is cosier than Quaglinos, but still glitzy – well coutured if not completely cutting edge. It generates a sense of occasion without formality and after so short a time in business, the assurance of the cooking and service makes it seem like an old hand.'*

By contrast, Emily Green of the *Independent* (15 October 1995) spoke disparagingly of both food and style *'Some sort of overcooked offal, kidney perhaps, was strewn over the top. Its taste and texture was akin to dried mud'* and in conclusion *'by plonking Mezzos here in Soho, Conran has crudely gone against the kind of shaggy cool that provides the potent local glamour'*.

Clearly, in terms of Foxall's 'Informational Reinforcement' 10 000-plus customers a week are here being given very different messages. In its early days, Mezzos had clear novelty value. In the longer term, potential customers seem to have adopted frequenting, rather than non-frequenting behaviour. It seems that the positive messages have won the day!

Source: authors

Post-modernism and product life-cycle

How does the post-modernist scenario of shifting sophisticated market demand fit with product life-cycle? The basic idea of product life-cycle is

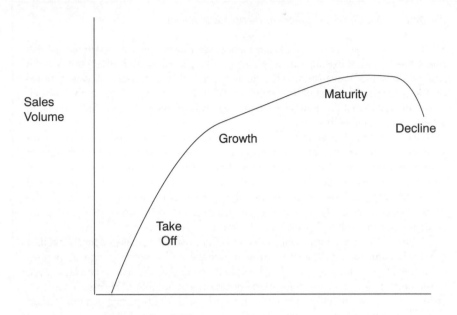

Figure 7.4 Product/service life cycle.

that demand for products and services can be shown to go through a number of clearly defined stages. These stages also correspond to the market's life-cycle (Figure 7.4).

Undoubtedly some of the markets associated with the hospitality, tourism and leisure industries are past the growth stage in the product life-cycle. Yet, even when markets are well into the mature phase, opportunities exist for introduction and growth of new concepts. Certainly, the hotel market overall is undoubtedly well into the mature phase. Yet, within it, as we have seen, different sectors decline and others emerge and grow. Chain operations, particularly in the budget hotel accommodation sector, continue to increase their market penetration. The much maligned bed and breakfast operation and guest houses have, in some instances, fought back against hotels by upgrading and introducing en-suite facilities. Furthermore, some have positioned themselves towards niches such as the non-smoking market, for example, and appear to be trading successfully, even in seaside resorts which may be in overall decline. In addition, there is always the possibility of a product/service re-launch (see Figure 7.5) to move the concept on into a new cycle. Demand for live viewing of football is a good illustration of how a re-launch and change in image can re-stimulate demand that may seemingly be in the mature or even decline phase (see opposite).

Other leisure concepts have not been so successful in establishing a new stage in the product/service life-cycle. For example, stand-alone ten pin bowling centres experienced very rapid growth in the 1960s and then declined equally as rapidly. They were re-launched in the late 1980s and seemed to be set for another major renaissance. This may still be the case. However, it now seems that their future may lie within the new concept of large multi-provision leisure centres offering customers a range of leisure

Illustration: live football, product re-launch and market re-positioning

The re-launch of the First Division as the Premiership, combined with extensive Sky television coverage, did much to promote a more exciting modern image for the game, at least at the top level. Television money has also enabled talented overseas players to be recruited to the British game, bringing additional flair and glamour. Consequently, attendances have re-assumed a strong growth curve. No doubt sustaining this in the longer term may be to an extent dependent upon the performance of the national team. But then there is always the opportunity of a pan-European league to re-launch it again! All very good news for the top clubs. But in the lower divisions, clubs are struggling as they are not viewed as having the same style and glamour.

Source: authors

activities. On the other hand, bingo has been much more successful in repositioning itself as a more stylish and exciting leisure pursuit. Investment in new, more luxurious surroundings, the promotion of food and drink as auxiliary service offerings, and the possibility of much more substantial prizes, have all helped to change bingo's image and broaden its appeal.

The overall message for entrepreneurs is that the idea of a product/service life-cycle inevitably following a course through the various stages to eventual decline and ultimate withdrawal of provision, is past its sell-by date! In fairness this was being said by Dhalla and Yuspeh as long ago as 1976! Within this vibrant post-modern society there is infinite opportunity for innovative ideas to be introduced which will re-position and re-launch products/services. Even within a broad aggregate market which is perhaps

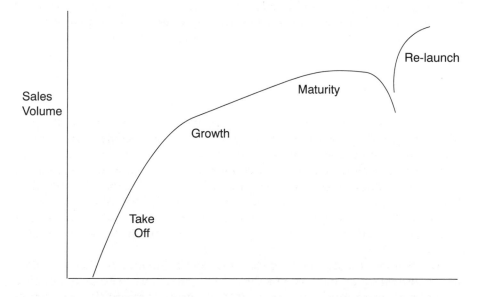

Figure 7.5 Modified product/service life-cycle

in maturity, some sub-sectors will be growing strongly whilst others decline. There is therefore continual opportunity to **de-couple** the individual concept's product/service life-cycle from the life-cycle of the aggregate market sector in which the service is located.

Pricing, value and concept flexibility

Price is an important component in the marketing mix and can be used to help position the concept towards different customer groups, or to encourage the same groups to use the service on different occasions. For example, customers may eat at a weekend mid-evening time for a socially based meal experience with friends. The same customers return mid-week **early** evening for a casual everyday eating experience – if the price is attractive. For the weekend occasion, the product/service being offered will probably be less price-sensitive than the mid-week one. Many restaurants increasingly have differentiated prices, frequently via promotional discounts, which reflect this reality, as is the case in the following illustration.

Illustration: Number Twenty Four, promotional discounts

Richard Hughes is a veteran of lunch-for-a-fiver schemes. As chef-proprietor of Number Twenty Four in Wymondham he now has three *Times* Eat Out for a Fiver promotions under his belt. For Hughes, the schemes have several benefits. They fill his restaurant for eight weeks, boosting the revenue for an otherwise erratic lunch trade. This year, Number Twenty Four achieved £400 every lunch time for eight weeks, with an average spend of £12. *'You would not get that money in January, February and March – they are quiet months. If I didn't do it, people would only go somewhere else'*, said Hughes. The promotions are perceived by the local people as good value for money. They create goodwill and the restaurant becomes a talking point.
Source: Fox, 1997b

Hotels and tour operators have, of course, been quick to recognize the perishability of their product and many adopt **yield management** practices to take account of variability in demand. However, Rogers (1995) carried out empirical research which showed that tourism attractions generally adopted very conservative and inflexible pricing policies. Compared with this, leisure attractions in the public sector have generally been quite innovatory in using differentiated prices to make activities more attractive to low-income groups at off-peak times, when there would otherwise be low utilization.

Price is undoubtedly a key aspect of market positioning. As Pavesic (1989) has identified, of all the business decisions which have to be made, pricing is one that causes much anxiety. There is a natural concern that in a price-sensitive market, pricing at too high a level will result in reduced customer counts and a shortfall in income. At the same time, prices which are excessively low will sacrifice profit. Nevertheless, the pricing decision has to be made. As well as being targeted at particular market segments and occasions, price should reflect all the factors which influence the purchase decision, such as product/service quality perceptions, ambience, and location convenience. Pavesic (1989) proposes that customers are actually quite sophisticated at weighing up different complex combinations of attributes which are offered by different organizations. He suggests that it is the buyer's perception of the **total relative value** of the product or service that influences their decision to choose between purchase alternatives and their willingness to pay the asked-for price. Customers may be tolerant of a businesses deficiency in providing some attributes, if the overall package is relatively attractive.

Intuitively most of us would probably agree with this. For example, when we are making a decision about where to go to eat, we probably have a short list of places that we are considering. Mentally, we will quickly go through an evaluation process in relation to the particular eating-out occasion which we have in mind. A wide range of perceived strengths and weaknesses may be, in some way, quickly weighed up before the decision is made.

Morgan and Dev (1994) investigated the place of brands in customer purchase behaviour and concluded that, in the USA hotel market, **competitive sets of brands** existed for particular business or leisure stay occasions. Hence, in the case of competition for business travellers, Holiday Inn were placed in the same competitive set as Ramada. For the leisure traveller market Holiday Inn competed with Marriott, Sheraton, Hilton and Hyatt. Consequently it is the relative value offered by companies within the competitive set for each market which is important. Morgan and Dev's work was very useful in that it established linkages between **competitive sets** and **customer segments**. Their findings were derived from extensive national sample surveys carried out by the National Family Organization in USA households. Linkages were therefore demonstrated at high levels of statistical confidence.

The implication of these issues for entrepreneurs is that it is important to identify the other organizations with which customers will be comparing their market offering. These may be different according to the occasion or purpose which is stimulating the purchase decision. Competitors for one occasion may be different from that of another. Competitive sets may

---

Illustration: competitive sets

Market research carried out amongst customers eating in the Café Bar at the Showroom (a multi-screen arts cinema complex in Sheffield) showed that the competitive set at lunchtime was different from that in the evenings.

At lunchtime, the main customer group was comprised of nearby workers, who compared the offering with pubs and wine bars serving food in the locality. In the evenings, people travelled to the Showroom from further afield and considered other 'destination' venues to be the competition.

Source: authors

operate if competitors are familiar with competing operations owing to brand recognition or some other reason. In comparing with organizations within the competitive set, consumers are probably quite sophisticated in evaluating total relative value represented by the different attributes offered by each of the respective businesses.

Differentiation and communication

If concepts need to be flexible in order to cater for different customer groups/occasions, marketing theory also tells us that they should also be **differentiated**. In an increasingly cluttered market place, it is important that a concept is obviously differentiated from others – that it stands out from the crowd. Only in this way will the consumers identify it, be swayed by its benefits and attributes, and arrive at their purchasing decision. If a concept is not differentiated – a **me too** type of product – then consumers will presumably be indifferent or purchase an alternative product/service which is more strongly differentiated. In the same way that it is desirable for concepts to be positioned so that attributes important to customers are given prominence, it is also desirable for importantly rated attributes to be used to differentiate it. After all, it is little use being perceived as different if the difference is not important! However, in today's demanding market place of post-modern consumers there is a certain tension between the need for flexibility and the need for differentiation which sends out strong, consistent messages. The following illustration is an example of a company which has successfully managed this tension.

Illustration: YSE Ski Operator, differentiation

Most regular skiers will have experienced the frustration of airport and transfer delays. With multiple operator use of charter aircraft and the vagaries of winter weather, it is far from unusual for flights to be considerably delayed whilst the arrival of another tour operators' clients are awaited. Such delays can be extremely frustrating, particularly on a busy winter Saturday, when all the world seems to be passing through airports such as Geneva and passenger facilities are pretty near stretched to breaking point.

YSE have differentiated their operation in important ways. They fill their own chartered plane, so that they are the only company transferring clients for the aeroplane departure. Since they only deal with winter holidays in Val D'Isere, there is no question of waiting for transfers from other resorts. When they get their clients to the airport, they know the plane can depart. Also they have based their holidays on Sunday departures, a considerably quieter day for air travel.

The sum total of these differentiating features is that the customer feels more confident that the company is likely to deliver hassle-free transport to and from the resort.

It is interesting that these same differentiating attributes are used throughout the season though the price charged for their holidays varies very considerably. Pre-Christmas and late-season skiers are generally getting in an extra fix of skiing and are offered an attractive price. The price for a peak season ski holiday week, when everyone wants to go for their main holiday, is over 80 per cent higher! This is a good example of 'yield' management being used alongside differentiation.

An illustration of the flexibility built into the concept is provided by the description of the sleeping arrangements at the company's Chalet Crête Blanche! The brochure puts this very amusingly:

> The bedrooms were recently refurbished to three-star standard. The sixteen rooms facing south, up Bellevarde, are spacious and sunny. They nearly all have baths, separate loos, and a double and a single bed. This lopsided-looking arrangement is ideal, catering for couples who share a bed, couples who don't, couples who think they might or pretend they won't, as well as couples with a child.

Interestingly, owners John Yates-Smith and Fiona Easedale were both initially involved in the ski holiday business with another operator in Val D'Isere. They gained experience of what was needed to run a specialist holiday operation there – and then used it to develop an improved customer-offering for their own company. A classic development, according to entrepreneurial theory.
Source: YSE sales brochure, 1996

Becker-Suttle *et al.*'s (1994) research has shown that differentiation can be made more difficult in that customers actually perceive groups, or clusters, of attributes. It may well be the total bundle that is being responded to, rather than a portfolio of individual benefits. In market research the technique of conjoint analysis can be used to separate out the relative importance of individual attributes from within the total benefit bundle. However, very little research has been carried out to date within the hospitality, tourism and leisure industries as to which attributes are most important. Such research is probably more achievable for large organizations and academics, than for individual entrepreneurs struggling to put a concept together within a short time-scale.

Such analysis may not, in any case, produce the empirical evidence required to predict effective benefit bundles useful in new concept design. Our view is that although functionality is considered very important, it is almost taken for granted by the majority of customers. More intangible attributes such as service quality and ambience may certainly be rated as less important. However, in a situation where product/service functionality is being delivered by a large number of professional organizations, it may be these **less important intangibles** which are actually being used by consumers to differentiate between competing offerings. Certainly this would explain the high profile given to quality of service by very many operators within the industry.

The following illustration tells how research activity was carried out in an attempt to identify the attributes which differentiated one restaurant from another. In this instance, it was the very attribute which is most difficult for the chain operator to consistently control which made the difference. Friendly service may not have been **rated** the most important attribute, but in a situation where all other desired attributes were being delivered it assumed the most important differentiating role. This may give independent entrepreneurs an edge over chain operators as it may be more difficult to maintain consistent service standards without the close attentions of a dedicated owner-operator. It appears that for the individual entrepreneur developing a new concept, differentiation remains as much an art as a science. It is probably this very uncertainty which makes the industry so appealing to entrepreneurs.

Illustration: market research, differentiation

Joanne Wallace, an undergraduate student, recently carried out a customer trail analysis at two competing chain restaurants. The trail involved benchmarking the customer experience from initial entry through to departure.

The two restaurants were both operating in interesting premises, very well-furnished and with good standard of decoration. They were pleasing to the eye. Products were similar with a good menu range priced in similar bands. Both wine lists were extensive and competitively priced. The ordering and service system worked well and did not demand a great deal from the customers. The actual food was well cooked, well presented, and efficiently served in both instances.

When it came down to it there was little to choose between many of the hard and soft system features. Differentiation in such a situation is very difficult for consumers. In Joanne's case the decision as to which restaurant she would return to was based purely upon the friendliness and attentiveness of the service.

Source: authors

Differentiation is partly a function of product/service delivery but, as Lewis (1990) has identified, advertising and promotion can also play a part through influencing customer perception. Images, benefits, and differentiation lie in the perception of the customer, not of management. However, customer perception is not static. It can be shaped by both actual service delivery and through the use of communication techniques and media. Whilst many entrepreneurs are gifted at developing new concepts, they frequently are disadvantaged when communicating with customers. Here, the corporations enjoy a considerable advantage owing to their economies of scale and scope. Furthermore, running multiple-unit operations makes expenditure on advertising and other marketing media much more feasible. Independent operators can counteract this by participation in marketing consortia, local tourism promotions, and free publicity via public relations activity. In this, the innovative, creative characteristics of the entrepreneur are a considerable strength as they can be mobilized to harness the multitude of low cost, effective methods in which to communicate with the market place. The following illustration uses the Consort Hotels Group as an example of a marketing consortia which can benefit independent hotel entrepreneurs.

Hylands Hotel illustrates how, with minimal financial investment, maximum media exposure can be achieved, successfully differentiating it as a lively, trendy place to go.

Illustration: Consort Hotels Group, market communication

Consort was established in 1981 as a marketing consortium. Currently, it has a membership of 180 independently owned and operated hotels spread throughout the UK. These are in a variety of styles, the majority are three-star quality level, but range from two-star to four-star. In terms of competitive positioning, it sees itself to be on a par with Best Western. The major strengths of Consort for independent owners is that it provides centralized marketing expertise and resources which they could never dream of affording individually. This includes participation in national and international promotion programmes, access to computerized central reservation systems, and all the hotels are featured on the Internet via HotelNet.
Source: Conway, 1997

Illustration: Hylands Hotel, creative communication

A touch of glamour heralded the opening of the new restaurant at Hylands Hotel. 120 local business and media people rubbed shoulders with the Champagne-swilling duo from the television comedy *Absolutely Fabulous*. The pair were, in fact, AbFab look-a-likes brought in to spice up the official opening and to project the lively, trendy image which general manger Lynne Kennedy is keen to promote.

To get the party going with a swing, Champagne was served and the bar was free. The cost – comprising £690 for the girls, £400 for canapés and £1250 for liquor – was written into the marketing plan.
Source: Mullen, 1997

Geographic dispersion and micro-demand

A significant, additional market factor worthy of consideration within the hospitality, tourism and leisure industries is that of geographic dispersion of service provision. Whilst in one geographic area a mature market demand may be satisfied, in another there may still be a lack of provision, as was the case for hotel accommodation in Sheffield.

As local economies develop in different ways and consumer needs evolve, there will always be specific locations where, for some reason or another, local market demand is not satisfied. Pockets of opportunity may exist for entrepreneurs, even within a macro-market whose needs have been broadly satisfied.

Illustration: hotel accommodation, geographic market dispersion

The overall growth in supply of UK hotel rooms is probably at an end. New developments such as budget hotels will most likely be at the expense of existing provision. However, certain areas of the country have extremely high occupancy levels and could sustain further general growth in the local room stock. This can be the result of development of new sources of business. For example, the event-linked business attracted to Sheffield as a result of its high-profile sporting facilities and University conference activity has resulted in one of the highest hotel occupancy levels in the country. As a consequence, up to six new hotels are currently seeking planning approval.

There are other areas, such as Oxford, London, and parts of Birmingham, where, for various reasons linked to the micro-economy in those areas, the hotel market is far from saturated.

Source: authors

Summary

In hospitality, tourism and leisure, we are dealing with industry sectors where different factors impinge together to provide a unique marketing context. The importance of concept intangibles, their significance to life-style and cultural preferences of customers in themselves represent a major challenge. Such intangibles may be more vulnerable to changes in customer perception than the physical aspects of product and service delivery. However, intangibles also present an opportunity for individual entrepreneurs to create alternative and differentiated concepts, based on their own view and intuition of what customers will find appealing.

The dispersed structure of the industry means that both demand and supply sides of the business equation can vary significantly, geographically, from location to location. The equation is also extremely volatile in that local fluctuations in either supply or demand can substantially impinge upon existing operations. For entrepreneurs, this results in a challenging, dynamic business environment in perpetual motion. Furthermore, such market fluidity creates tremendous entrepreneurial opportunity. For those entrepreneurial organizations and individuals whose innovations spark a purchasing decision from customers, success can arrive rapidly.

From the marketing perspective, there is a complex web of factors to consider when developing new product/service concepts. Undoubtedly, many entrepreneurs have developed very effective concepts without taking into account the range of theoretical and empirical issues which we have covered here. However, that is not to say that the theories are not valid. Our view is that successful entrepreneurs often have an intuitive affinity with the needs of the market, and have utilized this gut feel sense of what will work to put together a concept offering which has potentially strong market appeal. Having conceived a concept offering is one stage in developing the entrepreneurial venture. Taking it to the market place, and converting the concept into cash, is quite another. This is where the application of marketing theories and principles, combined with the qualities, traits, and expertise of the entrepreneur, has a vital role to play in the achievement and sustenance of business success.

Reflective questions

1 Discuss the proposition that marketing is central to the entrepreneurial process.
2 Identify examples of entrepreneurial new entrants to the hospitality, tourism and leisure industries. Using Porter's model 'Forces governing competition to an industry', shown in Figure 7.1, evaluate their impact on the competitive environment.
3 Consider the ways in which market dynamics, trends and conditions have currently generated fertile entrepreneurial opportunities within the hospitality, tourism and leisure industries.
4 Debate the extent to which market segmentation using socio-economic variables is relevant within the current business environment.
5 Discuss the impact of the post-modernist consumer challenge upon entrepreneurs' marketing activities within the hospitality tourism and leisure industries.

References

Almanza, B., Jaffe, W. and Lin, L. (1994) Use of the service attribute matrix to measure consumer satisfaction, *Hospitality Education and Research Journal*, **17**, No. 2, 63–75.

Anonymous (1995) Marketing strategies for industry, fast food UK, 1995, *Caterer and Hotelkeeper*, 2–8 November, p. 16.

Becker-Suttle, S., Weaver, P. and Crawford Welch, S. (1994) A pilot study utilising conjoint analysis in the comparison of age based segmentation strategies in the full service restaurant market, *Journal of Food Service Marketing*, **1**, No. 2, 71–91.

Brown, S. (1993) Post modern marketing, *European Journal of Marketing*, **27**, No. 4, 19–34.

Brown, S. (1995) *Post Modern Marketing*, Routledge, London.

Callan, R. (1995) Lodging preferences of female customers: an empirical study, *Proceedings of Council for Hospitality Management Education Research Conference*, April 19th–20th, Norwich Hotel School.

Conway, H. (1997) An inspector calls, *Caterer and Hotelkeeper*, 27 February, p. 60–61.

Cova, B. and Svanfeldt, C. (1993) Societal innovations and the post modern aestheticisation of everyday life, *International Journal of Research in Marketing*, **10**, 297–310.

Deloitte Touche (1997) *Market Prospects for Budget Hotels*, Deloitte Touche, London.

Dhalla, N. and Yuspeh, S. (1976) Forget the product life-cycle concept, *Harvard Business Review*, January–February, pp. 102–112.

Elliot, R. (1993) Marketing and the meaning of post-modern consumer culture. In *Rethinking Marketing* (D. Brownlie, ed.), Warwick Business School Research Bureau, Coventry, pp. 134–142.

Firat, A., Dholakia, N. and Venkatesh, A. (1995) Marketing in a post-modern world, *European Journal of Marketing*, **29**, No. 1, 40–56.

Fox, L. (1997a) Welcome to the food factory, *Caterer and Hotelkeeper*, 10 April, pp. 66–67.

Fox, L. (1997b) Lunch breaks, *Caterer and Hotelkeeper*, 5 June, pp. 69–70.

Foxall, G. (1993) Consumer behaviour as an evolutionary process, *European Journal of Marketing*, **27**, No. 8, 46–57.

Horner, S. (1997) The triumph of entrepreneurial hunch over marketing research, *Proceedings of Hospitality Business Development Conference*, November 1997, Sheffield Hallam University.

Hutcheon, L. (1988) *The Poetics of Post-modernism*, Routledge, London. (Quoted in Brown, S. *op cit*, 1995).

Kimber, L. (1997) Mail dominance, *Caterer and Hotelkeeper*, 24 April, pp. 82–83.

Lambin, J. (1993) *Marketing a European Perspective*, McGraw Hill, London, New York.

Lewis, R. (1985) The market position: mapping guests perceptions of hotel operations, *Cornell Hotel and Restaurant Administration Quarterly*, **26**, No. 2, 86–99.

Lewis, R. (1990) Advertising your hotel's position, *The Cornell Hotel and Restaurant Administration Quarterly*, **31**, 2, pp. 84–91.

Morgan, M. and Dev, C. (1994) Defining competitive sets of hotel brands through analysis of brand switching, *Journal of Hospitality and Leisure Marketing*, **2**, No. 2, 57–83.

Mullen, R. (1997) New restaurant sweetie, *Caterer and Hotelkeeper*, 3 June, p. 54.

Pavesic, D.V. (1989) Psychological aspects of menu pricing, *International Journal of Hospitality Management*, **8**, No. 1, 43–49.

Porter, M. (1985) *Competitive Advantage*, Macmillan, New York.

Rogers, A. (1995) Pricing practices in tourist attractions, *Tourism Management*, **16**, No. 3, 217–224.

Romm, D. (1989) 'Restauration' theatre: giving direction to service, *Cornell Quarterly*, **29**, No. 4, 30–40.

Searles, (1980) Quoted in *Marketing Principles and the Arts* (ed. Mokwa), quoted in Lambin, J. (1993) *Marketing a European Perspective*, McGraw Hill, p. 29.

Weaver, P.A., McCleary, K.W., Lepisto, L. and Damonte, L.T. (1994) The relationship of destination selection attributes to psychological, behavioural and demographic variables, *Journal of Restaurant and Food Service Marketing*, **1**, No. 2, 93–109.

8 Strategy and entrepreneurship

The objective of this chapter is to examine selected concepts, principles, and techniques from the domain of strategic management and to consider their implications for entrepreneurship. More specifically, the chapter will develop understanding of the:

- evolving nature of strategic management theory;
- implications of an entrepreneurial approach to strategic management;
- organizational structure and culture issues;
- impact of the market and general environment forces on strategy formulation;
- entrepreneurial strategies effective within the hospitality, tourism and leisure industries.

Introduction

Strategic management literature has moved forward in the same way as that of marketing. There is now a greater understanding of how significant developments and changes in direction happen within organizations. What follows is a consideration of three key aspects of strategic management which we believe to be most relevant to an entrepreneurial approach within our industry sectors. These aspects are: the entrepreneur playing a catalyst role in strategy formulation and strategic management; organizational issues, particularly relating to the involvement and motivation of employees; and the changing frame of reference relative to the future and its implications for the strategies employed.

The traditional view of strategic management was that a strategy for, say, a five-year period, was determined within a corporate planning department, agreed by the Board of Directors, and then implemented. Writers such as Mintzberg (1994a, b) have criticized this view as being dysfunctional to true strategic thinking, owing to its emphasis on quantitatively expressed fixed views of the future. Mintzberg believes that planners should not create strategies but that they can supply data to help line managers think strategically and then assist in programming the vision. He criticizes strategic planning as being the manifestation of a calculating/reductionist style of management. What is actually needed is a committing style of strategic management based, not on detached formalism, but on energetic participation. He further criticizes strategic planning as being inflexible. What is really required is the willingness to consistently adapt to the changing conditions of the market place, since it is impossible to predetermine the business environment for any appreciable length of time into the future.

In a forceful rebuttal of Mintzberg's criticisms, Ansoff (1994) has accused them of being based on an outmoded 1960s strategic planning view. He protests that strategic management has progressed in many ways that Mintzberg's thesis does not take account of, and that strategic planning is but one element in the strategic management process.

According to Ansoff (1994, p. 31), in best strategic management practice:

> ... general managers and implementors participate in developing plans, staffs play catalyst roles, the planning process is coupled with the design and management of discontinuous organizational transformation, the planning process blends creativity and rational analysis, the inevitable organizational resistance to change is anticipated and managed, and the key impact of the key managers' mind set and of the organizational culture is anticipated.

Certainly what Mintzberg is criticizing in strategic planning is the antithesis of entrepreneurial management. On the other hand, much of what Ansoff claims to be best strategic management practice would clearly be recognized as seeking to engender effective entrepreneurial behaviour.

The need for organizational transformation, already considered in Chapter 3 when we considered concepts of intrapreneurship, is also a major theme in contemporary strategy literature. Central to the strategic idea has been the need for organizations to be adaptive and to focus on staying close to and responsive to the consumer. Peters and Waterman (1982) have made a major contribution to the widespread recognition of the requirement to continuously change and improve. *In Search of Excellence* was a catalyst in establishing the pre-eminent requirement to deliver quality to consumers. Subsequent texts, *Thriving on Chaos* and *Liberation Management,* have focused on the challenge of doing this in a competitive environment where the pace of change is fast. An important dimension in Peters' prescription for success is freeing up and empowering managers to act and deliver what customers need. It is sufficient here to note that removal of bureaucratic obstacles and empowering management to act has been a widely adopted strategic practice, designed to create organizational conditions which enable employees to be more entrepreneurial.

Stacey (1993) adds to the debate in proposing that we revise our frame of reference on how organizations actually develop strategically. As depicted in Table 8.1, Stacey believes that the process of strategic development is shaped by the reality of the long-term future being substantially unknowable. He believes that since the future is unknowable, strategy is best formulated when spontaneously emerging from the inevitable chaos of challenge and contradiction. This corresponds to Schumpeter's (1934) theories of entrepreneurship emerging from situations in disequilibrium, and evokes echoes of the ideas discussed in Chapter 4 when considering the environment for enterprise.

The general theme of a complex unfolding situation depicted in Stacey's model is one with which we can identify. However, there are some elements which we challenge. Specifically, we depart from Stacey's view that a vision

Table 8.1 Changing the frame of reference for strategic management

Today's frame of reference	*A new frame of reference*
Long-term future is predictable to some extent	Long term future is unknowable
Visions and plans are central to strategic management	Dynamic agendas of strategic issues are central to effective strategic management
Visions: single shared organization-wide intention. A picture of a future state	Challenge: multiple aspirations, stretching and ambiguous. Arising out of current ill-structured and conflicting issues with long-term consequences
Strongly shared cultures	Contradictory counter cultures
Cohesive teams of managers operating in state of consensus	Learning groups of managers, surfacing conflict, engaging in dialogue, publicly testing assertions
Decision making as a purely logical, analytical process	Decision making as an exploratory, experimental process based on intuition and reasoning by analogy
Long-term control and development as the monitoring of progress against plan milestones. Constraints provided by rules, systems and rational argument	Control and development in open-ended situations as a political process. Constraints provided by need to build and sustain support. Control as self policing learning
Strategy as the realization of prior intent	Strategy as spontaneously emerging from the chaos of challenge and contradiction, through a process of real-time learning and politics
Top management drives and controls strategic direction	Top management creates favourable conditions for complex learning and politics
General mental models and prescriptions for many specific situations	New mental models required for each new strategic situation
Adaptive equilibrium with the environment	Non-equilibrium, creative interaction with the environment

Source: Stacey (1993, p. 12)

is too precise and should be replaced by a challenge comprising multiple aspirations. A vision provides a clear view of what an organization wishes to become, whilst still providing room for energetic debate as to the specific form which the vision will take and how exactly it will be achieved. The idea of individual strategic business units with their own cultures and aspirations is not incompatible with the idea of a vision to which all are, in different ways, committed. The following illustration clearly articulates the shared vision and ethos of Jarvis Hotels.

Jarvis's strategy seems to incorporate the freedom to innovate in a non-bureaucratic structure, but with the focus that comes through a strong sense of mission and clear boundaries. Jarvis believes that each hotel should have the freedom to develop its own personality. In the geographically dispersed hotel industry it is quite feasible to treat each individual hotel as a strategic

---

Illustration: Jarvis Hotels, flexibility to innovate within boundaries

The success of John Jarvis in launching a new hotel company in a recession is really quite remarkable. The following extracts from the 1995 annual reports provide a good illustration of the benefits of a clear mission and defined boundaries from within which an entrepreneurial approach is welcomed.

Our Business Aim
A clear strategy to dominate the middle market
To be a major player in your market sector, you first have to define its parameters, and we have a very clear view of ours. Like any market led company, we always describe our sector from the perspective of our customers.
Jarvis customers are looking for more than a bedroom at a price not more than they can afford. They want fully serviced friendly hotelkeeping with no pretensions, but without losing the sense of occasion a good restaurant or bar gives them. They're looking for new ideas that make them wonder why they've never seen them before, and innovation that they wouldn't expect to have at the price they're paying. They like to be surprised when it doesn't matter, they want to be impressed when it does, and most of all, they want their whole stay to be effortless – and that's the middle market.
Creating the difference through innovation
Our young company seeks to surprise, entertain and prove that hotels have a personality. We hire attitude and achieve service beyond that expected in a middle market hotel.
Most important of all, create a management structure that replaces traditional bureaucracy with individual initiative.

To this end, Jarvis' hotel management is organized along two fronts – Quality and Service, and Sales and Spend. Within the hotel units, Deputy and Assistant Managers have been abolished. In their place there is a Quality and Service Manager responsible for ensuring that excellent service is delivered and a Sales and Spend Manager responsible for increasing spend per guest.
Source: Jarvis Hotels, 1995 Company Report

---

business unit able, to a considerable extent, to express its own identity and establish its own culture. However, it is recognized that this may be at some expense to brand identity, and that the tension between entrepreneurial scope and consistency of delivery is very real. Jarvis is approaching consistency from the customer-output perspective, rather than via an approach which emphasizes standard operating systems.

So far in this chapter, we have established that there are contrasting views both as to the worth of strategic management and how it works in reality. From these contrasting views, where does contemporary strategic theory and practice now stand? In respect of the formulation of entrepreneurial strategy within organizations, key questions can be postulated, including:

• how can strategies be formulated so that they harness the energies and creative abilities of employees?
• what conditions will ensure the effective deployment of such strategies, engendering entrepreneurial behaviour?

- given an unknown future, to what degree should strategy formulation be spontaneous, reflexive, and evolving in nature?
- can strategy realistically incorporate the multiple aspirations of individuals in the organization or should the guiding vision of the founding entrepreneur(s) dominate?

In seeking to address these questions and associated issues, relevant and current strategic management literature is presented and debated along with illustrations from the hospitality, tourism and leisure industries. But first it is necessary to explore more closely the interface between entrepreneurs and strategy.

Entrepreneurs and strategy

Moore (1992) observed, relative to corporations, that strategy formulation is not the singular product of one person's mind, but a continuing organizational activity. The validity of this perspective requires further exploration within the domain of the entrepreneurial firm. In this context, for a small to medium-sized enterprise, the **one person** very often equates to the total organization, or may at least dominate its decision making. Therefore, the evolving strategy may, in fact, primarily be a product of one person's mind, albeit shaped by history, current management ideologies, environmental factors, available resources, competitive domain of operation, and distinctive competencies of the business (Chell and Haworth, 1991). As we discussed in Chapter 6, some entrepreneurs are capable of growing along with the organization, others are not. An entrepreneur's ability to develop effective strategies at different stages of the organization's development is crucial for sustained success. Alternatively, the entrepreneur needs to let go to the extent necessary to involve others who have the ability to contribute to strategy formulation.

Thus, it is necessary to understand the behavioural issues which underlie entrepreneurial strategy decision making. This requires an examination of the organizational and cultural contexts of the task environment, as well as the individual personal characteristics of the entrepreneur (Olsen *et al.*, 1992). Furthermore, such an understanding needs to recognize the interplay of personal and business objectives, and characteristics of entrepreneurial management which often defy rational economic decision-making philosophy. We have already observed that many small business proprietors have life style, rather than achievement or financial reward, priorities. Whilst such business operators may not be considered entrepreneurial, it does illustrate that the motivations of entrepreneurs and intrapreneurs are not necessarily straightforward.

Contemporary contributions to the strategy literature (Greenley, 1989; Kotler, 1991; Moore, 1992) consider strategic management as working towards developing and maintaining a strategic **fit**. This involves an effective combination of the firm's objectives; internal resources; resource application; management capabilities; external threats and changing market opportunities; strategic analysis, decision making, and implementation.

They consider that only with the achievement of this will success result. A considerable amount of entrepreneurship research has also focused on the achievement of such a **fit**.

Relative to the entrepreneurial firm the components can be regarded as:

- **entrepreneur(s)/intrapreneurs:** this component represents the prime managerial resource, the motivations, quality, and effectiveness of which will be influenced by the factors identified and discussed comprehensively in Chapters 1, 2 and 3;
- **organization**: it is the product of the decisions made by the entrepreneur(s) which have shaped the business. In a long-established organization it will be how it has been shaped by the previous entrepreneurs or intrapreneurs. Associated characteristics will include the established culture, structure, control, competencies, and capabilities, as explored in Chapters 5, 6 and 7;
- **environment:** the factors at work which promote and/or inhibit entrepreneurial behaviour arising from social, technological, economic, and political changes, which may alter market conditions and the possibilities for enterprise. These factors were investigated in Chapter 4.

These three components may be considered as overlapping or intersecting circles, as illustrated in Figure 8.1.

The point at which the circles intersect is where an **entrepreneurial strategy fit** can be achieved. Storey (1994) found that those firms which achieved this generally: shared equity with external individuals or organizations (e.g. venture capital providers); made conscious decisions relative to market position; exploited differentiated and quality advantages; introduced new products on a regular basis; and selected, motivated and retained individuals in the creation of a strong managerial team. These approaches imply an existence of a strategic awareness on the part of the entrepreneur, in that they are externally focused towards assistance and markets, and at the same time

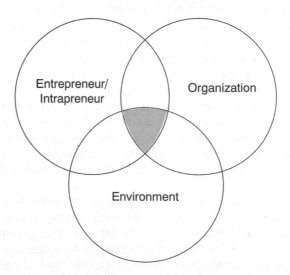

Figure 8.1 Entrepreneurial strategy fit

internally focused towards innovation, delegation, and team management, to the ultimate benefit of the organization.

Authors such as Greenley (1989) and Kotler (1991), have refocused general definitions of strategic management to incorporate the reality of the entrepreneurial firm. Specifically, this recognizes that decision-making motivation cannot always be assumed to be driven purely by perceived economic outcomes, and rational business growth objectives. In addition, it takes account of the dynamic nature of the entrepreneur, organization, and environment. Our description of entrepreneurial strategy, which we believe is particularly relevant to the hospitality, tourism and leisure industries reads as follows:

> A dynamic managerial process which operates within the realities of the market. It is about achieving strategic fit between the components of the entrepreneur/intrapreneur, organization, and environment, to bring about sustained business success.

Thus, we present a simple question which, to some extent, represents the essence of entrepreneurial strategy. Given the characteristics of the entrepreneur(s)/intrapreneur(s), organization and environment, what managerial actions, once the business has been created, are likely to be associated with the achievement of a strategic fit? In attempting to address this question we now turn to explore issues relevant to the organization and the environment prior to presenting a range of entrepreneurial strategies.

Organizational issues

Organizational culture

Support for the importance of culture in affecting organizational effectiveness comes from Morgan (1993). Figure 8.2 illustrates the proposition that organizational culture is affected by both internal and external influences. Since the mix of affecting variables will be unique to each organization, Morgan suggests that it is not productive to suggest one optimum culture. The implication of this is that culture should be managed in a contingent way, dependent upon the situation in which the organization finds itself.

This supports the contention that, rather than have rigid views of the way forward, the organization needs to learn through experience and exploration. Furthermore, to facilitate a learning organization it is necessary to have cultural and political conflicts within the organization, and to prevent the closed-mindedness which comes from a strongly defined corporate culture. This can be at odds with the entrepreneurial drive, energy, and focus required to set up and manage a venture. Though entrepreneurs need to adapt to changing situations, they also need to be determined and single minded to realize their dreams. Here we have a possible conundrum. Whilst closed-mindedness undoubtedly brings problems, too much conflict can also bring with it its own difficulties. Debate about the most advantageous way forward can be healthy, but too much organizational uncertainty can also internalize energies and inhibit or delay action.

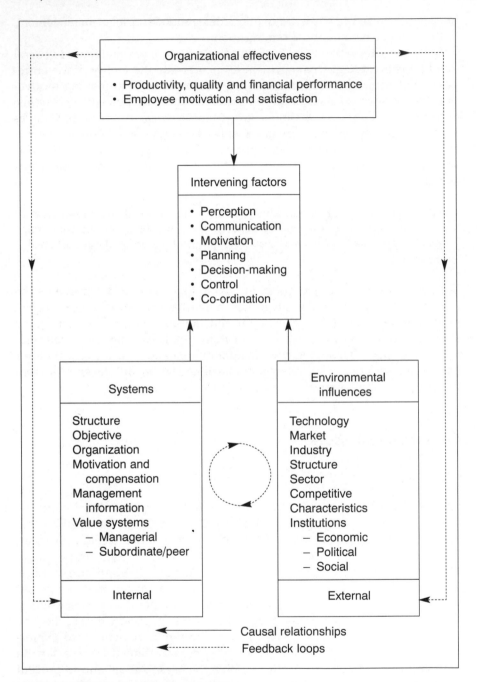

Figure 8.2 Analysing organizational culture
Source: Adapted from Morgan (1993)

Certainly the entrepreneur/intrapreneur will play a defining role in establishing and maintaining the intervening factors identified in Figure 8.2. Depending on the entrepreneur's own traits and motivations, the organization and its cultural norms will develop in very different ways. Whether or not the end result is effective will depend upon the degree of fit with the circumstances of the moment and the nature of the venture.

Organizational structure and control

Morgan's model appears highly plausible. However, in organizations within the hospitality, tourism and leisure industries there are a substantial number of additional variables which need to be brought together to launch a concept and then achieve efficient and effective service delivery. In a multi-unit situation we have previously argued that a control culture may be viewed as appropriate, to ensure consistent service delivery against corporate-wide standards. However, it is the authors' view that even within a standardized multi-unit operation, service delivery will inevitably involve unanticipated challenges, and these are best responded to by local initiative and creativity. The cultural management challenge is to design and incorporate systems, and standards of performance, in such a way that they are perceived as positive aids to effective action, rather than as obstacles and excuses for inadequate response. The following illustration describes one company's experience with organizational structure and control.

Illustration: Toby Restaurants, entrepreneurial unit managers

Toby Restaurants operates a range of restaurant brands for Bass PLC. The restaurant business seems to attract entrepreneurial individuals who often approach the running of their unit as if it were their own, rather than a company, establishment.

This is in many ways commendable. This kind of commitment is essential to success in the fast-moving restaurant business. However, it can also cause difficulties. One persistent 'problem' was managers introducing new dishes which they felt were right for their local market. Sometimes so many alternative dishes were introduced that there were effectively two menus running alongside each other – the brand's and the unit manager's! Corporate staff felt it resulted in brand image dilution. Managers felt it helped them to be responsive to the customers in their locality.

One solution was that when a new concept was rolled out, it incorporated within it scope for managers' specials, but to strict criteria and to a firmly controlled extent.

Perhaps an uneasy compromise, but there is undoubted tension between necessary control and harnessing of entrepreneurial spirit and it is not always easy to manage.
Source: authors

Here again parallels can be drawn from within entrepreneurship theory. Entrepreneurs have been shown as more likely to emerge from a social culture where there are positive entrepreneurial role models. Consequently, an enterprise culture, once established within an organization, has the potential to gain momentum as more individuals perceive that entrepreneurial behaviour is both welcomed and rewarded. Once established, an entrepreneurial culture will create a virtuous spiral where a **can do** culture positively reinforces itself.

Influencing the components of the intervening culture, including perception, communication, and motivation, is therefore a vital component of effective entrepreneurial strategic management. Systems need to support a

culture where enterprise can flourish, whilst at the same time exercising sufficient control to ensure consistent operating standards. It can be difficult to
get the balance right. In Chapter 3 we saw how one solution is to separate off
the totally new, unconstrained, entrepreneurial stream, whilst supporting
the culture which allows bounded change and development of the mainstream. The following illustration presents a powerful example of the need
to balance the freedom to operate entrepreneurially with the systems necessary to ensure consistent control and reliability.

Illustration: Queens Moat Houses PLC, entrepreneurial/control culture

One of the most radical approaches towards the establishment of an entrepreneurial culture was that adopted by Queens Moat Houses. The company entered into
incentive agreements with managers of its hotels. In essential terms, the agreements
granted managers the freedom to operate their hotel as if it were their own business.
The companies which the individual managers formed contracted to deliver a
certain amount of profit to Queens Moat Houses. If they made more profit than this,
they got to keep it. If they made less, their companies were supposed to make up
the 'guaranteed' level of profit.

Effectively, Queens Moat Houses became the holding company for many different businesses to which management responsibility had been devolved.
Consequently, the company was able to operate with an extremely small headquarters staff, which concentrated on strategic acquisitions, rather than business strategies and operational control of individual units. It made great play of this feature.

This was all well and good until the recession hit. Queens Moat Houses did not
have the detailed control over its individual hotel businesses to enable it to gauge
how they were really performing. Hence, profits were consolidated into accounts on
the basis of what managers were supposed to remit, rather than what they were
actually able to. Subsequently an announcement modifying the level of profits
achieved had to be made, after higher profits had already been reported. This in
turn questioned Queens Moat Houses' asset value at a time when property prices
were already tumbling. The company had neither the asset backing nor the cash
flow to support its highly geared borrowings and corporate disaster swiftly followed.
Source: authors

A further related perspective is presented by Stacey (1996) and his idea of
ordinary and **extraordinary** management. This seems particularly relevant
to the hospitality, tourism and leisure industries, with the need to practice
ordinary management in exercising the ongoing control to achieve
product/service consistency, and to manage functionally. Against this, in
such fast-moving industries there is also the need for extraordinary management to ensure that the business continues to develop dynamically
alongside its market.

Clearly, the task of maintaining both dimensions of management concur-
rently is considerable. Specifically, for the smaller independently owned
business units, achievement of this management balance presents significant
challenges. Furthermore, for individual entrepreneurs, directly responsible
for service delivery (often in a hands-on way), it can be almost impossible to
find sufficient time and energy to reflect and create. Some ideas as to how

these challenges can be met are provided later in this chapter.

Competencies and capabilities

In the same way as culture and organizational structure can provide the right conditions for entrepreneurship to flourish, so strategy can also be encouraged to emerge in such a way that the overall strategic direction of the organization is sustained. In this respect, strategy literature highlights the concept of feed-forward control. This takes on board the fact that strategies are often incremental, evolving gradually over time in response to experience, and that they can also be opportunistic. With opportunistic strategies, organizations may have a sense of what they wish to become (**vision**), but accept that in conditions of uncertainty and ambiguity, they can never be entirely sure how they will actually get there.

Feed-forward control, instead of the traditional form of control based on feedback, is based on organizational self-regulation. Such regulation is via monitoring of proposed new activities against the organization's core competencies – those core attributes which enable it to invent and shape consumer demand, enter new markets successfully, and generally keep ahead of the game. Strategic decisions would therefore be tested for consistency in maintaining and developing these core competencies. Band and Scanlon (1995) have discussed how focused alignment of organization culture, structure, human resource management, and information systems – the strategic architecture – with the aim of sustaining and fostering these core competencies, can assist in steering the organization towards strategic decisions congruent with its core expertise. It would also encourage a focus on businesses that are known and understood rather than unfocused diversification.

Furthermore, the concept of feed-forward control can be related to findings within the entrepreneurship literature. Many successful entrepreneurs have spent time within a particular industry sector, referred to as an **incubator organization** (Chapter 2), and later set up their own organization within the same sector. In this way, the expertise which they have developed in one organization has guided the setting up of another, as can be seen from the following illustration.

Illustration: Restaurants at Work, incubator organization

Restaurants at Work, the new contract catering enterprise of David Jenkinson, ex-managing director of the Catering Guild, has started winning its first contracts with blue-chip clients. The company was set up when Jenkinson branched out on his own following the acquisition of the Catering Guild by Sutcliffe in 1995. '*We are turning over £400,000 a year and are on target to reach £750,000 and 12 contracts by the end of 1996,*' said Mr. Jenkinson. '*Our long-term aim is to be as big as the Catering Guild within five years – with 100 contracts.*'
Source: Anonymous, 1996

In acquiring contextual skills and competencies within a specific sector, Jenkinson had developed his competencies in such a way that they were in focused **alignment** with the organization, and business environment. In so doing he has achieved a strategic fit which enables the creation of a defensible competitive position. It also sits comfortably with the concept of many entrepreneurial ideas and projects being arrived at serendipitously, and opportunistic events triggering entrepreneurial achievement for individuals as well as companies.

Moreover, the concept of feed-forward control, aligning competencies to the capabilities needed for organizational development supports the idea of **sticking to the knitting**. If entrepreneurial activity is not focused within manageable boundaries of activity and expertise, then the organization can become too diffuse. The follow-through necessary to successfully carry out the development of entrepreneurial activities will not be available. In this situation, the organization's capacity to manage and control has been exceeded, as Emil Malak found to his cost.

Illustration: Emil Malak, sticking to the knitting

Emil had been in hotels all his working life. He had also been educated in the management skills needed to run them via an Ed Exel Higher Diploma and ongoing exposure to the management controls and disciplines of a large organization.

His great charm, charisma, and enthusiasm meant that he had the persuasive skills necessary to convince people with capital to back him in his own ventures. As reported later in this chapter, these were initially extremely successful. Unfortunately, Emil did not stick to what he had demonstrated he was good at. Rather than the rewards of running a successful business, he went for the more speculative rewards possible through property development. A series of planning applications went against him. He even tried his hand at currency dealing! He lost everything! Presently he is building a new hotel business in Canada. We are sure he will bounce back – if he remembers to **stick to the knitting**!
Source: authors

Bakker *et al*. (1994) identify that, as well as competence, organizations also need the capability to succeed in new business development. Whilst relevant technological competencies may exist, important broader based capabilities needed for the new venture may not. Functional areas such as marketing and financial management may not be equipped for the different scale of operations. In the past, this was the case with Stakis PLC as referred to in the following illustration.

Overall, Stakis has performed strongly since returning to the areas in which it had proven competence and capability, acquiring inspirational leadership. Its rehabilitation is complete and, as referred to in Chapter 3, it is now able to look towards developing its third related business area – leisure.

The challenge therefore is to provide the organizational culture and structure which support innovation and the ability to embark on new strategic challenges. At the same time there is a need to ensure that these challenges are within the organization's core competencies and management capability. In essence this is no different whether it is applied to the entrepreneurial activity of corporations or individual entrepreneurs. However, this does not

---

Illustration: Stakis PLC, sticking to the knitting

In 1991 Stakis PLC were in a state of crisis. A period of rapid expansion during the 1980s had seen the company over-extended both financially and managerially. Technically the company was illiquid.

The appointment of the experienced company doctor, Sir Louis Robertson, as Chairman, and subsequently David Michels as Managing Director, enabled a rescue programme to be agreed with the company's bankers.

A period of retrenchment followed where the company's interests in nursing homes, off licences, public houses, and computer software were divested. This left the company operating in its traditional areas of hotels and casinos.

David Michels' hotel expertise has been used to strongly improve hotel operating performance on the back of a general recovery in the hotel market. Yield management techniques have been used aggressively to improve the occupancy and achieved room rates combination.

The company is now back on a growth tack, cherry picking new hotel acquisitions, together with more substantial take-overs and using its core competencies to add value. It has also built upon its experience of operating leisure facilities in its hotels to launch a new leisure division.

Whilst casinos have not been expanded in the same way as hotels and leisure, the company is well placed to take advantage of any relaxation in the gaming laws which may occur in the future.

Source: authors

---

take place in a vacuum. As is now discussed, it is affected substantially by the business environment.

Environment for entrepreneurial strategy

Competitive advantage and market positioning

One of the most powerful concepts in the domain of strategy formulation has been Porter's (1985, p. 3) concept of the need to secure competitive advantage. He states that competitive advantage:

> … grows out of the value a firm is able to create for its buyers that exceeds the firm's cost of creating it. Value is what the buyer is willing to pay, and superior value stems from offering lower prices than competitors for equivalent benefits or providing unique benefits that more than offset a higher price. There are two basic types of advantage, cost leadership and differentiation.

The concept of competitive advantage therefore underpins the marketing idea of positioning, as discussed in Chapter 7. In looking at the relevance of competitive advantage, we are exploring the fuzzy boundary at the interface of the marketing and strategy literature. It is sustained competitive advantage which will bring about long-term success and secure survival beyond the short term. This is one of the main challenges for an individual entrepreneur or any entrepreneurial organization. Often, there is the temptation to pursue short-term gains at the expense of long-term capability. If this is at the expense of long-term sustainability, then it is a pyrrhic victory.

This need to retain a long-term future orientation with regards to competitive advantage is emphasized by Hamel and Prahalad (1994). As they point out (Table 8.2), in a time of such rapid change, if the answers to the **future** questions are not different from the answers today, there is little prospect of sustaining competitive advantage. Continuous improvement of the product/service offering may be incremental rather than revolutionary, but such improvements do need to amount to significant and meaningful benefit to customers.

Table 8.2 A future orientation

Today	*In the future*
Which customers do you serve today?	Which customers will you serve in the future?
Through what channels do you reach customers today?	Through what channels will you reach customers in the future?
Who are your competitors today?	Who will your competitors be in the future?
What is the basis for your competitive advantage today?	What will be the basis for your competitive advantage in the future?
Where do your margins come from today?	Where will your margins come from in the future?
What skills or capabilities make you unique today?	What skills or capabilities will make you unique in the future?

Source: Hamel and Prahalad (1994, p. 127)

Miles and Snow (1978) classified organizations based on their intended rate of product/service market change (Table 8.3). This is related to whether organizations are more internally or externally focused. Though obviously long-established, more recent research by Dev and Olsen (1989) has identified that there may be reason to believe that within the hospitality industry, success can be correlated with adoption of strategic behaviour corresponding to the Miles and Snow classifications. Particular strategic behaviour can be associated with success in certain market conditions.

Using the Miles and Snow classification, strategy types are primarily differentiated by the manner in which each solves the entrepreneurial challenge of how to strategically manage its product/services – the market interface. The classifications are, of necessity, broad generalizations. Organizations which may have a tendency towards one classification in most aspects of their operations will doubtless also exhibit behaviour more appropriate to another.

The concept of entrepreneurship seems to fit more comfortably with the classification of **prospector** with its emphasis on new market opportunities and innovation. Certainly, this is the classification where entrepreneurial behaviour is most widespread and has a dominant role in forming the culture of the organization. However, we would also argue that entrepre-

Table 8.3 Different types of organizational culture and their influences on strategic decision making

Organization type	Characteristics of strategic decision making		
	Dominant objectives	Preferred strategies	Planning and control systems
1. Defenders	Desire for a secure and stable niche in market	Specialization; cost-efficient production; marketing emphasizes price and service to defend current business; tendency to vertical integration	Centralized, detailed control; emphasis on cost efficiency; extensive use of formal planning
2. Prospectors	Location and exploitation of new product and market opportunities	Growth through product and market development (often in spurts); constant monitoring of environmental change; multiple technologies	Emphasis on flexibility, decentralized control, use of *ad hoc* measurements
3. Analysers	Desire to match new ventures to present shape of business	Steady growth through market penetrations; exploitation of applied research; followers in the market	Very complicated; co-ordinating roles between functions (e.g. product managers); intensive planning

Source: Adapted from Miles and Snow, 1978

neurial behaviour can be, and is, exhibited by organizations which are **defenders** and **analysers**. The following illustration raises the question of at what stage a defender's or analyser's innovatory behaviour generates sufficient new market potential for it to be thought of as a prospector?

Illustration: pub retailing, entrepreneurial behaviour

Following the Monopolies and Mergers Commission report in 1989 the 'Beer Orders' ordered the reorganization of the pub industry. This freed a large proportion of the tied estate resulting from the brewing companies also owning public houses and, therefore, the retailing activity. The large brewing companies were required to free of tie 50 per cent of pubs they owned, over and above the ceiling limit of 2000, by November 1992.

Consequently, the large brewing companies who were also pub retailers were faced with a considerably reduced tied estate from which to produce their retail profit. Though probably classified as defenders or perhaps analysers, they have exhibited considerable entrepreneurial/innovative behaviour in an attempt to generate more business and profit from a reduced number of outlets.

Examples of innovation have centred around increased differentiation of pubs to attract different market segments for different social occasions. New food concepts have been rolled out, children's play facilities developed, electronic games introduced, 'computer pubs' set up, and sophisticated café bars developed.
Source: authors

From Chapter 2, we know that attempts to establish a desirable blue print for an effective entrepreneur have not been at all conclusive. Entrepreneurs come in many different forms, as do the organizations they create. The same applies to their behaviour in the form of the strategies employed. This seems to us to reinforce the importance of the concept of strategic fit, as presented in Figure 8.1 which individualizes entrepreneurial strategy given the factors at work in the combination of entrepreneur, organization, and environment.

Furthermore, the hospitality, tourism and leisure industries are sufficiently diverse as to be able to offer a wide variety of market conditions within each of its sub-sectors. It is hardly surprising if, as a consequence, different types of entrepreneurs and organizations can find areas where they can operate successfully. This all adds up to the richness of the industry sectors and goes some way towards explaining their appeal to such a variety of individuals, who have all been triggered in some way to become entrepreneurs within it. At the heart of this entrepreneurial activity, whether by corporations or individuals, is the presence of change in the business environment and the resultant opportunities. One implication of this fast-moving maelstrom of activity is that it becomes increasingly important to have a clear sense of what is happening in the environment. For existing businesses, what are the developments in the environment which can affect the business both positively and negatively? For potential new businesses, are the market conditions such that an opportunity exists for the proposed new venture? Effective environmental scanning and analysis can assist in answering these questions.

Environmental scanning and analysis

Strategic management literature contains useful models of environmental analysis. Potentially, a structured approach to environmental analysis can ensure that a more balanced and less biased view of developments is gained. As already argued, this should not be at the expense of the entrepreneur's/intrapreneur's intuition, since the subjective response is part of the generation of the opportunity. However, scanning the environment is an important entrepreneurial strategic management activity, as was identified in Chapter 1. Failing to undertake it can result in an inadequate or non-existent response to threats as well as missed opportunities.

If the marketing concepts and techniques discussed in Chapter 7 are so powerful and effective, how is it that consumers have not all been satisfied long ago? That there remains scope for new opportunities to be identified and developed is clearly demonstrated by the continuous supply of new ventures and innovations which come along, in all areas of business. Why is this so? Given so many proficient practitioners, why is it that all possible new opportunities have not long since been identified and taken up?

One reason is that many existing organizations, for understandable reasons, tend to concentrate on evolving their existing activities. This results in a tendency to focus on the interface of existing operations with the market. Current performance indicators such as sales trends are very influential and research targeted towards fine-tuning existing provisions, within reasonably short time horizons, occupies management attention. It is the short-term pressures which are given greater prominence. Olsen *et al.* (1992) described this as a tendency to concentrate on the **task** environment, that is, the environment connected with their immediate operational imperatives. This reinforces the importance of our earlier discussions concerning the mainstream and the newstream and the need to practice extraordinary management alongside the ordinary.

Pinto and Olsen (1987) discovered that environmental scanning by financial directors of hospitality firms tended to be a largely informal process based primarily on networking. Where external sources were used, similar ones tended to be selected, leading to a rather narrow, congruent view of the external environment. The implication of this is that most organizations will end up having the same, rather blinkered view of what is going on in the world. A large part of the answer also lies in the constantly changing business environment in which organizations operate. As society evolves so, as we have already demonstrated in Chapter 7, consumer behaviour and expectations are also modified. At the same time, technical innovations can enable organizations to adopt more effective and efficient ways of going about their business.

Such **macro** or society-wide changes can impact considerably. The extent of macro-changes in the overall operating environment can be wide ranging and their pace dynamic. Viewed in entirety all these different influences can appear so extensive and complex that they are bewildering for entrepreneurs. In these circumstances it is possible to feel so overwhelmed that inertia results. It is difficult to know where to begin, so the easiest option is not to start at all! How can all this change possibly be responded to?

Changes are much more manageable when viewed as a series of specific events, trends or influences at both macro- and micro-levels. Thus, to help identify macro-trends affecting organizations, it is useful to consider changes in different broad areas of focus. These factors have been suggested by a variety of authors as being Social, Technological, Economic, and Political. Investigating these involves undertaking a **STEP analysis**. Other writers, perhaps reflecting a more cynical view of the world, refer to it as a **PEST analysis**. Depending on your world stance, you could use either! The following two illustrations provide examples of fortuitous and calamitous outcomes arising from the impact of macro-STEP factors.

Illustration: Emil Malak, environmental opportunities

Sometimes different environmental factors can combine to produce extremely turbulent operating conditions. These can be fortuitous as well as calamitous.

In 1982 British Rail were selling their Transport Hotels. This was as a result of **political** developments. The sale was part of the government's privatization programme. At this time various **economic** conditions were also conspiring together and were on the verge of bringing about very considerable and rapid inflation in commercial property prices.

A **problem** with British Transport Hotels (BTH) was that they were heavily unionized and had high staffing costs owing to over-manning and higher-than-the-norm pay rates. This depressed their value, but for anyone willing to set about the task of reforming them, here was a wonderful **opportunity!**

Emil Malak was an ex-Forté hotel manager, who had branched out on his own, taking on one or two pub leases with fairly modest success. At the time of visiting the North British Hotel Glasgow (one of BTH's hotel properties) to look it over with a view to purchase, Emil was extremely hard up (I know because I did his feasibility study for free!). Once having seen the hotel, Emil was extremely enthusiastic about it, so much so that he found a millionaire business partner, put in a bid, and became its owner!

Just over eighteen months later, the hotel was sold on – at a price £2.5 million higher than he had paid for it! As you already know, the results of this good fortune were regrettably soon to be lost.

Source: authors

Illustration: demise of Michelin three-star restaurants, environmental threat

'*For the second time in less than a year, a French three-star Michelin restaurant is threatened with closure*' (*European*, 12–18 September 1996). The report explains that a combination of high interest rates (12 per cent) and lower meal prices have impinged together to create considerable financial problems for this sector of the French restaurant industry. '*Businessmen can't very well take clients and partners to ruinously expensive restaurants when at the same time they are downsizing their companies, cutting jobs and slashing overheads. The climate has changed.*'

'*Top restaurants in France have had to face the new realities of changed spending attitudes and act accordingly.*' The report goes on to say that prices have, in effect, been reduced by one-third to one-half, through the offering of previously unthinkable modified A La Carte menus and business lunch formulas.

With a changing macro-environment even three Michelin stars are no guarantee of automatic success. Many of the top Michelin chefs have invested huge sums at a time when money has become more expensive and the consumer market has turned against them.

Source: *European*, 12–18 September 1996

As well as these macro-trends, organizations are also affected by **micro**, or more localized, trends. The hospitality, tourism and leisure industries are often particularly exposed to these, since so many of their services are delivered through thousands of individual units dispersed over wide geographical areas. Whilst overall macro-trends can be similar for all these establishments, at the micro-level, broad trends operate alongside specific localized market developments. It is the combination of macro- and micro-trends which impinge upon individual units and/or create new market opportunities. Often the micro-changes in individual local markets can be more dramatic in their effect than the wider macro-trends, as the following illustration shows.

Illustration: hotel market in Sheffield, micro-trends

In 1989, the Sheffield hotel market was already suffering owing to the general reces-sion. Reduced occupancy levels were hitting profitability and those hotel businesses with high levels of borrowings were struggling to generate sufficient cash flow.

Into this already struggling market, a new build Novotel was launched, offering modern hotel and leisure facilities in a city centre location. New beds were brought on stream overnight. Sheffield Novotel opened with an aggressive opening price strategy that directly competed with existing two-star hotels. Most of these two-star hotels were dated conversions of Victorian villas. Facilities and ambience did not compare favourably with those of the new Novotel. Over the next two years, three of the Victorian two-star hotels were forced into liquidation or shut, with disastrous personal consequences for their owners.

Micro-conditions in the Sheffield hotel market had combined with macro national economic trends to bring about a fundamental deterioration in the com-petitive position of the older two-star hotels. Their market had effectively been destroyed overnight.

As we have previously noted, eight years on the market is now transformed. Sheffield is one of the cities where there is now substantial under-provision of hotel rooms.

Source: authors

STEP analysis targeted towards the hospitality, tourism and leisure indus-tries therefore needs to be implemented from a perspective that considers both significant macro- and micro-trends. West and Olsen (1988) carried out empirical analysis which demonstrated that, despite the difficulty of carry-ing this out, organizations undertaking environmental scanning and analy-sis perform better than those which do not. This could, however, be because they were being better run generally, rather than because they practised scanning.

At this stage it is important to consider just who will be carrying out the STEP analysis. A method is only as good as the people implementing it and the resources which they bring to the task. Different individual entrepre-neurs and intrapreneurs may view the same situation very differently when it comes to assessing it. Interesting insight into the effect of individual per-ception is provided by systems theory. Carter *et al.* (1985) describe how indi-viduals viewing the same empirical event will interpret it very differently according to their **weltanschauung** or **world view**. We have probably all seen the visual manifestation of this phenomenon, where a drawing can either be interpreted as an old hag or a beautiful young woman. The same perceptual filter process also applies when a wider spectrum of information stimuli is being considered. The identical information may invoke a com-pletely different response, depending on the analyst who is interpreting it! This is where the opportunity-spotting capability of the entrepreneur or intrapreneur is so important.

It would certainly not be in keeping with the spirit of entrepreneurship to suggest that information should be interpreted in a certain way. However, one generalization is that a broad awareness is preferable to a narrower per-spective. The danger of this view is that too much awareness can also be dangerous. For example, given a situation where 80 per cent of restaurants can close within three years, who will be courageous enough to open one? Perhaps in some instances ignorance is bliss, but generally speaking it is better to be aware than unaware! The 80 per cent of people who had to close down their restaurants would probably agree with this, perhaps the 20 per cent who remained trading under the same ownership would not! They may not have embarked upon their venture had they known the extent to which the odds were stacked against them.

What steps can be taken to generate this awareness? In systems terminology, the entrepreneur or intrapreneur needs to be an open system, widely and sensitively scanning the environment, interpreting the feedback signals, and acting upon them. Yet within the strategic management literature, there is very little material on *what* should be scanned. Rather the emphasis is on how to analyse what has *already* been scanned.

Figure 8.3 summarizes the activities which we believe prospective and actual entrepreneurs and intrapreneurs should be undertaking on a regular basis to effectively monitor both micro and macro operating environments. Whilst not in itself guaranteeing an informed view of trends and developments, it does at least ensure that the entrepreneur is exposed to a range of different opinions and information sources. How these are interpreted and what the entrepreneur chooses to do about them is quite another matter.

No doubt many of the activities suggested in Figure 8.3 are undertaken by actual and prospective entrepreneurs anyway. Those who are already employed in the industry and who choose to branch out on their own have often arrived at the identification of a market gap as a result of a detailed knowledge of the way in which a particular industry sector operates. They will have a sensitivity towards how customer requirements can be better met, or where needs have not been fulfilled at all. A danger exists where those without this awareness nevertheless feel that they have something new and wonderful to offer, and that customers will beat a path to their door. Sometimes they will. Often not!

Analysis of the external environment and its **opportunities** and **threats** is important, but so is a recognition of the **strengths** and **weaknesses** of the actual or prospective business organization in relation to them. This is referred to as **SWOT analysis**. In the same way as the environment is scanned, so the potential of the actual or intended organization to react to it should also be evaluated. We have already noted instances, in the form of Stakis and Malik, where organizations and individuals identified opportunities but lacked the core competencies and capabilities to be able to successfully capitalize on them.

Once environmental analysis has been gained and evaluated, inevitably a level of uncertainty will still remain. One technique which has been proposed to cope with this uncertainty is **scenario planning**. Foster (1993) comments that, despite the aversion to strategic planning often evident amongst entrepreneurs, the uncertainty inherent in the future still needs to be confronted. He maintains that **scenario building** is a viable technique for the individual entrepreneur as well as for larger, relatively resource-rich, corporations.

Foster defines a scenario as 'a description of a possible future based upon a set of mutually consistent elements within a framework of specified

Action	To find out	Regularly	Sometimes	Not at all
READ ■ Local press	Planning applications, competitor developments, and local economic outlook			
■ Business section of quality national daily newspaper	What the big boys are up to, general economic outlook			
■ *The European*	A wider horizon of business activity and social trends			
■ Trade journals	New innovations, competitor developments, and food and accommodation trends			
LISTEN TO ■ Radio	Development and financial information			
■ Television	New innovations and what the competition is up to General and local economic outlook			
TALK TO ■ Supplier representatives	Generally who is up to what			
■ Local officials dealing with planning enterprise and commerce	Economic and tourist outlook, details of big new developments			
■ Tourism officers	New initiatives, outlook, and marketing opportunities			
■ Local hotel, restaurant and tourism providers	New initiatives, outlook			
■ Tourism/hospitality colleges	New ideas			
■ Your workforce	Who is doing what when?			
■ Customers	Where else they are going What they are impressed with			
PARTICIPATE IN ■ Local branches of charitable organizations ■ Industry representative bodies ■ Local hospitality associations ■ Social and business networks	Generally market and local intelligence			

Figure 8.3 Potential environmental scanning activities

Key factors

Identify the key environmental STEP factors

Assumptions

Identify assumptions implicit in scenario

Sources

Identify sources of information for key factors

Issues

Identify issues arising from conflicting sources

Pictures of futures

Generate internally consistent pictures and development pathways

Figure 8.4 Stages in scenario development. **Source**: Derived from Foster (1993, p. 125)

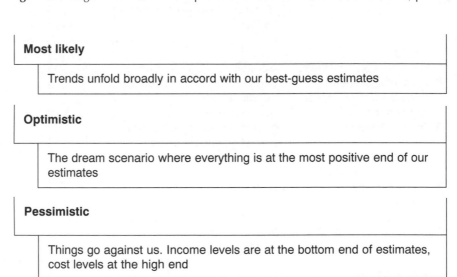

Most likely

Trends unfold broadly in accord with our best-guess estimates

Optimistic

The dream scenario where everything is at the most positive end of our estimates

Pessimistic

Things go against us. Income levels are at the bottom end of estimates, cost levels at the high end

Figure 8.5 Types of strategic scenario. **Source**: Derived from Foster (1993, p. 126)

assumptions' (p. 123). He suggests it should encompass both quantitative and qualitative elements. A simplified methodology to develop scenarios is shown in Figure 8.4.

The model illustrates how scenarios can be derived from the information gained during STEP and a SWOT analysis. The information can be pieced together in consistent ways to form different types of scenarios, as indicated in Figure 8.5.

Foster's paper also proposes a fourth category of **surprise-free** scenario, but this seems to be so close in concept to the **most likely** scenario that we do not consider it worthwhile to develop it separately. Changes in markets and the internal organization inevitably occur and it seems preferable to conject what they will be in the **most likely/best guess** scenarios, rather than to anticipate a state of status quo equilibrium which is unlikely to occur. The **most likely**, **optimistic** and **pessimistic** scenarios should, in themselves, provide a wide divergence of prospective futures. This approach was discussed in Chapter 5 relative to finance and business planning.

Scenario building can also be complimented by undertaking **flexibility analysis,** an example of which is presented in Figure 8.6. In this, Johnson and Scholes (1993) have illustrated how the organizational response to recognized areas of uncertainty can be identified. The required response can be compared with the available existing response capability. Problem areas, represented by gaps between the desirable and available response, can then be identified and appropriate action considered. This avoids the pitfall of responding in ways outside of the organization's or individual's competence or resource capability.

Thus, while we accept that the future environment within which the entrepreneur(s) will operate is largely unknown, ambiguous, and uncontrollable,

Major areas of uncertainty	Flexibility		Comments
	Required existing response	Available response	
Demand for service to an extent uncertain	Ability to increase/decrease scale of operations	Ready supply of part-time casual labour Core staff are a fixed cost as cannot operate without them	Safe up to –20 per cent below best-guess projections Below that into negation of cash flow
Supplier uncertainty Heavily dependent upon one specialist supplier May loose supply or increase costs substantially	A competitive alternative supplier	No alternative supply available within immediate geographic vicinity	Investigate feasibility of paying for transportation from London
Head Chef may (almost certainly will!) resign at some stage	Need to have trained replacement ready	Sous Chef not yet ready to take over	Need to build in extra resources to enable training to take place
Overdraft may be called in	Alternative source of cash facility	None	Could negotiate short-term loan to replace overdraft facility

Figure 8.6 Flexibility analysis – an example. **Source**: adapted from Johnson and Scholes (1993, p. 149)

we do not believe that this justifies abdicating responsibility, nor turning a blind eye. Indeed, what is essential is as close to twenty-twenty vision as is humanly possible, in order to gain and sustain a strong market position and competitive advantage.

Entrepreneurial strategies

With such clarity of vision, appropriate entrepreneurial strategies can be devised and implemented to fit the interface represented by the entrepreneur, organization, and environment. A useful framework for differentiating such strategies is provided by Norburn *et al*. (1988). They note that a wide range of strategies should initially be considered, and that some organizational forms involve transcending traditional corporate boundaries. They classify different entrepreneurial approaches according to the dimensions of sovereignty (ownership) and the degree of control which the organization retains over the new operation. The position along these dimensions is certainly open to debate. In addition, specific examples of each type of approach potentially differ substantially as well. However, the matrix does provide a useful illustration of how different ways forward can have varying impacts on the originating organization and its future.

Furthermore, effective entrepreneurship may involve using more than one of these alternatives as the business makes transitions throughout its lifecycle. Each represents a way by which organizations can deploy deliberate strategies to bring about entrepreneurial development. Most involve the setting in motion of a train of events to bring about predetermined entrepreneurial outcomes. The remainder of this chapter will consider each of the

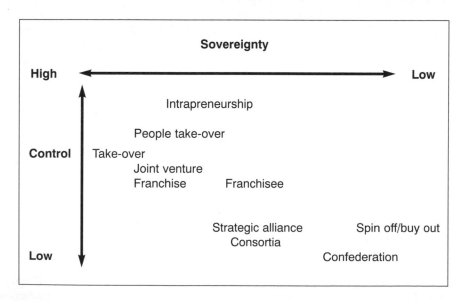

Figure 8.7 Entrepreneurial strategies. **Source**: adapted from Noburn, D., Manning, K., Birley, S. (1988, p. 47)

entrepreneurial strategies identified in Figure 8.7 in more detail, with the exception of intrapreneurship, which was comprehensively addressed in Chapter 3.

Franchising

Franchising was introduced in Chapter 1 as a context for entrepreneurship. It is relevant to entrepreneurial strategy from the perspectives of both franchisors and franchisees. A **franchisor,** the originator of a concept, can roll it out to additional markets and locations, harnessing the motivation, expertise, flair, and capital of individual entrepreneurs. This may enable a very rapid growth rate to be achieved and enhance return on capital. **Franchisees** can access new business opportunities through the acquisition of technical and business know how, enabling them to grow new businesses in areas which may not otherwise be possible.

The hospitality industry is the one of the most prolific areas of **Business Format Franchising**. According to Preble and Hoffman (1995, p. 80) :

> ... business format franchising is designed to have a franchisee replicate in different locations, the entire franchisor's business concept including the marketing strategy and plan, the operating manuals and standards and quality control.

Furthermore, they describe the major international business format franchising markets and state that:

> ... fast food, food retailing and non-food retailing are areas of rapid franchise growth. Additionally France and the Netherlands reported that the hotel industry was an important growth sector in their countries. (p. 83)

Franchisors normally appoint sole or master franchise rights to a business concept. A sole/master franchisee is responsible for rolling out the concept, establishing new outlets and managing them. They will take responsibility for finding and appointing other franchisees, perhaps building in a further layer through the appointment of regional franchisees. Entrepreneurial opportunity is therefore provided for different organizations and individuals as the franchise is rolled out.

Illustration: Bass Leisure and Dave and Busters, expansion through franchising

Bass Leisure Entertainments have secured an exclusive master licence for the UK operation of Dave and Busters. The multi-million-pound **leisure boxes** feature a mix of restaurants, food outlets, and bars, plus virtual reality games including racing car, jet fighter, and golf simulators, areas for shuffle board and billiards, bowling, Karaoke, and gambling for fun. The aim is to appeal to all ages and incomes, with the emphasis on family entertainment. Clearly Bass felt that a franchise licensing agreement was the best way to achieve the know how required to operate such a large-scale and multi-faceted leisure outlet.
Source: Dave and Buster promotional literature

Cultural and physical proximity are often two important criteria for initial expansion of franchise concepts into overseas markets. This can be important owing to the standardized business concept. However, as we have seen with McDonalds, the increasing globalization of culture, together with more liberal world-wide economic conditions, means that high-profile franchises effectively have world-wide market potential.

It is a widely accepted belief that franchises are between four and seven times less likely to fail than independently conceived and operated small businesses. This is due to the concept having already been tried and tested both in terms of market response and the operational viability. There is consequently less risk and a new franchisee simply needs to roll out the formula in a new location.

However, recent research in the USA suggests that the situation may not be so clear-cut (Bates, 1995). Remarkably, the findings of his study indicate that new franchise businesses had a higher failure rate! He stated (Bates, 1995, p. 26), on the basis of a very rigorous and extensive sample frame, that:

> Findings of this study indicate that young franchise start-ups exhibit both higher rates of firm discontinuance and lower mean profitability than independently established businesses.

However, franchises should not necessarily be dismissed out of hand. It may be factors other than the franchise itself which cause the poor performance. In earlier research, Bates had found that owner traits associated with **greater** likelihood of survival include: owners working full time in the firm, highly educated owners, and large financial investment in the firm by the owner at formation. In the owner education category, franchisees were significantly less well educated than people who formed independent businesses.

The fact that a franchisor can point to successful franchises does not necessarily mean that the risk for a specific new franchisee is diminished. As Bates has clearly demonstrated, there are other factors which can be shown to be related to success in starting a new small business. Unless the entrepreneur, market conditions, and capitalization arrangements are all also right (strategic fit) the franchise concept may not work, no matter how well the business format has performed elsewhere.

Business and people take-overs

Business take-overs are a common occurrence within the hospitality, tourism and leisure industries. They provide opportunity for established organizations to move into new business areas. At the same time, entrepreneurial individuals who have built up businesses can sell out, capitalize on their success, and generate considerable wealth.

Motivations for take-overs are many. Perhaps not all are entrepreneurial, in the sense that they do not involve the acquisition of something new and different for the acquiring organizations. For example, Whitbread's purchase of the Bright Reasons restaurant chain was inspired as much by the acquisition of new sites to extend outlets of its existing Pizza Hut, Café Rouge, and Dome brands than to buy specific expertise or the new brand opportunities represented by Bella Pasta. Nevertheless, business take-overs do provide valuable opportunity to keep pace with a rapidly changing industry. In this respect they can be said to be entrepreneurial, whether or not acquisition of new business areas or new expertise is involved.

Change is endemic within the hospitality, tourism and leisure industries and established organizations constantly need to anticipate and respond to it. One of the themes of the late 1990s is the increasing emergence and importance of brands. Business take-overs are certainly a means of expanding the brand portfolio, and perhaps also acquiring new expertise en route, as illustrated in the following Whitbread PLC example.

Illustration: Whitbread PLC, expansion through take-over

In 1995 Whitbread bought Scott's Hotels, a chain of sixteen UK hotels from Scott Hospitality, a Canadian company. It is likely that the fact that Scott's had the UK franchise for Marriot hotels was far more important than the acquisition of the properties which Scott owned.

Marriot is a major long-established USA hotel group, with almost 900 hotels in the USA and a fast expanding portfolio of more than 100 overseas. It is an extremely well known and respected international brand, but Scott's had not really capitalized on the opportunity which the UK market represents for Marriot. The purchase gave Whitbread both a strong brand name and also access to Marriot's world-wide reservations systems and sales office. Access to major central reservation systems (CRSs) is likely to be extremely important strategically for hotel companies in the future. It enables direct customer access to these systems and the important business market will increasingly make reservations through them. Whitbread will also gain access to Marriot's hotel bed space sales expertise. Marriot claims that in the USA home market their occupancy rates are 10 per cent higher than competitors'.

The purchase of Scott's, therefore, unlocked the door to both a strong brand name (which will sit well alongside Whitbread's Travel Inn brand), and also Marriot's established expertise in CRSs and hotel room marketing. The purchase makes sound sense for both Whitbread and Marriot and appears to be an extremely astute move.
Source: authors

In other instances, a take-over presents opportunity for moving into a new business area. In this case, as Block (1983, p. 30) has pointed out, the new venture should fit with the existing **venturing base** of the firm. He defines this as:

> ... those characteristics of the firm (areas of knowledge, skill, technology, market position, distribution channels) which can serve as a major resource for starting new businesses.

Other authors, for example Bakker *et al.* (1994), refer to the organization's core competencies and the need to have a **critical mass** of these to bring about the success of a new venture, as we have previously emphasized. This applies whether the venture is developed in-house or is a new acquisition.

In each instance, the new business will both prosper and integrate to a greater extent if it fits in with the organization's existing capabilities. We again refer to the importance of strategic fit. This is not to say that something new should not be acquired. After all, extension of capability is presumably one of the prime motivations for the take-over. However, the new business should build on existing corporate strengths and contribute towards the achievement of the company's strategic intent, as was the case with Stakis's take-over of Living Well.

Illustration: Stakis PLC, expansion through acquisition

Stakis PLC had experience of working with Living Well, who operated leisure and fitness facilities within some of their hotels. Living Well also had seven Premier Health Clubs in city centres and was a leisure facility operator for Hilton. Through this association Stakis came to realize that there was a major business opportunity for the company in this area, both in terms of enhanced positioning for their own hotels and extra profit and return on capital in a new business area. They also recognized that operating leisure clubs involved specialist expertise which they did not currently have within the company. One way forward would have been to buy in individuals with the expertise. However, rather than this, they decided instead to buy Living Well.

In May 1996, Stakis acquired Living Well for £19.75 million with a view to building on the existing leisure businesses within hotels and to developing a national chain of health and leisure clubs as a third leg of the group (the other two being hotels and casinos). An early task was to integrate the Living Well leisure clubs into all of Stakis's suitable hotels. The next phase will be to rapidly develop the Premier Health Clubs nationally. The acquisition therefore presented opportunity for both further developing the existing hotels business and also moving into a new, but related, business area.

The new venture has involved Stakis in restructuring company management responsibilities as well as planning for a major corporate investment programme spanning the next three years. Such a substantial initiative would not be possible without careful financial and business planning. However, the development represented a logical extension to the company's existing activities and capabilities, consequently it was more readily able to be taken on board.

The move represents a considerable contrast to the period of the late 1980s when Stakis expanded rapidly into different business areas to form a mini-conglomerate. Some of its ventures had only a tenuous link with existing capability. New initiatives, such as the move into computer software, though they could perhaps be regarded as being extremely entrepreneurial, were not successful. Furthermore, they helped to bring the company close to ruin.

Source: Stakis PLC 1996 Company Report

Though the hospitality, tourism and leisure industries can be asset-intensive, they are also employee-intensive. Sometimes it is the expertise resting in people that is being sought, rather than physical assets. In situations where a company has identified a need for specific expertise to move the business forward, it may consider that its existing human resource capability is not adequate. In this situation, it could make more sense to hire the people with the expertise than to buy the businesses in which they are currently based. Nowhere is this more evident than in the culinary field, where expertise and reputation count more than the aesthetics of a particular location.

The contract catering area of facilities management is particularly competitive. Currently, this industry sector has low barriers to entry. In the main, contracting-out organizations own the asset base and the contractor uses this in providing a specified service. In such a situation it is the expertise of the catering operator that provides the added value for their clients. Consequently it is hardly surprising that, in an attempt to establish credibility, contract caterers have established links with high profile chefs, such as Gary Rhodes in the following illustration.

Illustration: Gardner Merchant and Gary Rhodes, people take-over

Gary Rhodes is probably the most well known of chefs. He established his credentials as head chef at the Greenhouse, which achieved three Michelin stars. He has also had considerable media exposure in a series of television food programmes. Gary's link with Gardner Merchant provided the contract catering company with the opportunity to demonstrate its serious intent with regards to the provision of high-quality exciting food for its clients. Gary was initially used in a training and development capacity, with the company also making use of his considerable public relations skills. Training sessions for the company's chefs were set up in a series of regional training days. The end result of each of the training days was a dinner hosted by Gary. Such occasions provided the opportunity for Gardner Merchant to invite along their important corporate clients and impress them with their efforts to achieve still higher standards of performance. The occasions also provided a valuable opportunity to inspire and motivate the company's own chefs through the opportunity to work directly with Gary and learn more about his approach.

The company have now invested over £500 000 in developing a public restaurant 'City Rhodes' in their London headquarters. The venture makes good sense for both parties. The company gains a high-profile venue which can be used for impressing existing and potential clients as well as for continuous training of the company's staff from around the country. Added benefit will come from the considerable media exposure resulting from the initiative. Gary Rhodes also has the opportunity to generate serious wealth without associated financial risk (though he is risking his reputation in starting a new venture). Exact details of the financial arrangements have not been made public. Gary does not have capital tied up in the venture, but undoubtedly has a well-structured incentive scheme which will ensure that he shares in the restaurant's success.

Other organizations have been quick to follow Gardner Merchant in negotiating similar associations with other celebrity chefs. A good example of imitative entrepreneurship! Even small companies have managed to achieve good links. Everson Hewett is a contract catering company with a first year turnover of £1.75 million. The company was started by two ex-Sutcliffe managers in January of 1996, in a classic case of employees leaving a large organization to set up on their own in the same line of business. The company have entered into a collaborative agreement with Pierre Hoffman, executive chef at the three-Michelin-starred La Tante Claire. Pierre Hoffman's agreement includes a monthly retainer. He will also gain percentage of the income from contracts on which he advises. The association has the

> potential to add credibility to Everson Hewett's sales pitch as it attempts to grow and win more contracts.
>
> At the time of writing, Gary Rhodes is in the process of displaying his own entrepreneurial credentials by setting up a national programme of high profile 'Rhode' shows, taking cooking firmly into the domain of live entertainment.
>
> **Source**: authors

People take-overs might be considered to have advantages over business take-overs, in that it is seemingly easier to integrate individuals than entire organizations. However, as has been discussed in Chapter 3, if entrepreneurial individuals are to flourish, they need freedom to operate in terms of organizational structure and culture. If this is not forthcoming then buying in expertise may not be effective. Entrepreneurial individuals often find it difficult to operate within the confines of large organizations anyway. Whitbread acquired David Lloyd along with the David Lloyd leisure centres, but he stayed with them for less than a year following the take-over of his business! Stakis also acquired Frank Reed along with Living Well, but he too did not thrive in the large company environment.

Acquisition of people expertise is not restricted to culinary skills. As can be seen from the following Queensborough PLC example, broader based commercial expertise can also be taken on board.

> *Illustration: Queensborough PLC and Michael Guthrie: people take-over*
>
> Queensborough is a leisure company operating a theme park and a series of mobile-home-based holiday parks in UK and France. It decided that it wanted to set up a third core business in the chain restaurant area, but did not have the necessary know how. Michael Guthrie has extensive expertise in building restaurant brands, including Bright Reasons, the pasta chain which was sold to Whitbread. He was a prime candidate for Queensborough, but his services did not come cheap.
>
> Queensborough went to their shareholders at the end of 1997 to seek approval for a substantial incentive scheme to be offered to Michael Guthrie and his development team. The scheme effectively shares all profits in excess of a 15 per cent return on capital equally between Guthrie and Queensborough. There is also the provision for share incentives. The company have acquired a proven entrepreneur and his team, by giving them substantial opportunity to participate in the rewards of what they are being asked to create. Guthrie has available the resources of Queensborough which should enable him to develop his new business quickly and without the associated financial risk.
>
> **Source**: Queensborough PLC Shareholder approval document, 1997

Spin offs/buy outs

Spin offs and buy outs are mirror images of acquisitions. Here, rather than creating added value for shareholders and owners through acquisitions in new areas of business, the decision is taken to focus on fewer business areas instead. Alternatively, an organization may consider that the opportunity cost of continuing in a particular business area is too great in terms of alternatives which are being foregone. It may not just be a question of capital scarcity. There is also the issue of management competencies and capabilities. Being spread across too many business areas means that attention can be diverted from the major areas of opportunity. Whatever the motivation, a decision is taken to spin off company assets. This was the case with Forte and one of its strategic business units. The outcome was a management buy out.

Illustration: Forte and Gardner Merchant, spin off

Gardner Merchant, the contract caterer and facilities management company, was a strategic business unit within Forte for many years. However, Forte decided that shareholders interests were better served by selling the company at an advantageous price rather than continuing to own and operate it. The company established its independence via a venture-capital-supported management buy out by the experienced incumbent management team, led by Gary Hawkes. In this new form, the company traded independently very successfully until bought out by Sodhexo, a French facilities management group.

Interestingly, divestment was also a major plank of Forte's strategy when attempting to resist the hostile bid from Granada. The basic idea was again that shareholder value could better be unlocked through selling business assets at inflated prices, rather than having the benefit of ongoing income from operating them.
Source: authors

Spinning off of non-core business activities was also a major plank of the last Conservative Government's strategy to transform the national economy, as was discussed in Chapter 4. Within local government, organizational areas such as catering and leisure services were formed into direct service organizations and forced to bid for the right to continue operating their service. If successful in winning the contract, such organizations established a new kind of business relationship, that of customer/client, and the service area had been effectively spun off.

The broad thrust of this policy seems set to continue under the new Labour Government via its Best Value rules. In this situation, the public sector becomes a service specifier rather than a service operator. This brings a number of potential benefits. The public-sector organization specifying the service is obliged to think through exactly what it wants and how much it is willing to pay for it. Direct service organizations delivering the service are subject to competition and have to carefully consider how to provide their services cost effectively. The area of business opportunity has also theoretically been extended to entrepreneurial private-sector businesses. However, where it involves substantial capital requirement, such as in Private Finance Initiative (PFI) situations, it is likely to mean that it will be the more established businesses, strategic alliances, and joint ventures which will primarily benefit.

Strategic alliances and joint ventures

Strategic alliances and joint ventures occur when business organizations come together for a common purpose. They may or may not form a new organization. The fact is that they have arrived at the conclusion that they can achieve more through collaboration than through their separate individual efforts. Such alliances represent entrepreneurial activity since they involve each party of the alliance in looking beyond their existing scope of activities and accepting that some form of relationship with other businesses is needed, if they are to progress. This is therefore an innovatory response to a perceived business problem or opportunity. One such response was evidenced by a strategic alliance initiated by Hilton and Ladbroke, as indicated in the following illustration.

Illustration: Hilton Hotels Corporation and Ladbroke PLC, strategic alliance

Rights to the Hilton brand name have for many years been in the hands of two separate companies. This has impeded the development of what is possibly the world's best known hotel brand. Hilton Hotels Corporation owned the right to the brand in the USA whilst, resulting from a past sale of the international part of the Hilton business, the British-owned Ladbroke PLC owned the right to the name in other parts of the world.

Clearly, the fact that there were two companies separately operating the Hilton hotel businesses did not make sense from the customer's perspective and was likely to result in customer confusion and antipathy. The prospect of not being able to book a Hilton room in the UK from a Hilton property in the USA, or vice versa, was not likely to create a favourable impression with either company's customers. Yet, for many years, this was the situation. In fact, the two organizations were on constant bad terms, with law suits being a feature of their dialogue.

In early 1997 the two organizations broke the mould and made a formal agreement to enter into a far-reaching alliance. The alliance has the objective of making Hilton appear as one company from the guest's perspective. Three jointly owned companies have been established to cover marketing, reservations, and the Hilton H rewards scheme. Certainly, the alliance to undertake these activities on a worldwide basis makes sound business sense for both companies.

Source: Leisure Opportunities, 24 January 1997

In a fast-changing, global scene in which information technology (IT) is playing an increasingly important role, we are probably going to see a proliferation of IT-motivated business alliances which will bring about added value for both businesses and customers. The widely recognized power of electronic access and distribution systems is forcing companies to either enter into strategic alliances to harness the power of IT or risk getting left out in the cold. The illustration at the top of the following page provides an example of an IT-motivated strategic alliance.

As specialist focused businesses become increasingly global in their scope of operations, they move into new markets. Initially such moves have been shown to be most effective when the overseas market has a similar culture

---

Illustration: Pegasus, strategic alliance for IT

Pegasus systems, parent company of Travelweb, is owned by fifteen of the world's major hotel and travel companies. These include Best Western, Choice, Intercontinental, ITT Sheraton, Marriot, and Westin Hotels and Resorts. *Travelweb* allows travellers the opportunity to check air fares and purchase tickets from 300 airlines twenty-four hours a day from anywhere in the world via the Internet. Tickets are delivered within seventy-two hours via Federal Express.

Travelweb also offers customers the opportunity to make credit card guaranteed reservations at more than 8000 hotels, in more than 125 countries around the world. Since March 1996, hotel room sales via the Internet have increased at a monthly rate of around 40 per cent. The company plans to produce one-stop travel operations by adding the largest car rental companies to the airline and hotel information.

Source: Travelweb 1996, *http:www.travelweb.com/thisco/global/twebnews.html*

---

to that of the host country. However, with globalization, hospitality, tourism and leisure companies are increasingly involved in setting up operations in different cultural contexts. This provides further incentive for setting up joint ventures with partners who understand local operating conditions. Such ventures can also provide opportunity for sharing the required capital contribution and associated risks, as is the case for the Tussaud's Group.

Illustration: Pearson PLC, leisure joint venture

The Tussaud's Group (a division of Pearson PLC) already operates three theme parks, the latest being Port Aventura in Spain. Tussaud's strategy is to develop an international range of successful visitor attractions. The company is currently carrying out a feasibility study with Sahaviriya City, a Thai company, with the aim of developing a £100 million theme park in Thailand. Michael Jolly, Tussaud's Chairman and Chief Executive, recognizes the need to adapt and combine his company's experience and creativity with local markets and cultures. The intention is that, if the project goes ahead, Tussaud's will have a 10 per cent equity stake in the venture. Tussaud's are therefore gaining both local expertise and the ability to expand with only limited capital outlay.

Source: Leisure Opportunities, 24 January 1997

From the above illustrations it can be seen that organizations enter into strategic alliances and joint ventures for a variety of motives. In a business environment that is so dynamic, the competencies necessary for business success are constantly evolving. Entrepreneurial companies recognize when their development aspirations are such that entering into an alliance brings greater likelihood of success than operating alone.

Consortia

Consortia are a form of strategic alliance which have special importance in the hotel industry and are therefore worthy of particular mention. The fragmented nature of the industry sector means that many individual businesses do not have the financial clout to take advantage of opportunities. As such, they may choose to join with other hotels in a consortium, in order to pool resources and benefit from economies of scale. Such consortia need not necessarily be entrepreneurial in nature or behaviour, though they undoubtedly were at some stage in their development. Consortia such as Leading Hotels of the World or Best Western are often subscribed to because of their established marketing or purchasing expertise, rather than for their development of new initiatives. However, it can be argued that the individual organizations joining consortia are certainly being entrepreneurial. They are recognizing that their membership will offer added value for them in acquiring access to services, resources and distribution systems that they are incapable of accessing independently. Consortia can either be a co-operative venture, established for mutual benefit, or a commercial initiative which is created for the profit of the founder. In the illustration below, the consortium can certainly be described as entrepreneurial.

Illustration: Golfotels, consortium for profit

Golfotels was conceived by Graham Wilson who recognized that independent hotels with golf courses were each having to spend considerable amounts on marketing expenditure to attract golfing-related business. He recognized that if he could attract golfing hotels of a similar standard, there was considerable added value to be gained from collaborative marketing. In particular, Wilson believed that a consortium would be able to more effectively reach the corporate golf market.

A main criterion for membership of the consortium is that hotels should have an eighteen-hole golf course with a par of at least sixty-eight. They should also have a minimum of three crowns, or equivalent, for their accommodation. To date, Golfotels has enrolled some very impressive venues, including such renowned course and hotel combinations as Slaley Hall, Selsdon Park, and Hawkstone Park.
Source: *Caterer and Hotelkeeper*, 1–7 August 1996

Confederations

Furthest away from the organization in terms of sovereignty and control is the confederation relationship. In this relationship, the initiating organization has neither ownership interest nor direct control over new developments. Initially this relationship was identified and described by Handy as a **network of loosely linked commando units drawn together to solve problems in a task culture.** Though Handy described it as operating **within** organizations, the concept of a confederation also has utility as a descriptor for intra-organizational collaboration.

Owing to the very nature of the relationships, such collaborations will often be based around issues of common interest, rather than economic gain.

A contemporary example is the coming together of leading chefs from competing restaurants, speaking out about the need for pure, unadulterated food. They are campaigning for quality and safety to be the main driving influence in all matters to do with the food chain, rather than profit and yield. The collaboration is intended to bring both influence and innovative energy to the task, and an output of their lobbying has helped bring about Government action.

Absence of direct economic gain is not always the case. In the Guinness illustration below, profit was clearly the incentive. However, there were particular legal obstacles which meant that the Company chose to collaborate with independent retailers in a loose, rather than more structured, manner.

Illustration: Guinness PLC, Irish pub confederation

In the late 1980s Guinness World-Wide Ltd was finding it difficult to maintain export sales. The Company clearly needed a major retailing initiative to reverse a potential decline in the sale of Guinness, its main product. However, in important markets such as the USA, legislation prevented brewers from also operating liquor distribution and retailing establishments. There was therefore a dilemma between what the company was allowed to do by law and what was required strategically for success.

In 1992 Guinness decided that, rather than marketing Guinness, it should put a major effort into exporting the Irish pub concept. It decided not to do this directly, but indirectly through the encouragement of entrepreneurs. Such was its success that Guinness's Retail Development department now has a staff of around forty people helping independent entrepreneurs open Irish pubs at the rate of one a day throughout the world. Assistance takes the form of a five-day class in all operational aspects of running an Irish pub, as well as covering the important financial aspects. Guinness also has a 'preferred' pub fitting-out company, the Irish Pub Company, which offers five types of ready-to-operate Irish pubs: Victorian Dublin, Gaelic, Irish Brewery Pub, Irish Pub Shop, and Irish Country Cottage. The Irish Pub Company advises potential investors on capital requirements and potential returns. Other spin-off companies have also set up, including an 'Irish' satellite television company, an employment agency, and a musicians booking agency.

As a result of all this support, over 1000 Irish pubs have opened in thirty-five countries in the last four years. They have been a great marketing and financial success. There are plans to open up an additional 600 in the USA alone during the next five years. The independent entrepreneurs are not tied to Guinness in any formal business relationship, although they have been supported to put together the mix of tangibles and intangibles which constitute a good Irish pub. Neither are the entrepreneurs linked to Guinness by any kind of franchise or management agreement. They operate their businesses on their own terms. However, Irish pubs do sell Guinness and in large quantities!

Guinness has enjoyed around 100 per cent growth in its overseas sales of stout in each of the last four years. The support it has given to the development of Irish pubs has therefore delivered considerable profit through increased liquor sales. The loose confederation of Irish pubs world-wide clearly brings considerable business benefit to the company, despite all the individual businesses being independent and outside of its control. Independent entrepreneurs have enjoyed the retail success and Guinness the brewing success, as Irishness has become a fashionable commodity throughout the world.

Source: *Asian Wall Street Journal*, 26 October 1996

Summary

From current strategic management literature we have distinguished that entrepreneurs and intrapreneurs have a catalytic role to play in entrepreneurial strategy formulation. This is through their own involvement and also through harnessing the strategic ability of others within and outside their organizations. Through establishing a culture where an enterprising approach is valued, the organization can enjoy the vitality brought about by employee commitment and motivation. Such adaptability and responsiveness is recognized as having particular value as businesses increasingly operate within changing frames of reference. The future is full of ambiguity and uncertainty and this can also be true of the way in which strategy emerges. Sometimes this may be from chaos and disequilibrium, but we have argued that it is important to maintain a clear vision amidst this uncertainty.

An investigation of the relationship between entrepreneurs and strategy generated an understanding of the interface between the components of the entrepreneur/intrapreneur, organization, and environment which results in the achievement of an individualized strategy fit unique to each entrepreneurial business. Clearly, this interface of the entrepreneur, organization, and environment is at the heart of entrepreneurial endeavour. It will be explored further in the concluding chapter. The strategies employed at the interface fit may take a wide range of forms, and will adapt and change as the entrepreneurial business inevitably works through various transitions at different stages in its life-cycle. We gave examples of a range of strategies frequently employed within the industry sectors.

Our investigation of entrepreneurial strategy is summarized in the following model in Figure 8.8 which provides the strategic scaffolding on which to build an effective entrepreneurial strategy designed to create and sustain competitive advantage with a strong orientation towards the future.

Overall, the evidence therefore seems reasonably strong that contemporary strategic management has changed from its traditional form. The essence of the change in approach is that organizations have sought to be more entrepreneurial in their strategic development. In so doing, they employ a range of strategies which often involve working with other organizations and individuals in a variety of business relationships. They also pay attention to organizational structure and culture to provide the conditions in which enterprise can thrive.

There are robust echoes of entrepreneurship theory within the current strategy literature. At the same time, there are important lessons for the entrepreneur regarding the need to be adaptive, the importance of core competencies and capabilities, and the significance of strategic fit in deciding which opportunities to give birth to and which are better not to be conceived.

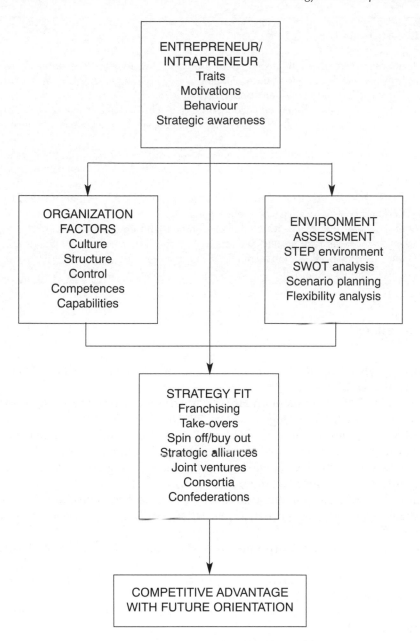

Figure 8.8 Entrepreneurial strategy formulation

Reflective questions

1 Successful entrepreneurial strategy in the hospitality, tourism and leisure industries owes nothing to long-term planning and everything to the short-term challenge of chaos and contradiction. Debate.
2 Identify entrepreneurial behaviour issues which underlie strategic decision making and conject as to how they may impact upon the effectiveness of formulated strategies.
3 In the context of entrepreneurial organizations within the tourism, hospitality and leisure industries, discuss the concept of 'strategic fit' and its significant components.
4 Consider issues associated with organizational culture, competencies, capabilities, and control, relative to entrepreneurial firms.
5 Discuss the key ways in which the environment and entrepreneurial firms interact to shape strategy. Identify the range of approaches which can be adopted to effectively manage this interaction.

References

Anonymous (1996) Restaurant at work scoops blue-chip deals, *Caterer and Hotelkeeper*, 21 March 1996.

Ansoff, H. (1994) Comment on Henry Mintzberg's rethinking strategic planning, *Journal of Long Range Planning*, **27**, No. 3, pp. 31–42.

Bakker H., Jones W. and Nichols, M. (1994) Using core competencies to develop new business, *Journal of Long Range Planning*, **27**, No. 6, 13–27.

Band, D. and Scanlon, G. (1995) Strategic control through core competencies, *Journal of Long Range Planning*, **28**, No. 2, 102–114.

Bates, T. (1995) Analysis of survival rates amongst franchise and independent small business start ups, *Journal of Small Business Management*, **33**, 26–37.

Block, Z. (1983) Can Corporate Venturing Succeed?, *Journal of Business Strategy*, **3**, No. 2, 21–33.

Carter, R., Martin, J., Mayblin, B., Munday, M. (1985) *Systems Management and Change – A Graphic Guide*, Harper and Row.

Chell, E., Haworth, J. and Brearley, S. (1991) The Entrepreneurial Personality, Routledge, London.

Dev, C.S. and Olsen, M.D. (1989) Environmental uncertainty, business strategy and financial performance: an empirical study of the US lodging industry, *Hospitality Education and Research Journal*, **13**, No. 3, 79–87.

Foster, M. (1993) Scenario planning for small businesses, *Journal of Long Range Planning*, **25**, No. 1, 123–129.

Greenley, G. (1989) *Strategic Management*, Prentice Hall, Englewood Cliffs, NJ.

Hamel, G. and Prahalad, C. (1994) Competing for the future, *Harvard Business Review*, January–February, pp. 107–114.

Johnson, G. and Scholes, K. (1993) *Exploring Corporate Strategy*, 3rd Edition, Prentice Hall, Englewood Cliffs, NJ.

Kotler, P. (1991) Marketing Management, Analysis, Planning and Control, 2nd Edition, Prentice Hall, Englewood Cliffs, NJ.

Miles, R. and Snow, C. (1978) *Organizational Strategy, Structure and Procession*, McGraw-Hill, New York.

Mintzberg, H. (1994a) Rethinking strategic planning, parts I and II, *Journal of Long Range Planning*, **27**, No. 3, 12–21, 22–30.

Mintzberg, H. (1994b) The fall and rise of strategic planning, *Harvard Business Review*, July/August, pp. 122–128.

Moore, J. (1992) *Writers on Strategy and Strategic Management*, Penguin, London.

Morgan, M. (1993) How corporate culture drives strategy, *Journal of Long Range Planning*, **26**, No. 2, 110–118.

Norburn, D., Manning, K. and Birley, S. (1988) Why large corporations must change, *Journal of Management Decision*, **26**, No. 4, pp. 12–19.

Olsen, M.D., Tse, E. and West, J.J. (1992) *Strategic Management in the Hospitality Industry*, Van Nostrand, New York.

Peters, T. (1987) *Thriving on Chaos*, Macmillan, London.

Peters, T. (1992) *Liberation Management*, Macmillan, London.

Peters, T. and Waterman, H. (1982) *In Search of Excellence*, Macmillan, London.

Pinto, E.S. and Olsen, M.D. (1987) The information needs of finance executives in the hospitality industry, *Hospitality Education and Research Journal*, **11**, No. 2, 181–190.

Porter, M. (1985) *Competitive Advantage: Creating and Sustaining Superior Performance*, Macmillan, New York.

Preble J. and Hoffman, R. (1995) Franchising systems around the globe: a status report, *Journal of Small Business Management*, **33**, 80–89.

Schumpeter, J. (1934) History of Economic Analysis, Oxford Uni. Press, New York.

Stacey, R. (1993) Strategy as order emerging from chaos, *Journal of Long Range Planning*, **28**, No. 1, 10–17.

Stacey, R. (1996) *Strategic Management and Organizational Dynamics*, 2nd Edition, Pitman, London.

Storey, D. (1994) *Understanding the Small Business Sector*, Routledge, London.

West, J.J. and Olsen, M.D. (1988) Environmental scanning and its effect upon firm performance in the food service industry, *Hospitality Research Journal*, **14**, No. 1, 87–100.

9 Entrepreneurship, an overview

The purpose of this short final chapter is to provide an overview of entrepreneurship and to encourage further reflection about the range of factors which impact upon it. Specifically, the chapter will:

- review important issues raised in previous chapters;
- consider interlinking themes;
- further develop critical awareness of factors likely to influence entrepreneurial success;
- provide an overall perspective.

Introduction

In the preceding chapters of this book, we have considered entrepreneurs and entrepreneurship, the entrepreneurial environment, and a wide range of relevant management concepts and techniques. Readers will now be aware that the domain of entrepreneurship is complex and involves drawing upon different perspectives and functional disciplines. It is about judgements and possibilities more than absolutes.

In deliberating upon the conditions likely to bring about entrepreneurial success we have, in the main, tried to avoid a prescriptive approach. In industry sectors which offer such a wide spectrum of varied entrepreneurial opportunity, best practice is always likely to be situationally specific, rather than in the form of general tenets which can be applied across the board. Nevertheless, in looking back with the benefit of an overall perspective, we are now able to draw some general conclusions. As well as reviewing important individual issues, we will link together different areas and develop additional insight into entrepreneurship within the hospitality, tourism and leisure industries.

The process of entrepreneurship

In examining the process of entrepreneurship we learned that it took place in many different dimensions and contexts. As a process being essentially concerned with innovation and the bringing about of new economic activity, it can originate from within all sizes and types of organization. Some of these will be new start-ups operated by independent individual or team entrepreneurs. Some will be new ventures started by established organizations. Entrepreneurship may or may not be carried out for profit.

There are both pull- (opportunity oriented) and push- (lack of alternative) based factors which stimulate entrepreneurship to take place, perhaps in association with some triggering event. It is infinitely variable in scale. In any event, we learned that within the literature there are different views of what constitutes entrepreneurship. Some commentators confine it to the setting up of a new venture, others apply the term to enterprising behaviour in general.

Perhaps of more importance than its scope is the spirit in which it is approached. The process involves creativity and change. It is debatable whether some life-style-based businesses operated by independent proprietors are really concerned with entrepreneurship. They do not encompass this change dimension. Clearly some large established organizations are extremely entrepreneurial. There is therefore profit to be gained from studying the process in both its independent and established organizational contexts.

In seeking to understand the process, we considered different approaches and perspectives. Some emphasized different dimensions, such as innovation or economic aspects. Some adopted an integrative approach. In deconstructing entrepreneurship, we learned that there are a number of elements contained within the process, all of which can substantially affect it. Already at this early stage, we learned of some of the complexities and intangibles inherent in entrepreneurship.

Such elements are brought to bear upon the entrepreneurship process in extremely heterogeneous ways. Given this, it is inevitable that entrepreneurship is an unstable process with uncertain outcomes, some of which may not be desirable. If it is debatable whether entrepreneurship is a force for equilibrium or disequilibrium, what is absolutely certain is that it has an enormous impact on society, both economically and in terms of the quality of life within it. In the hospitality, tourism and leisure industries, the process of entrepreneurship is often bound up with meeting cultural and social needs. It plays a vital role in satisfying the 'higher level' needs of consumers, as well as itself helping to shape them.

Entrepreneurs

If entrepreneurship as a process is difficult to define, then so are entrepreneurs. Many contributions have sought to define the entrepreneurial personality, by seeking to identify entrepreneurs' traits, attitudes, behaviours, and motivations. Whilst there is some degree of overlap amongst the different research-based contributions, divergent views also exist. This is hardly surprising, given the different views of what constitutes entrepreneurship, there is also no common ground as to who entrepreneurs are. Consequently, research sample frames vary enormously and differences in findings are bound to result. In any event, it is our view that entrepreneurs come in very different forms and to seek homogeneity is unrealistic.

As well as debate on the existence and composition of personal qualities in entrepreneurs, there is also controversy as to the extent to which such qualities are present genetically, influenced by society, or developed through learned behaviour.

If these identification and composition difficulties were not sufficient, the measurement of such traits and qualities is also extremely problematic. We are therefore left with a portfolio of possible personal qualities which may or may not be present to uncertain extents! Given these uncertainties the idea of some fixed entrepreneurial personality and capability blueprint seems ridiculous and is rejected.

Neither can the entrepreneur be considered in isolation from the entrepreneurial opportunity. The ideal entrepreneur for one opportunity may be less than perfect for another. In industries as varied as hospitality, tourism and leisure, different combinations of personal qualities and capabilities are required for the varied entrepreneurial contexts. There is also the point that entrepreneurs increasingly form themselves into teams and that individuals within the team can have complimentary strengths. An effective team entrepreneur may not survive if acting individually.

Our conclusion is that there are a wide range of factors at work which help to develop entrepreneurs, and that becoming an entrepreneur is potentially open to anyone. Having arrived at this conclusion, the point also needs to be made that whilst the make-up of entrepreneurs is full of uncertainty in terms of exactitude, in general terms what is needed to succeed in many situations and contexts can be identified. Clearly, prospective entrepreneurs need to reflect upon the reality of who they are and what they are good at in relation to the demands presented by the available opportunity.

Whilst entrepreneurs now have a much more favourable image within society, the reality is that many fail. Whilst the role of the entrepreneur has now been legitimized, the personal and societal cost of failure needs to be balanced alongside the rewards of success. The downside to entrepreneurship is often overlooked. This notwithstanding, it is apparent that the entrepreneur plays an important and growing role in national prosperity and has a vital part to play in bringing about constant change in the fast-moving hospitality, tourism and leisure industries.

Corporate entrepreneurship

We have established that entrepreneurship is relevant to established organizations as well as to new ventures set up by independent entrepreneurs. Chapter 3 set out to examine the challenge of developing the newstream whilst at the same time managing the mainstream efficiently and effectively. The challenge is manifested by the need to continuously improve the mainstream as well as just maintain it in existing form. Intrapreneurship literature has evolved to encompass continuous improvement and innovation of continuing operations as well as the development of new ventures.

Researchers in this area recommend different approaches. One school maintains that since change is now so endemic, organizations need to constantly re-invent themselves. Intrapreneurship therefore needs to be embedded throughout the entire organization. We made out a case that, since the hospitality, tourism and leisure industries have specific features that make them extremely difficult to control, adopting an organization structure which places responsibility for new ventures within a separate business development department is perhaps preferable. Systems could also be set up within the mainstream business to enable business improvement ideas to be gathered in, evaluated, and acted upon.

Intrapreneurs seem to share many of the characteristics of entrepreneurs, but they operate within the context, constraints, and opportunities presented by the organization. Since established organizations usually have greater resources than independent start-up entrepreneurs, they can potentially take more risks without threatening their ongoing existence. Evidence was presented that the hospitality, tourism and leisure industries are intrinsically entrepreneurial. In fact, organizations within these industries successfully overcome many of the potential obstacles to corporate entrepreneurship.

Environment for enterprise

Having considered the nature of entrepreneurship and the role of entrepreneurs and intrapreneurs within new and established organizations, Chapter 4 set out to consider the environment for enterprise. Given the widespread recognition of the importance of entrepreneurship to the competitiveness of nations, there is also considerable interest as to how entrepreneurs can best be encouraged and supported. This includes both demand-side activities which ensure that markets are open, substantial, and fluid, and supply-side activities which help entrepreneurs come on stream and operate effectively.

Since the election of the 1979 Conservative Government there has been continuous and substantial political intervention to encourage and support enterprise. This has included active social and cultural engineering to develop fertile entrepreneurial conditions, as well as economic support, industry restructuring, and vocational education and training programmes to help develop entrepreneurial skills. Similar policies are continuing under the new Labour Government. However, direct support for our industries seems destined to be focused on removal of supply-side obstacles, such as the restrictive licensing laws, rather than by positive assistance through measures such as grant assistance.

We consider structural promoters and inhibitors of entrepreneurship in some detail together with their impact. Despite benefiting from much of this general support activity, hospitality, tourism and leisure industries' entrepreneurs have also suffered from the peaks and troughs of economic cycles. As fast-moving consumer industries, they are always likely to fluctuate disproportionately as a result of changes in the general economy. In particular, interest rate instability and the collapse of discretionary spending and property values during the recession hit many entrepreneurial ventures hard. These industries are always going to suffer disproportionately from stop–go policies designed to win elections rather than provide a stable economic base. The environment for enterprise within these industries has therefore been inconsistent in its support, but is currently very favourable.

Finance, business planning and entrepreneurship

In part two of the book, we moved on to consider aspects of functional management particularly relevant to the entrepreneurial process. Careful business planning and sound financial management are particularly important in industries as fast moving and volatile as hospitality, tourism and leisure. The low barriers to entry in these industries mean that resource poverty is frequently a major issue, despite the availability of start-up capital and the generally favourable predisposition of many capital providers towards these industries. We identified sources of start-up capital for independent entrepreneurs and ways in which undercapitalization could be avoided, even if at the cost of some dilution of ownership.

Unfortunately, the use of the Government's Loan Guarantee Scheme is no longer available to many new ventures within the hospitality, tourism and leisure industries. This is perhaps a backhanded compliment to the industries' entrepreneurs who are presumably considered to require less encouragement than those in other industry sectors. It is perhaps also a sign of the continuing lack of recognition of the importance of these industries to the national economy and overseas earnings.

Resource poverty is also a question of expertise as well as funding. The fact that entrepreneurs without formal qualifications guaranteeing an element of technical and business management expertise are able to readily set up in business is surely an important reason for business failure.

Sound ongoing financial management is also very necessary given the volatility of these industries. The importance of a professionally specified management accounting system and of keeping records up to date, despite the many competing calls on the independent entrepreneur's time, was emphasized. Building adequate working capital requirements into the business plan to take account of the time often needed to build up trade is important if the dreaded resource poverty is to be avoided.

Operation and management

Chapter 6 identified the wide range of skills and expertise needed to successfully operate and manage entrepreneurial businesses. These competencies are not necessarily the same as those required to conceive and set up a business. Entrepreneurial managers in the hospitality, tourism and leisure industries typically have to exercise a wide span of control over a number of functional areas. Managing activities so that adequate attention is given to each area is in itself a challenge.

There is also the factor that, owing to the nature of these industries, many entrepreneurs are involved in their businesses in a hands-on way. This can involve long and anti-social hours and can lead to fatigue. It can be difficult to sustain performance at an adequate level, given such a wide range of physically and intellectually challenging responsibilities.

Furthermore, entrepreneurial businesses change in nature as they grow and the expertise required to manage them also changes. Entrepreneurs who are successful in the early days cannot necessarily make the transition to effective management of more complex organizations.

Marketing and entrepreneurship

Chapter 7 reviewed some of the contemporary thinking in marketing from the perspective of the entrepreneurial venture. Competition in the hospitality, tourism and leisure industry sectors is intense and the low barriers to entry mean that competitors can quickly come on stream even when conditions seem favourable. The demand/supply-side equation is seldom in equilibrium.

There are entrepreneurial opportunities both in growing and declining markets. Even within growing markets, the supply-side competition needs to be carefully evaluated. A market may be well supplied locally, even if it is growing nationally. Conversely, pockets of unsatisfied demand may exist even within mature or declining markets.

The emergence of the post-modernist consumer may present opportunities, particularly for independent entrepreneurs. Intangibles seem to be becoming increasingly important. It may well be that affinity with markets and the use of intuition and flair in devising and managing concepts to satisfy them is more important than development based on traditional marketing research.

Strategy and entrepreneurship

In the fast-moving markets in which the hospitality, tourism and leisure industries operate, organizations and independent entrepreneurs need to select effective strategies. They also need to constantly review them and to look to the future as well as take care of the present. This can be particularly challenging for the individual entrepreneur who will inevitably be bound up in the task environment. Opportunities for reflection are hard to come by when the demands of keeping the show on the road are so challenging. Such difficulties are not confined to individuals. Established organizations can also find it difficult to think long term rather than short term.

A number of potential strategies particularly appropriate to today's fast-moving and competitive conditions were reviewed. Some of these involved operating outside of traditional organizational structures in collaborative relationships. Such arrangements can bring to bear a wider range of resources and establish greater market presence than can be achieved by a single organization operating on its own.

Rather than prescribe particular strategies, Chapter 8 emphasized the importance of strategic fit which takes account of the entrepreneur/intrapreneur, the organization, and the market context in which the strategies are being deployed. Again, we are developing the theme that there is no simple formula which will lead to entrepreneurial success. It is about making judgements as to the best way forward from amongst an infinite number of alternatives.

End view

Whilst we have reviewed individual sections of the text, clearly successful entrepreneurial performance involves operationalizing an appropriate approach from amongst the array of personal, organizational, industry, and management variables potentially impacting. The concept of fit has already been introduced in Chapter 8 and we feel that this is at the heart of the matter. The most effective entrepreneurial approach will be one which successfully takes account of the dynamic components which are present in the specific situation.

The assumption underlying this is that there is no entrepreneurial blue print available, either in terms of an ideal entrepreneur or in terms of an ideal course of entrepreneurial actions. However, what is available is an increasing corpus of knowledge about, and relevant to, entrepreneurship. Concepts and techniques from many domains of research can be creatively combined to bring about a favourable outcome. This can help us to make wise decisions as to the best way forward given the specific situation in which we find ourselves.

Research which demonstrates this most effectively has been carried out by Robert Baum (1995), who investigated the relevance of twenty-two variables which had received the most extensive theoretical support as being important to venture success. Entrepreneurs were asked to evaluate the impact of these variables and LISREL structural equation modelling was used to establish direct and indirect antecedents of venture growth. The result is an effective presentation of these antecedents grouped together into clusters (Figure 9.1). The model shows how some entrepreneurial variables impact upon

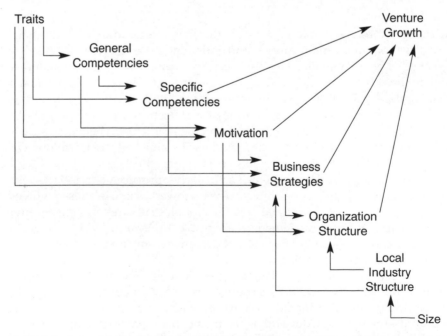

Figure 9.1 A reconfigured entrepreneurship model. **Source**: adapted from Baum 1995, p. 558

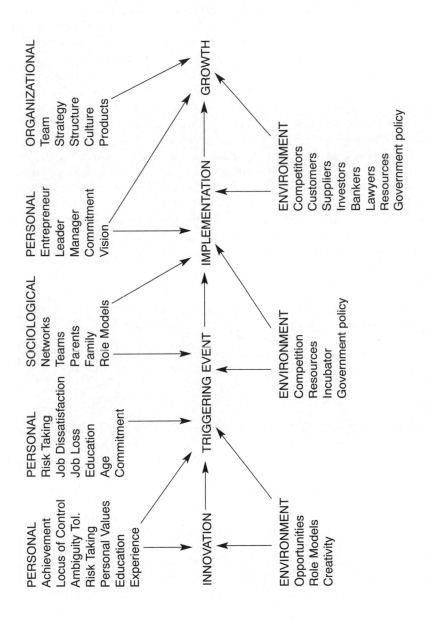

Figure 9.2 Moore's model of the entrepreneurial process. **Source:** Bygrave *et al.* 1997, p. 39

others and combine in a synergistic way to impact upon venture growth.

An alternative view of the entrepreneurship process was modelled by Moore (1986). As with Baum, Moore's model also depicts a range of factors which impinge upon the entrepreneurial process and influence whether it is successful. As shown in Figure 9.2, her model highlights the presence of innovation and the importance of some triggering event in causing the entrepreneurial start up to take place. Essentially, although the models use different words and emphasize different things, they both share a view of the antecedents of venture success as being complex and variable.

Rather than being disappointed by the absence of an entrepreneurial blueprint, we are actually excited and encouraged! At the end of the day, despite the close attentions of very many academics across the world, entrepreneurship remains an art as well as a science. This makes it a stimulating area to be involved with and gives hope to all those amongst us who think that we might just have the best entrepreneurial idea yet! Whilst no nearer to a definitive statement of what brings about entrepreneurial success we are in a position where we can provide useful signposts as to which ways forward may prove to be productive.

We hope this text has provided useful insights for all those involved in the entrepreneurship process, particularly those already embarked upon entrepreneurial careers and those who are being brave enough to consider it.

Reflective questions

1 Evaluate an entrepreneurial business against the antecedents of venture growth identified in Baum's model. To what extent do you consider the individual antecedents are significant in impacting upon performance?
2 Critically evaluate Baum's and Moore's models in terms of their congruence with entrepreneurship theory.
3 In terms of your own capability to launch a new entrepreneurial venture, what antecedents are sufficiently in place and which require further development?
4 Given the range of influencing factors, can the likelihood of a new venture's success be predicted?
5 Does vocational education do sufficient to prepare students for an entrepreneurial career?
6 Given the high failure rate amongst new ventures in the hospitality, tourism and leisure industries is it ethical to encourage entrepreneurial careers in these business sectors?
7 If you were asked to advise someone intending to start up a new hospitality, tourism or leisure venture, what are the key things you would say?

References

Baum, J.R. (1995) The relation of traits, competencies, motivation, strategy and structure to venture growth. In *Frontiers of Entrepreneurship Research*. (P. D. Reynolds et al, eds.), Washington pp. 547–561

Moore, C.F. (1986) Understanding entrepreneurial behaviour, Academy of Management Best Paper Proceedings, Chicago. Quoted in Bygrave, W., D'Heilly, D., McMullen, M. and Taylor, N. (1996) Toward a not for profit analytical framework. In *Frontiers of Entrepreneurship Research*. (P. D. Reynolds et al, eds.), Washington pp. 30–39

Index